For Party or Country

FOR PARTY OR COUNTRY

Nationalism and the
Dilemmas of Popular Conservatism
in Edwardian England

FRANS COETZEE

New York   Oxford
OXFORD UNIVERSITY PRESS
1990

Oxford University Press

Oxford   New York   Toronto
Delhi   Bombay   Calcutta   Madras   Karachi
Petaling Jaya   Singapore   Hong Kong   Tokyo
Nairobi   Dar es Salaam   Cape Town
Melbourne   Auckland

and associated companies in
Berlin   Ibadan

Copyright © 1990 by Oxford University Press, Inc.

Published by Oxford University Press, Inc.,
200 Madison Avenue, New York, New York 10016

Oxford is a registered trademark of Oxford University Press

Library of Congress Cataloging-in-Publication Data
Coetzee, Frans, 1955-
For party or country : nationalism and the dilemmas of popular
conservatism in Edwardian England / Frans Coetzee.
p. cm.   Includes bibliographical references.
ISBN 0-19-506238-8
1. Great Britain—Politics and government—1901–1910.
2. Nationalism—England—History—20th century.
3. Conservatism—England—History—20th century.
4. Conservative Party (Great Britain)—History.   I. Title.
DA570.C64   1990
320.941—dc20   89-48518

2 4 6 8 9 7 5 3 1

Printed in the United States of America
on acid-free paper

For my family

Preface

Unlike much recent work on British Conservatism, this book was not prompted by Mrs. Thatcher. When I began research a Labour government was in power, and although the intervening decade of Conservative rule has stimulated inquiry into the Conservative party's history, the nature of the relationship between the party and its constituency has yet to be entirely resolved. This study seeks to clarify that relationship by exploring the often bitter debates between party stalwarts and a series of associational activists who were animated by the conviction that, in the early twentieth century, temporary party advantage was no longer enough.

My sense of relief at finishing this book is mingled with satisfaction at the opportunity it affords to thank all who contributed to its completion. For while archival work often seems a solitary affair, the preparation of a book is a collective enterprise. I am grateful to the staffs of the various archives and libraries in England and Scotland for their assistance, and to the American Council of Learned Societies and the Fulbright Commission for their financial support. I should like to thank the following institutions and individuals for permission to quote from material in their custody: the Keeper of Manuscripts, British Library; the Archivist of the British Library of Political and Economic Science; the Clerk of the Records, House of Lords Record Office; D. McKenna and the Archivist, Churchill College, Cambridge; the University of Birmingham; the Warden and Scholars of New College, Oxford; the Bodleian Library; the Secretary, Army Museums Ogilby Trust; the Deputy Librarian, University of Sheffield Main Library; A. J. Maxse, Lord Egremont, and the Archivist, West Sussex Record Office; the Director of the Conservative Political Centre; Mrs. R. M. Stafford and the Scottish Record Office; the Trustees of the Bedford Estates and the National Maritime Museum; the Archivist, Wiltshire Record Office; the Archivist, Northumberland Record Office; and the Guildhall Library, London.

Lutz and Pamela Haber's hospitality made an initial year in London even more enjoyable. Peter Clarke, Emmet Larkin, and Geoffrey Searle have helped in many ways, not least by reading the manuscript and offering many suggestions for its improvement. Even if it is conventional, it is nonetheless entirely appropriate to absolve them of responsibility for any errors that remain. Jean Mosher typed the final draft with speed and accuracy, while the staff at Oxford University Press, especially Nancy Lane, have dealt with the manuscript in an exemplary manner.

Two other individuals also deserve special thanks. William Becker contributed in so many ways to the eventual publication of this book that any acknowledgement is bound to be inadequate. The same is true of Paul Kennedy, whose advice, encouragement, and assistance have been instrumental.

My most profound debt, acknowledged in the dedication, is to my family. I have been especially fortunate, for without my parents', grandparents', and in-laws' respect for and love of learning, and without their support in a variety of ways, I would never have been in a position even to begin this book. And without my wife and fellow historian, Marilyn, I would never have finished it. That admission, however, still does not reveal how she has contributed on every page, cheerfully if undeservedly sharing her life with an intrusive, untidy array of notebooks, papers, and boxes. Unfortunately, she knows it may only get worse.

New Haven, CT   F.C.
Spring 1989

Contents

Contents

For Party or Country

Introduction

In April 1908 Winston Churchill, standing as the Liberal candidate in a Manchester by-election, was defeated. He promptly ascribed this unfamiliar and unpalatable verdict to the assistance rendered his Unionist opponent by no fewer than thirteen separate Conservative pressure groups distinct from the regular party machine.[1] Associational proliferation on this scale prompted a Conservative observer to suggest that "if past eras have been known as the stone age, bronze age, and iron age, surely the present period in our history might be known as the league age. For new leagues and associations rise on every side with startling rapidity."[2]

Pressure groups or similar voluntary associations were, to be sure, already a prominent feature of the political landscape well before the Edwardian era. Though John Wilkes and Christopher Wyvill may be accounted pioneers, the apparent success of Richard Cobden and John Bright's Anti-Corn Law League in the 1840s spurred a host of eager imitators hoping to shape that league's now validated methods to their own varied interests. Overwhelmingly, such "faddists" and their organizations tended to be Liberal.[3] The Liberal party partly resembled a federation of pressure groups and derived from that association much of its diversity and dynamism even while requiring a unique leader to harness that energy effectively. Above all, Liberal pressure groups represented British Nonconformists, who found in them a means of collective action to compensate for the authority and privilege defended by the Conservatives. As the party of the establishment, the Conservatives had no need of recourse to such pressure groups because they already possessed access to institutions adequate for the defense of their interests within the existing sociopolitical framework. In the 1840s the politics of deference was not ineffective.

Even by the 1870s Conservative ranks had been swelled by the addition of only a modest number of church defense or brewers' associations, and the party leadership could congratulate itself on having avoided what appeared to be a peculiarly Liberal affliction. Formation of the Liberty and Property Defence League in 1882 barely disturbed this situation, for it failed to articulate a distinctive policy or to attract a substantial membership.[4] More gener-

3

ally, however, the 1880s marked the beginning of a significant upsurge in pressure groups with a Conservative complexion, such as the Fair Trade League (1881) and the Imperial Federation League (1884).[5] Neither league survived, but each gave initial organizational impetus to sentiments that remained prominent until the First World War. Many of the Fair Trade League's arguments presaged those of the Tariff Reform League, especially with regard to the necessity for tariffs to induce more equitable terms of trade from countries already secure behind tariff barriers of their own. The Fair Traders tapped a vein of protectionist sentiment latent in the Conservative party, and many local associations, and eventually the National Union itself, adopted resolutions in favor of fair trade. But Lord Salisbury, despite considerable personal sympathy, proved to be an insuperable obstacle for the Fair Traders because he would not risk the threat their policy posed to party unity. That Salisbury was able to defuse the issue was testimony to his grip as party leader, the as yet incomplete social transformation of his party, and the failure of the Fair Traders to find a spokesman of comparable stature. On all three counts, Salisbury's successor, Balfour, would not be so fortunate.

Whereas the Fair Trade League put protection before empire, the Imperial Federation League put empire before protection. Proposing some form of imperial federation as the best way to secure imperial unity, the league attracted a few prominent Liberals such as W. E. Forster and Lord Rosebery, but it failed to recruit a mass base. Insufficient funds and Rosebery's characteristically diffident leadership contributed to the league's dissolution in 1893. But the primary reason was an intractable split among the membership, who could not agree whether to concentrate first on measures of preferential trade or mutual defense.[6] In this instance, too, Salisbury successfully distanced himself, though the issue did not simply fade away.

For what followed, in increasingly rapid succession, was the foundation of an unprecedented number of Conservative pressure groups. The launch of the Navy League in 1895 opened the floodgates to a string of similar associations: the National Service League in 1902, the Tariff Reform League in 1903, the Union Defence League in 1907, the Imperial Maritime League and the Anti-Socialist Union in 1908, and the Budget Protest League in 1909. These ancillary organizations were often a valuable supplement to the party's electoral agitation (as Churchill ruefully noted), yet not infrequently a divisive impediment to concerted action. It was this latter inflection that "a hopeful Unionist" had in mind when he complained that "the Unionist party suffers in the main from the multiplicity of organising bodies."[7] To the professional party agent, as well, it was evident that the "legion of leagues" led to unnecessary duplication and undesirable friction. "Why then," the agent (identifying himself only as M. N. S.) asked his fellow Conservatives, "should we be divided within our ranks when we are all of one opinion on Home Rule, Socialism, Tariff Reform, the necessity for a big Navy, and kindred questions?"[8] Evading his own question, the agent preferred to dwell on the deleterious effects of proliferation, presuming that squabbling Unionists would suspend their individual efforts if only they were alerted to the folly of their duplication.

And thus the question remains why, after only a handful of examples up to the 1880s, so many Conservative-oriented pressure groups were founded in the two decades prior to the First World War and, therefore, why—if they were periodically disruptive—the Conservative party itself was apparently unable to contain them. It is not surprising that the party professionals found these questions difficult to confront, because their party preferred to project an image of consensus, as in the successful effort to avoid an open challenge in 1911 for the party leadership between Walter Long and Austen Chamberlain by compromising on the third choice, Andrew Bonar Law. The picture for public consumption was one in which the leaders were in harmony with the naturally Conservative temperament or inclinations of the rank and file.

The often turbulent history of these pressure groups affords an opportunity to penetrate behind the smug rhetoric, to investigate the ways in which the Conservatives really conducted business, to explore the process of confrontation, negotiation, and accommodation between party elites and local activists, between diehards and moderates. The reward of this approach is a fresh perspective not only on the mobilization of groups ultimately sympathetic to the Conservatives in Edwardian England, but also on the broader features of the Conservative party's development from a loose conglomeration of agrarian interests to the predominant party of government in urban, industrial Britain.

For, misleading enough as a self-image, the Conservative party's supposed affinity with the social psychology of the electorate was frequently elevated into a spurious but widely accepted account of its allegedly stable history. Admittedly, there is a sense of familiarity about a party whose persistence over the past century contrasts with the changing fortunes of its various rivals on the left. But to many Conservatives the longevity of their party in an industrial, democratic age was an occasion for self-congratulation rather than surprise. Their explanation of partisan survival was preening rather than probing. Thus Lord Hugh Cecil was moved to proclaim in 1912 that the "Conservatism of the Conservative Party, modern Conservatism, as we may say, is of course largely recruited from and dependent on the natural Conservatism that is found in almost every human mind."[9] His fellow peer, Lord Willoughby de Broke, articulated much the same sentiment, secure in his belief that "instinct rather than intellect" lay at the core of the "Tory tradition," which stretched back unbroken a century or more to Burke.[10] *Permanence, stability, tradition,* these were the words with which Conservatives sought to reassure themselves that politics might be reduced to a matter of temperament and that a party preaching continuity might compete successfully with those that promised change.

The "stupid party" was John Stuart Mill's famous label for the Conservatives, and he ridiculed their pretensions to stability and tradition as nothing more than obsolescence and obfuscation. Yet, in so doing, he reinforced the prevailing image of the Conservative party as inflexible, regardless of whether one considered its immobility to be its foremost virtue or its paramount vice. In fact, however, the party's fortunes were by no means as consistent as (and its evolution considerably less tranquil than) Cecil, Willoughby de Broke, or even Mill's ritualistic incantations implied. In the late 1840s and 1850s, in the wake of Peel's repeal of the Corn Laws, the party's immediate prospects were dim and its adherents divided. Furthermore, as English society industrialized and urbanized, a party committed to articulating the interests of the countryside might be thought to be backing the wrong horse. Landowners like Willoughby de Broke, to whom such sporting metaphors were especially dear, preferred not to dwell on the party's erratic development: its isolation from effective power for the middle third of the nineteenth century, its subsequent recovery (based in part on its increasing strength in urban constituencies), and its internal contortions over the extension and popularization of the party machine (exemplified in the struggle over the National Union in the 1880s).[11]

Upon closer inspection, then, the Conservative party's performance belied both the predictions of its imminent demise current at midcentury and the image constructed for it and reiterated a half century later. The Edwardian era was marked by a surge of Conservative tracts, many of which lovingly detailed the party's unique relationship to the cautious English temperament, but their mixture of nostalgia and unrepentant self-righteousness imperfectly concealed their authors' doubts. The sudden, unprecedented surge of Conservative pressure groups in the same era, then, indicated that Conservative politics was turbulent and factious, not tranquil and assured. Yet that associational proliferation also pointed to new sources of support whose eventual accommodation, and to new issues whose resolution, would ultimately modify the party itself and help to equip it for the challenges of postwar politics.

On the whole, these extraparliamentary associations have escaped systematic research, largely because the traditional focus of the historiography of British Conservatism has, until very recently, reflected the party's priorities by emphasizing the leadership at the expense of the broader membership.[12] Accordingly, biographies of the party's prominent politicians abound, but, when it comes to demonstrating how initiatives from above were translated and implemented on a popular level, the focus shifts only so as to include the more formal aspects of party structure and organization.[13]

The pressure groups occupied an intermediate position at the intersection of "high" and "low" politics. They provided an arena for both established elites and their critics, for the replication of time-honored practices at Westminster, but also for the articulation of regional and local sentiments. Their political and economic programs often carried an antiparty charge, and yet they also sought, eventually, to locate their prescriptions within the framework and traditions of the party (the Conservatives) they felt was ultimately the better guarantor of their interests.

Nonetheless, it is not my intention to provide a labored narrative of the minutiae of each association, for their significance is as a collective phenomenon. Interrelated in terms of members and policies, the individual associations only take on full meaning when considered in conjunction with the others. Collectively, they threw into bold relief many of the issues central to the Edwardian era: national defense, economic competition, and the relationship between state and society. As a result, three associations—the Navy League, the Tariff Reform League, and the Anti-Socialist Union—will receive what might at first seem disproportionate attention, but this focus sheds light on significant aspects of Conservative development that a zeal for greater comprehensiveness might obscure.

The pressure groups collectively constituted a nationalist agitation. They would probably have adopted the terms *patriotic* and *patriotism* to describe their chosen means and eventual object. I have preferred the term *nationalist*, though, partly to avoid the erroneous implication that only these individuals, on the right of the political spectrum, were patriotic; partly because the political practices and ideological precepts they pursued (however varied) went well beyond the identification with king and country; and partly because their exaltation of a shared culture led them to devote particular attention not just to the condition of the nation, but to the question of what characteristics of behavior entitled one to claim or to exercise membership within that national community.

Efforts to define and to mobilize what amounted to a variant of popular Conservatism in turn created two dilemmas, one that might be labeled strategic, the other tactical. Attempts to implement a nationalist agenda were constrained by existing political realities that in practice entailed defining the relationship between party loyalty and nationalist sentiment. The various pressure groups all confronted the issue of whether a patriotic Englishman and a staunch Conservative were always identical, or if the identification might prove ambiguous and thus susceptible to frequent redefinition. The tactical dilemma stemmed from the potential disjunction between efforts to mobilize widespread working-class support and those to preserve, albeit selectively, elements of a conservative political tradition. Could a greater degree of popular participation be harnessed to a defense of significant elements of the status quo? In short, the issue of "for party or country" raised the questions of which party (if any) and whose country?

The nationalist agitation, having emerged in the 1890s, developed in several successive phases. The first lasted until roughly the conclusion of the Boer War, was dominated by the naval issue, and was animated by perceived threats from France and Russia. In the second phase, from 1902 until 1906, the agitation expanded in two important ways, by now addressing questions of domestic military defense and economic security and by risking more directly an antagonistic relationship with Conservative party elites. The magnitude of defeat in the general election of 1906 and the unfamiliar task of bracing against a Liberal administration inaugurated a third phase. This period, which lasted until 1911, was marked by the temporary return to prominence of the naval issue, but also by the emergence of fresh initiatives (the concern with Socialism, hitherto implicit, became explicit) and by the intensification of prior efforts to modify Conservative party policies and practice. After 1911, and the spectacular defiance by the so-called Diehards during the constitutional crisis of that year, it became increasingly clear that the nationalist agitation was losing whatever sense of independent momentum it had once possessed. Exhaustion, fragmentation, and recrimination all contributed, but the essential point was that the party itself had adjusted and thus circumscribed the former independence of the agitation. It effectively rendered the pressure groups superfluous and, in so doing, apparently resolved the dilemmas that the agitation had posed. But the terms on which this eventual accommodation was conducted were to influence the subsequent course of Conservative politics.

1

An Isle Now Vulnerable

When new Conservative pressure groups began to appear during the 1880s, their emergence heralded the fact that some Englishmen were beginning to perceive an unwelcome deterioration in their country's relative position as a military, economic, and imperial power. Their pessimistic appraisals colored domestic politics as well as foreign affairs. For example, home rule for Ireland, long opposed, could now appear even more odious as an incentive to the disintegration of the empire and a harbinger of the erosion of British power. But perhaps the greatest anxiety over British security, that which animated the early development of the nationalist agitation, concerned British sea power.

It had not always been so. Once Napoleon had been defeated in 1815 and exiled to St. Helena, there were no compelling reasons to fear for the country's safety. Indeed, the grounds for satisfaction seemed only to increase as the century progressed. There were, it was true, disturbing revelations of inefficiency within the army in the wake of its mediocre performance in the Crimean War. But the defense of England ultimately rested not with the army, but with the Royal Navy, which had resisted the best efforts of the French emperor, whose forces had subdued, at one point or another, virtually every power on the European continent. Nothing had suggested that this glorious tradition of English naval supremacy would, in any significant way, be threatened. Both the conduct and the material of naval warfare had changed little during the past two centuries, and England therefore had accumulated a satisfying superiority in numbers and experience that seemed unlikely to be challenged. And if this were insufficient, the country's imperial primacy and industrial supremacy (not to mention its commercial and financial superiority) further sustained British power. To find an appropriate parallel one might well be forced to delve back as far as ancient Rome; indeed, this was the comparison suggested by Palmerston's famous invocation of the *Pax Britannica* during the 1850s.

In 1859 this complacency was temporarily shattered by Napoleon III. It appeared that his aspiration to duplicate the triumphs of his famous uncle would again threaten England's naval supremacy and thus, ultimately, its security. But the interruption was brief, and the nephew, undistinguished, despite his illustrious pedigree. After a flurry of defensive preparations, including construction of new ironclads and formation of volunteer units of dubious military value, anxieties for the island's safety again subsided. With the ascendancy of Gladstone, the naval issue sank even further from sight. Committed to limiting state expenditure and infusing public life with a high moral tone, the Liberal prime minister was determined to resist any increase in the naval estimates. He succeeded in this regard, in eliciting not only the support of the bulk of his party, but also the acquiescence of much of the Conservative opposition on naval matters. Until the mid-1880s, then, neither the politicians nor the public bestirred themselves over the question of whether the Royal Navy could be counted upon to repeat its glorious triumphs of the now distant Napoleonic era.

Even the Admiralty itself appeared to have succumbed to the pervasive sense of apathy and indifference: the "Admiralty's Dark Ages" is one scholar's apt designation of the period 1869–1885.[1] Those officers who possessed combat experience had gained it against ill-equipped opponents during the various "little wars" in Africa and Asia, which did not prepare the fleet for the defense of the British Isles and British commerce against European rivals. Accordingly, not much in the way of systematic thought had been given to the strategic aspects of the country's naval situation. Mobilization plans were nonexistent, and the Admiralty's attempts to gather intelligence about potential opponents were woefully inadequate: the Naval Intelligence Department was not founded until 1886, and naval attachés were spread too thinly to be of much use. Little wonder then that, upon becoming First Lord in 1886, Lord George Hamilton noted that he found the Admiralty in "a state of chaos."[2]

Likewise, prevailing tactical thought drew upon the traditions of the Nelsonian era, with its emphasis upon coming to grips with the enemy at the closest possible range and eventually boarding, apparently oblivious to the technological innovations that had rendered this concept obsolete. Yet boarding procedures with cutlasses and pikes were still rehearsed until 1905, while ramming remained a topic of intense wardroom discussion.[3] Gunnery standards, according to an acknowledged expert, were "deplorable" and often subordinated to cosmetic considerations (a struggle of "gunnery vs. paint" in Arnold White's memorable phrase).[4] Effective gunnery was also hampered by the Admiralty's failure to undertake a thorough overhaul of naval ordnance, for, apart from the variety of calibers with their attendant complications of supply and coordination, one-third of Britain's battleships were still armed with inferior muzzle-loading weapons as late as 1898. Combined maneuvers were unnecessarily difficult, hampered by the hodgepodge of ships with dissimilar characteristics (such as speed or turning radius) that officers found under their command. The most dramatic illustration was the collision of two battleships in June 1893, resulting in the loss of *H. M. S. Victoria*. There seemed to be far too much truth, then, in the *Contemporary Review*'s satirical portrait of "an English Admiral with ships that he cannot control and guns that he is afraid to fire."[5]

If the Royal Navy was ill-equipped and unprepared, what was being done to remedy the defects? Some of these matters came to public attention in late 1884. A series of inflammatory articles purporting to reveal "the truth about the navy" appeared in the *Pall Mall Gazette* in September of that year, attributed, ominously, to "One Who Knows the Facts." The author was in fact the *Gazette's* editor, W. T. Stead, who had been primed with information by an ambitious young naval officer, Captain John Fisher.[6] The cumulative impact of Stead's articles was to suggest that the Royal Navy was ill-prepared for a modern conflict and that it was incumbent upon the government to correct the fleet's deficiencies without delay. Historians frequently stress how rapidly public opinion erupted over the naval issue, precipitating the "navy scare of 1884" and persuading an initially reluctant Liberal government to spend more money on the fleet. Indeed, the tangible results seem impressive—an additional outlay of over £3 million for new construction over the next 5 years beyond what had already been allocated by the naval estimates. Equally significant, however, and perhaps even more striking in light of the breadth of accusations, was the rapidity with which the furor subsided. Though contemporaries did not at first appreciate it, a pattern had been initiated whereby naval scares arose at roughly 5 year intervals, each scare to be followed by brief bursts of remedial legislation and longer periods of indifference. In 1888 and again in 1893, as in 1884, a clamor arose that Britain's naval defenses had been neglected and should be put right. But it was not until the scare of 1893, or, more precisely, in its wake, that the critics seriously contemplated means of rendering their scrutiny more effective and more permanent.

Navalist critics finally coordinated their efforts in the winter of 1894–1895 by founding the Navy League. The league's foundation highlighted three aspects of the 1893 scare that differentiated it from previous scares and that finally displaced the prevailing inertia.[7]

In the first place, attention was focused less on the qualitative defects of an ill-prepared navy and more on the fact that Britain faced threats both beyond its shores, in this case in the Mediterranean, and against not one but two European rivals, France and Russia. Or so the public was led to believe. In August 1893 it was revealed that a Russian squadron would visit the French port of Toulon, and this disclosure was then interpreted to presage Franco-Russian naval cooperation and a permanent Russian presence in the Mediterranean that would threaten Egypt and ultimately India. Nonetheless, the press "relapsed into indifference" until the end of October, when William Laird Clowes, the respected naval correspondent for the *Times*, gloomily reported from Toulon about the extensive French naval facilities there and concluded that British commerce in the Mediterranean depended entirely on French amity.[8] For the next several months pessimistic predictions were bandied about. Skeptics queried the extent to which the French or Russian fleets contemplated united action, the extent to which such action actually could be undertaken, and the ends to which such action, if feasible, might be directed. It was by no means certain that England was the intended target; a number of observers suspected that a Franco-Russian show of strength might be intended to impress Italy or Austria-Hungary. The lack of reliable information upon which to base an intelligent estimate of comparative naval strength contributed to the volatility of debate, as did speculation about the French and Russian projected naval programs.

One cannot argue, therefore, that the new permanence of the naval issue after 1893, which found institutional expression in the Navy League, simply reflected the irresistible and cumulative force of supporting argument. Indeed, at times there seemed to be no consensus among navalists. The Navy League was founded not because the appeal it expressed could no longer be resisted, but largely because resistance was all too easy. The various conflicting arguments and the cyclical, boom-or-bust pattern of navy scares could be utilized by skeptics to argue that the big navy proponents were erratic scaremongers, not judicious, well-informed patriots.

Public attention, however, was more malleable because of the second fresh development, namely, the impact of Captain (later Admiral) Alfred Thayer Mahan's famous study of *The Influence of Sea Power Upon History*, first published in 1890. Although Mahan addressed his arguments initially to an American audience, he drew many of his examples from British history to demonstrate a causal connection between sea power and national prosperity.[9] In the English audience, Mahan's book stimulated a renewed awareness of Britain's rich naval heritage and its traditional dependence on an unchallengeable command of the sea. Translated into various languages, the book's historically grounded interpretations were rapidly and widely regarded as prescriptions for sound future foreign policy. To less subtle or discriminating minds it might well appear that Mahan had revealed a sure path to national success that, if adhered to, would enable a country to destroy British supremacy as surely as the British had succeeded to the maritime primacy once enjoyed by the Dutch Republic.

Nonetheless, it did not require someone of Mahan's genius to recognize the importance of the Royal Navy to British security. Even the most rudimentary knowledge of British geography and history would suffice in that regard. During the scares of 1884 and 1888, observers were not insensitive to the implications of both the defeat of the fleet itself and the interruption of seaborne commerce. Thus neither inevitable momentum nor clarity of argument will suffice to explain the emergence of the Navy League; nor will antedating the German threat. For, whatever misgivings navalists may have harbored about the power of Germany's army or economy in the early 1890s, its modest fleet aroused far less concern than the navies of France and Russia. The third critical ingredient was not foreign, but domestic, namely, the realities of politics at home.

For, despite the scare in 1893, the Liberal government appeared to be impervious to the navalists' dire warnings. In several parliamentary speeches during that November, Gladstone pronounced himself "perfectly satisfied as to the adequacy and capacity of the British Navy to perform all the purposes for which it exists," and he denounced those who persisted in the mistaken belief that Britain's naval supremacy would not be maintained.[10] Now in the twilight of a remarkable career, Gladstone was unwilling to accept what he regarded as a repudiation of his lifelong commitment against militarism, and many of the Radicals within the Liberal party agreed. His critics charged that the aging prime minister's addiction to thrift and fixation on the passage of a home rule bill for Ireland led him willfully to disregard the nation's legitimate security requirements. Although not all Liberals accepted the Gladstonian position, as the battle lines came to be drawn, the partisan outlines were unmistakable. The Liberal cabinet claimed to detect the allure of partisan gain rather than patriotic concern as the primary motivation of the alarmists. It was true that the majority of those who supported increased naval estimates were Conservatives. They focused on the inadequate defense measures of the current Liberal government and avoided an abstract debate about how the fleet should be reformed or redistributed. Numbers of ships constructed and pounds sterling allocated were the issues, and on both counts the Liberals were to be found wanting, all in contrast to a Conservative administration during which, it was implied, any such deficiencies would not be permitted to occur.

Such, on the whole, were the arguments rehearsed in the Commons in December 1893. Gladstone decided to treat criticism of his naval policy as a question of confidence in the government itself. Although he was assailed by the Conservatives for thus making the naval issue a partisan one, the prime minister responded, with some justification, that his opponents had already done so and that he was merely following their lead.[11] When the cabinet met to discuss the matter in January 1894, however, a majority was prepared to support an increase in the naval estimates in accordance with the Admiralty's recommendations. Again the obstacle was Gladstone, but his growing isolation on the issue and failing health sapped his effective resistance. The best he could manage was to have his subsequent resignation (on 1 March 1894) attributed to failing eyesight rather than to an irreconcilable difference of opinion about the navy. When Rosebery succeeded him, the Liberal government approved an increase of some £3 million, which included provisions for at least seven additional battleships. As in the previous two scares, the subsequent increase in the estimates was a compromise.

Far from being satisfied with the course of events leading to the new naval estimates, navalists urged continued vigilance. Unaware of the cabinet's confidential discussions, Gladstone's critics perceived the eventual increase as a very close-run thing, as an unexpected and providential reversal of policy rather than as the confidently anticipated product of a consistently "big navy" policy such as they hoped to substitute. If Gladstone's health had been better, they asked, would England's defenses still have been strengthened? Moreover, apart from Gladstone's obstinacy, there had been the bitter partisan aspects of the entire affair. There were, then, especially to those suspicious of French and Russian intentions, deeply disturbing implications for the provisions for Britain's defenses. People who believed that national defense was an issue that merited consideration "above party lines," in a spirit of harmony and common purpose, could take no comfort in the obvious lesson that the differing fiscal and philosophical priorities that divided the parties on other issues divided them over the navy as well. Others might disdain any display of nonpartisanship on defense as mere camouflage. They were likely to suspect that most Liberals (as "Little Englanders") were temperamentally incapable of ensuring the maintenance of British power. If so, they faced the unappetizing prospect of frequent Liberal governments reversing the indispensable efforts of Conservative administrations to strengthen the fleet. From two orientations, often reinforcing but potentially conflicting, there emerged support for devising a means of ensuring that the naval issue remained current, that it did not lapse into periodic oblivion.

Any effort to do so, however, was shaped by the new configuration of politics produced by the cluster of electoral reforms in the mid-1880s. These included the extension of the franchise by the Third Reform Act in 1884, the introduction of more stringent legislation to limit electoral corruption in 1883, and the redistribution of many parliamentary seats in 1885. The new system appeared to be more open, with the former ascendancy of landed elites challenged by new voters in the counties and with even modest prosperity enfranchising more working men in the boroughs. What appeared more open also seemed more volatile and unpredictable; anxious patricians feared that the decisive influence in elections might be exercised by the less propertied, less educated, more capricious elements of the electorate. These new conditions, often subsumed under the label "mass politics," dictated a response different from that of the politics of deference, which had proven effective in the past.[12] Mass organization was necessary to mobilize the electorate, especially on issues about which it had been indifferent and uninformed. Many Conservatives worried over how their party could adapt to so uncongenial an atmosphere. To them it was scant consolation that the electorate seemed intent on permitting the parties to alternate in power. But this only served to reinforce the urgency of finding a way to pressure the Liberals to maintain the nation's defenses during those inevitable periods when they were secure with a parliamentary majority. One could not—and this was the key point—simply wait until the next election forced the Liberals out and then put matters right.

A note of urgency intruded because political change was compounded by the shift in Britain's entire military position. The industrialization both of the Continent and of warfare itself threatened to eclipse the supremacy Britain had long enjoyed. Until the middle of the nineteenth century warship design had changed little; thus a lead accumulated over decades was satisfyingly durable. But with the revolution in naval architecture—in the use of iron and later of steel, in weaponry, and in propulsion—ships built a decade earlier might prove distinctly inferior to the latest design. Thus the emphasis shifted to the future, to careful long-range planning, which, given the pace of technological innovation and the scale of financial limitation, was indispensable. On precisely these grounds, the response by the Royal Navy appeared inadequate unless the Admiralty was supported (and occasionally prodded) by firm governmental commitment and consistent public pressure. Given both the mediocre performance of the British economy when compared with the spectacular industrial growth of Germany and the substantial gains of other rivals, a few years squandered might in the long run prove disastrous. Any industrial power was a potential naval rival, and to maintain an adequate margin of safety in naval terms would require extraordinary measures.

Launching the Navy League

A proposal for some form of navalist organization was first broached in rather general terms by Sir George Clarke in late January 1894. Only the force of public opinion, he suggested, applied "steadily, persistently, and uniformly" by an "organization adapted to the purpose," could secure "continuity and sufficiency" in British naval policy.[13] Nonetheless, Clarke's recommendation attracted little interest, for several prominent navalists who might otherwise have pursued his idea had chosen to follow another course. Sir Charles Dilke, the foremost Liberal exponent of a large navy, originated the notion of preparing a letter elucidating certain indispensable principles of defense policy. Cosigned by counterparts from other parties (Sir George Chesney of the Conservatives, H. O. Arnold-Forster of the Liberal Unionists, and Spenser Wilkinson as a neutral civilian expert), it would be directed to the leading politicians, Gladstone, Salisbury, Balfour, Chamberlain, and Devonshire.[14] When published, the results would, Dilke anticipated, form a basis for informed discussion of future defense policy. Perhaps it might persuade the parties to compose their differences, but, at the least, it might elicit their intentions. Dilke and Wilkinson spent much of January 1894 correcting successive drafts, though one of the quartet, Chesney, already had misgivings about the project, which he expressed to Dilke:

> I would say that I doubt if the public generally can be trusted to take in the scope of the proposals in the somewhat abstract form presented. They are plain enough to the expert, but the man in the street needs to have the case put very plainly, and I fear he would hardly grasp the constitutional points, clear though they be to the skilled official. Yet it is the public whose attention has to be caught.[15]

Ironically, in his more candid moments Dilke too was pessimistic, expecting little from the party leaders to whom his proposals were ostensibly directed. Gladstone, he presumed, would give "no particular answer," while Balfour, though sympathetic, was deemed "lazy" and thus unreliable insofar as a prompt and explicit statement was concerned.[16] When, late in February, the letter was published and official replies began to filter in, Dilke's suspicions were largely borne out. Only Chamberlain expressed interest in the proposals, and he preferred to remain noncommittal. It was evident that any effort to limit the politicians' future leeway by committing them to particular policies was unlikely to prove effective, especially if, as in this case, that appeal reflected the opinions of only four men.

The initiative thus passed to Spenser Wilkinson. He had established an enviable reputation as the military correspondent for the *Manchester*

Guardian and as the coauthor (with Dilke) of studies of the problems of imperial defense. Accordingly, when Wilkinson published a series of articles in the *Pall Mall Gazette* in October 1894 on British sea power, he was not content merely to restate Mahanite maxims as they applied to the island nation. Rather, he sought to go beyond indicating that Britain required a navy in order to explain exactly what kind of navy was necessary. Above all, he hoped to apply to naval administration the organizational structure that he believed had been responsible for the Prussian victory over France in 1870–1871. He urged the Admiralty to model itself upon the German General Staff and, in particular, to single out one professional adviser—a "naval Moltke"—to bear ultimate responsibility to the cabinet. In his final article in the series, Wilkinson concluded that an effective navy could "only be obtained by taking the proper means—that is, in this country, by organizing votes."[17] Five days later, on 16 October, the *Pall Mall Gazette* published another appeal, attributed to "Four Average English men," to form a league. The *Gazette*'s editor, Henry Cust, was impressed by the number of letters the appeal had elicited, and he offered his services and arranged an initial meeting in his office between Wilkinson and the "four."[18]

By 11 December 1894, sufficient contributions had been received (about £243) to proceed with founding the new association. A preliminary meeting was held at the Westminster Palace Hotel in London at which Spenser Wilkinson was selected to chair a provisional committee to draft a constitution and prepare a list of names to be submitted for election to the league's executive at the first general meeting. A month later, on 10 January 1895, the Navy League was officially founded. The constitution adopted on that occasion embodied the new league's goals. It would disseminate general information about the Royal Navy, emphasize the interrelationship between naval supremacy and the welfare of the British Empire, and seek to impress these matters upon "public men" in general and parliamentary candidates in particular.[19] Given the initial prominence of Wilkinson in the preliminary administrative matters and the dominance of his conception of the league's future role, the meeting also endorsed his quest for a single responsible professional adviser (stipulated in clause 2c of the constitution). To many potential league supporters, however, this peculiarly personal crusade of Wilkinson appeared irrelevant, for the lesson of recent events seemed to have less to do with conflicting opinions in the Admiralty than with the relationship between domestic political realities and naval strength. Partisanship, civilian budgetary policy, and periodic public indifference were the issues. Initially Wilkinson's clause 2c was tolerated, because the fledgling league could ill-afford to lose someone of his stature.

Inauspicious would be the best way to describe the Navy League's early efforts. After a preliminary ripple of donations, the league soon faced the financial difficulties that would plague it for more than a decade. It encountered similar problems in its search for a luminary to serve as president. Lord Lansdowne, the executive committee's first choice (a peer and, as a Liberal Unionist, perhaps less offensive to potential Liberal supporters), declined the nomination. The fact that an active politician was initially approached in preference to a more obviously nautical personality suggests that the parties, no less than the navy itself, were the targets intended by some league members. Several other prospective civilian candidates also refused; Wilkinson therefore approached Admiral Sir Geoffrey Phipps-Hornby,[20] one of the most respected officers in the fleet. Hornby accepted the invitation to serve as Navy League president and thus lent the weight of his professional reputation to Wilkinson's campaign to reform the Admiralty. Within a month, however, in March 1895, the elderly Admiral died, and his loss was a blow. As one member recalled, "Admiral Hornby's death made a terrible difference in the authority with which we spoke in those early days."[21]

In the wake of the Admiral's death, the league's internal divisions rapidly came to the fore. Both the league's advocacy of the single adviser issue and its avowedly political agenda raised difficult questions about the basis for such actions. Whom did the league seek to represent, on what grounds could it justify the choices it made, and how would it accommodate indifference or dissent? Almost immediately, the league began to reconsider its public position on the naval adviser issue (clause 2c). A triangular struggle ensued in which the executive committee found itself caught between substantial sentiment among the general membership for dispensing with clause 2c and Wilkinson's insistence upon retaining it. Several executive committee members were not unsympathetic to Wilkinson's position, but, as dissatisfaction mounted, even they had to concede that Wilkinson's prominence had become a liability rather than an asset. Many league members regarded his campaign as an unwarranted intrusion by a civilian into military affairs. Already in early March the executive considered "points of disagreement with regard to the aims of the league."[22] Although the committee never resolved whether Wilkinson's view, in principle, was right or wrong, it could not evade the fact that the league was seriously short of money and members. Both deficiencies were promptly attributed, with considerable justification, to the league's endorsement of the single adviser issue. The executive committee concluded that "it is obvious that in consequence of clause 2c of the constitution in the propaganda of the Navy League, the growth of the league does not progress and is not supported as expected."[23] Two weeks later, on 27 March 1895, the committee resolved to substitute for clause 2c a milder phrase concerning the need "to call attention from time to time to such measures as may be requisite to secure adequate preparation for the maritime defence of the Empire."

Wilkinson soon resigned, as did several other members. The executive committee implored him to reconsider and, far from denying the validity of his arguments, cited an unfavorable climate of opinion. Although Wilkinson was persuaded to attend the league's first annual meeting in January 1896, he subsequently had little further contact with the league, believing that it had erred fatally by deviating from its original purpose. Even those members who conceded the force of his arguments, such as W. L. Ainslie (one of the original four "Average English men"), chided him for pressing on when "public opinion is not yet ripe" with "strategically faulty and tactically disastrous" results.[24]

The implications of Wilkinson's departure were important insofar as they contributed to the definition of the naval issue. His rebuff was, in part, a blow to those of a "national efficiency" cast of mind who argued, frequently on the basis of the presumably superior German model, that the country's institutions must be modernized.[25] The events of 1893–1896 indicated that criticism of the Admiralty was to be off limits and that those who elected to use it as a focus for agitation would be ostracized as lonely voices in the wilderness. Clearly, then, the responsibility for an inadequate navy had to be shifted elsewhere. But where? One possible avenue would be to stress public or even official ignorance of the extent of Britain's dependence on the fleet, a position that pointed logically to educational efforts as the solution. Conversely, one might presume that politicians, once in office, were inevitably committed to limiting public expenditure, even if this meant denying the senior service. In this case, only sustained public pressure, exercised with inescapable regularity at the ballot box, would ensure the proper maintenance of the fleet.

No sooner had the Navy League drafted and amended its constitution to avoid dissension than the country in July 1895 faced a general election. The controversial single adviser issue had, it seemed, been laid to rest, but differences of opinion reemerged in the course of the campaign. The league simultaneously stressed its intentions to secure parliamentary candidates pledged to its aims and to remain "absolutely distinct from all party politics."

Faced with incompatible ends and hampered by unsubstantial means, the executive committee contented itself, albeit at relatively short notice, with preparing a single test question. If the candidate answered in the affirmative, by pledging himself "to urge upon the Government, irrespective of party, the necessity for naval estimates adequate in the opinion of the Admiralty" to protect British commerce, maintain the nation's food supply, and "guarantee the command of the sea under all probable contingencies of war," he would be entitled to the league's official support.[26] Precisely what that support might amount to was another matter. Having done little yet to establish local branches or the machinery for effective political intervention, the league was reduced to addressing its members through its monthly journal and to urging them to act on an individual basis. "All who consider the safety of the Empire more important than any party question," the *Navy League Journal* prompted, were encouraged to undertake the task of putting the test question to local candidates and publicizing the results.[27] Local initiative, on a sporadic, ad hoc basis, was the best the league could do to substitute for a coherent and comprehensive electoral policy implemented consistently and convincingly.

Even this limited effort, however, met with criticism, from within the Navy League as well as from without. Some internal critics deplored the feebleness of the league's electioneering, but a more prevalent complaint was that the league had been deflected from its proper educational focus. Herbert Wrigley Wilson, the editor of the *Navy League Journal*, dismissed charges that the league had blundered into partisan politics:

> It was perhaps only to be expected [he wrote in the journal] that the Navy League would be criticized for its action in the election, but it is hardly fair that this action should be misrepresented. . . . 'Political' has two senses. In the first sense it means 'relating to public affairs,' in the second 'relating to party.' In the first sense the Navy League is, and always must be, political, since after all the Navy is a public affair, and not the private preserve of the service papers. In the second, and now more accepted use of the word, the Navy League is non-political.[28]

The first few months of the Navy League's existence, then, were hardly encouraging to navalists. United in their desire to secure the strong navy that historically had made Britain great, they found little in the past that suggested how they might achieve consensus in the future. All were agreed that the navy scare of 1893 was proof that the navy's condition and funding must be dependent on careful planning and continuous public interest rather than on provisional arrangements hurriedly conceived during the occasional spasms of public indignation. Both the pace of technological change and the array of industrialized potential enemies dictated that the British must work harder to maintain their naval supremacy. This common ground, however, was nonetheless too slender a basis upon which to ensure that the strength of the navy remained a permanent issue in British public life. For how far was the naval issue to reach? To Spenser Wilkinson, institutions as well as attitudes required reform. But, as the modification of clause 2c demonstrated, most league members were content with less drastic measures. A cleavage similar, though not identical, to that between interventionists and noninterventionists developed between "educationalists" and those who sought to augment an educational approach with political action. Yet those who espoused political action were not of one mind. To one group of navalists, the naval issue offered a promising platform on which to overcome partisan conflicts: under its unifying grip Liberals and Conservatives might set aside their lesser differences and—on the issue of naval security, which ultimately affected them all—unite for the common good. Pro-navy Liberals would be welcome, lukewarm Conservatives unacceptable until their navalist convictions had stiffened. Even Conservative governments might be susceptible to the politicians' natural affinity for budgetary pruning without due regard to the effective military consequences, and, with these possible failings in mind, an ecumenical approach was best.

Such an outlook was hopelessly optimistic, even delusory, to navalists within Conservative ranks. Although they conceded that the naval issue had erupted during Lord Salisbury's administration in 1888–1889, they regarded the primary lesson to be the persistent obstinacy of Gladstonian Liberals, not once, but twice, in defiance of the clear necessity for naval expansion. Political action was certainly appealing, but not in employing the naval issue as an umbrella sheltering otherwise disparate groups. Rather, it afforded a means of stigmatizing and defeating the exponents of Little Englandism. Properly utilized, the naval issue would sharpen rather than blur distinctions, by exposing the unpatriotic. In 1893, or even by 1895, these positions had yet to evolve toward their logical conclusions. They had progressed far enough to support the formation of a permanent navalist association, but little further. The various positions would be sharpened only by the more persistent and immediate sense of urgency that stemmed from the revelation of an enemy with incontestable aggressive intentions and by the recovery of a Liberal party united and determined to reshape state and society.

The remedial legislation enacted in 1884, 1889, and 1895 was predicated on the assumptions that Britain might face more than one enemy and that the minimum margin of safety required was a fleet as powerful as the combined strength of the next two strongest naval powers. The so-called two power standard was given a respectable ancestry by being attributed to the younger Pitt. Yet it reflected the anxieties of the late nineteenth century, for it had not been the specified guiding naval policy during the intervening period. In the early 1890s, the most threatening combination appeared to be France and Russia, as indeed the *Times* correspondent (Clowes) had linked them in his reports from Toulon. Whether these hereditary enemies could cooperate effectively, however, was a matter for conjecture. In the wake of the 1893 scare, information filtered out suggesting that the offensive capabilities of the French and Russian fleets had been exaggerated.[29] Few at this time apprehended any particular threat from Germany; the rise of German power two decades earlier had been applauded as a necessary counterweight to France, and there were various dynastic, cultural, and religious affinities as well between England and Germany. Yet, from 1897 onward, it would be German action that would transform English opinion on the naval issue.

Germany increasingly appeared to represent the dangerous combination of motive and opportunity. Without the stabilizing presence of Bismarck, Kaiser Wilhelm II was an impetuous, impulsive monarch who sought the flattery of sycophants rather than the advice of experts. The Kaiser's unfortunate penchant for pursuing his egocentric and erratic course was dramatized when he congratulated the Boers over the collapse of a bungled coup in South Africa, the Jameson Raid. Thus the Kaiser's "Kruger Telegram" in January 1896 suggested that he harbored a particular enmity for the island nation. If such suspicions were temporarily set aside during the mood of self-congratulation of Queen Victoria's Diamond Jubilee in 1897, they recurred with a vengeance in 1898 when the German government inaugurated a major naval building program. The Fashoda crisis with France of the same year, it is true, prevented Germany from being perceived as the sole threat to British security. But contemporaries did recognize that Germany represented a potentially more formidable foe in light of its superior industrial capacity. As Paul Kennedy has noted, "historians grappling with the overall alteration in Anglo-German relations have before anything else to confront the fact that whereas Britain produced over twice as much steel as Germany at the beginning of this period (the 1860s), it produced less than half at the end of it."[30] Moreover, it was not simply the fact that Germany was catching up, but that the sectors in which it was doing so were most prominently and precisely those with critical military significance—among them steel, chemicals, and optics.

Definition of a Public Role

The greater the extent to which a massive German naval construction program menaced Britain, the greater became the apparent justification for the Navy League. From its inception, the league faced a struggle for legitimacy, namely, to forge a coherent policy and to win acceptance as a recognized authority on naval matters. Crying wolf in 1884, 1888–1889, and again in 1893 was deemed insufficient, partly, of course, because it was feared the wolf might attack his prey before the alarm was raised again. The Navy League's intent was to publicize the wolf's predatory designs and the fateful consequences thereof. However, some of its members wished further to demonstrate that existing measures to stop the wolf were all wrong. But, by attempting to keep the naval issue in constant focus, the Navy League ran the risks of boring potential supporters and of alienating them with a barrage of unfulfilled or irrelevant promises—in short, scaremongering.

Wilkinson's efforts with regard to clause 2c suggested to a number of observers that indeed the league suffered from the delusions of civilians who presumed in their arrogance to instruct the professionals. It became readily apparent that, whatever the shortcomings of the fleet, blaming the Admiralty would not generate the consensus necessary for sustained consideration of the naval issue. Shedding its meddlesome image, however, required the league's constant attention. In June 1896, it reemphasized that it "was not working against the authorities" and lamented that "misapprehension still existed as to the league's real aims."[31] The *Times* commented on "the misguided aims" that had done "so much to alienate some of the best friends of the Navy."[32] Shortly afterward, the league again found it necessary publicly to "repudiate any desire to reconstruct the Board of Admiralty."[33] In 1898, the league's offer of prizes for accurate gunnery occasioned further comment and a brisk refusal from the Admiralty.[34] Two years later, a strident campaign to persuade the navy to withdraw the last of its remaining muzzle-loading battleships (which featured the use of sandwichmen at Whitehall) antagonized professionals and civilians alike. Sensitive feelings were also bruised by the Navy League's inquiry during 1900 into delays in shipbuilding in which the league rejected the Admiralty's explanation and advocated, among other "reforms," a reduction in the business British shipyards undertook with foreign governments.[35] Further controversy erupted when journalist Arnold White, after visiting the Mediterranean fleet in 1901 with league president Robert Yerburgh, published a confidential letter from Lord Beresford critical of the fleet and subsequently embellished it with his personal criticisms.[36]

On the whole, these particular issues reflected the specific concerns of a handful of publicists whose greater visibility and activity should not lead their arguments to be mistaken for the sentiments of the general membership. Local branches sought less abrasive policies that would reach beyond the occasional navalist zealot who shared the publicists' passion for the displacement and firepower of the latest ships or the Admiralty's deployment of them. Effective policies entailed framing the naval issue so that "average Englishmen" could relate it to their personal situations. Two approaches proved to be promising, by virtue of stressing what Englishmen shared: their common geographic isolation as members of an island nation and their rich heritage of naval accomplishment, which was deemed inseparable from the triumphant pageant of English history.

Geographic chance—being an island—had proven a blessing by insulating the English from the follies of their less fortunate and less remarkable continental neighbors. On this score, the league would have encountered little, if any, dissent from the membership. But as the Navy League was at increasing pains to point out, what remained a privilege and a source of satisfaction now concealed potential vulnerability. There was, of course, the obvious possibility of seaborne invasion, dismissed by Earl St. Vincent during the Napoleonic Wars in his famous pronouncement, "I do not say they cannot come my lords, only that they cannot come by sea." When the naval issue was discussed for much of the nineteenth century, the discussants tended to share St. Vincent's definition of the problem, if not always his self-confidence. England was vulnerable because her beaches would be exposed to an invader if ever the British fleet lost control of the surrounding sea. Protection of the coastline by the fleet was in a sense the British equivalent to the fortifications that continental countries required. Englishmen had been doubly privileged, for English soil had not reverberated with the tramp of foreign conquerors since 1066, and it had avoided becoming a "garrison state." Geography and English seamanship obviated the necessity of maintaining a large standing army at home. This was a strong point in the navy's favor, and money for the fleet could be justified as a kind of insurance policy that permitted the allocation of resources to commercial and industrial ventures instead. Furthermore, some naval enthusiasts went so far as to claim that the threat of retribution from the Royal Navy sustained "free trade," that its ships kept the sea lanes free to the benefit of the whole world.[37]

It was as this point in the argument that the Navy League entered an important qualification. While the traditional danger of invasion persisted, the country now had to consider the specter of starvation as well. Why was England now susceptible to starvation? In part, the league argued, the difficulties encountered by British agriculture since the 1870s and the consequent reduction in the acreage sown with grain ensured that a high proportion of the population—too high for complacency—relied for sustenance upon imported foodstuffs. Estimates varied as to exactly how much of the wheat consumed in England, for example, was imported, but that the proportion had increased since 1815 was incontestable.[38] In 1897, therefore, two Navy League members brought the food supply issue before Parliament. Henry Seton-Karr, an MP for St. Helens, introduced a motion that urged the government to consider the "wholly inadequate production of food supplies with the area of the United Kingdom in relation to its large and increasing population."[39] Seton-Karr, seconded by Robert Yerburgh, raised the question of possible damage from commerce raiders (such as that inflicted by the Confederate marauder

Alabama during the American Civil War or that advocated by the *Jeune École* school of naval thought in France) or from embargoes against Britain by grain-exporting countries.

While stressing possible external threats, Seton-Karr and Yerburgh were nonetheless groping toward an implicit analysis of a perceived internal threat. In the subsequent debate their position was clarified, and it did not require a keen intelligence to discern that "food supply" was a coded way of broaching the issue of working-class loyalty. From the Navy League's inception, a number of members were concerned by developments within the working class, and as a consequence they sought to develop a domestic resonance to the naval issue. The survival of substandard living conditions—as revealed by Booth and later by Rowntree—suggested to suitably inclined minds the similarities between the working-class life and those of savages and animals. Darwin's theories could be cited to lend support to such assumptions, and, when they were combined with an appreciation of both the debilitating or atomizing nature of modern urban life and the political stirrings exemplified by the formation of the Independent Labour party in 1893, the result was often increased anxiety. To the league's publicists, Britain appeared to be degenerating into a race of weaklings, perhaps unwilling to defend the legacy bequeathed by sturdier and more patriotic forebears or, possibly, incapable of doing so even if willing.[40] These were delicate points to bring out, however, without appearing too reactionary.

Already, in the initial issue of its journal, the Navy League had stressed that "there is the working man to be converted. His clubs echo with socialistic denunciations and detractions of an imperial policy. He is only half convinced of the value of our Empire and but a lukewarm supporter of larger naval budgets. We must be at him and teach him. It is the duty of the better educated amongst us . . . [and] our end is to strengthen that England which has made us what we are."[41] Herbert Wrigley Wilson, the journal's editor, had distinguished himself as a military journalist and as a naval historian, yet his fears for the nation's domestic situation were never far from the surface. "Our national character has probably softened since 1815," thought this son of a Yorkshire clergyman. He attributed this deterioration to several developments: "the operation of inevitable causes crowding the robuster country population into the towns, . . . socialistic legislation which has weakened the old self-reliance of the Englishman, . . . [and] the long reign of peace and the essentially unmilitary character of the people."[42] To find the least offensive way of conveying the ultimate implications of such appalling conditions, the Navy League adopted the language of contingency and hypothesis. Rather than condemn the working class outright, despite the wealth of evidence that demonstrated to the satisfaction of anxious minds that workers could no longer be counted among the patriotic strata, the league preferred to speculate upon the consequences of any sustained interruption of imports.

Should the navy, weakened by the misplaced economy of Little Englandism, somehow temporarily lose command of the sea, Britain's imports of food would be sharply curtailed. Those with sufficient pluck would, in the best

English tradition, bear up under the strain. But what of the majority? On this score Yerburgh was especially pessimistic, predicting "a sullen, discontented population, ready to take to riot and pillage under the stress of hunger and fear of starvation." There would be "no recourse," he feared, "but unconditional surrender and the loss of empire."[43] The Navy League's pamphlets reiterated this message, as in Wilson's "The Meaning of Defeat" in which the loss of naval supremacy inevitably culminated in "grass-grown streets, ruined mills, bankrupt cities, social revolution."[44] Among the precautions Seton-Karr, Yerburgh, and other Navy Leaguers proposed were the storage of surplus wheat in national granaries and some form of commercial federation with the empire. Presumably the latter tactic would spur colonial wheat production, though what use this would be if England were blockaded was not addressed. Seton-Karr advised his parliamentary colleagues that "free trade was a question, not of principle but of expediency," and Yerburgh expounded upon this theme in recommending the introduction of a registration duty upon imported wheat to finance the construction of national granaries.[45] In pursuing this line of argument, though, the two Navy Leaguers had gone further than many of the general members were willing to go. For one of the attractions of navalism was its insistence that sufficient expenditure could preserve security and prosperity without in any way compromising traditions of voluntarism. With a strong navy there would be no need for either conscription or protection. Indeed, opposition to these proposals emerged from all quarters, and the sharpest rebuke came not from the Liberals but from the front benches of the Unionist party. Arthur Balfour was a devastating critic, who reminded Yerburgh that his scheme of national granaries would place the exchequer in an intolerable position as the country's major dealer in wheat, would unjustifiably interfere with trade, and would aggravate rather than eliminate popular discontent.[46]

If not pushed to extremes, however, the problem of food supply was an attractive issue, respectable and yet indistinct. Moreover, the food supply lent itself to treatment in the way that league members felt the naval issue could most effectively be promoted. Implicit in these discussions was the notion that the working class could only be reached on a "knife and fork" issue. George Chesney had suggested as much in January 1894 when he argued that "the man in the street" had little use for the "finer constitutional points" of national defense.[47] Likewise, Wilkinson's clause 2c could be criticized for dissipating energies better focused on the economic aspects of navalism rather than the arcane byways of the Admiralty. Only on the most elementary level could the crude minds of the populace be forced to recognize the extent of their debt to adequate British naval strength. The April 1898 issue of the league's journal reflected the way the food supply issue was to be packaged for popular consumption:

> The Navy League has today to preach as great a cause as did Cobden and Bright. They demanded cheap food for the people. It is not now the question of the cheapness of the food, but that there shall, under all circumstances, be

food to eat. What the Anti-Corn Law League did the Navy League can do if you help it. The poorest and richest in the land can give their mite or their gold to support this national cause.[48]

The appeal to the precedent of the Anti-Corn Law League was not unusual. Although that league certainly had not been the primary factor in the repeal of the Corn Laws in 1846, it was nevertheless presumed to have been instrumental, and therefore it frequently served as the model for subsequent pressure groups. Bright was more revered than, for example, Salisbury or Balfour among the social strata that the food supply question was intended to reach, and the Navy League's appropriation of his legacy was another aspect of its effort to broaden its own impact. Implicit in the preceding statement was also the assumption that the naval issue, presented properly, could dissolve class barriers: the "poorest and richest," prompted by the realization that they were in the same boat, so to speak, could cooperate in a glorious national cause.

In an attempt to supply its economic analysis with a cultural dimension, the Navy League complemented its emphasis on food with veneration of the anniversary of the great naval victory at Trafalgar on 21 October 1805. Given the premise that most workers responded less readily to intellectual stimuli, an appropriately simple and tangible form had to be devised to convey so diffuse a subject as the country's naval heritage. Accordingly, the Navy League concentrated on Admiral Lord Nelson, in the belief that he could personify a glorious past, and thus invented a tradition of celebrating his greatest victory. Every 21 October parades and speeches commemorating the event would be held. The focal point, of course, was London's Trafalgar Square, festooned with Nelson's famous signal, but similar ceremonies were organized throughout the country by local league branches.[49]

A Nelsonian focus to league ritual promised several benefits. His image harmonized with the league's professed nonpartisan stance, for Nelson did not evoke the political overtones that might be associated with more contemporary figures. Nor did he appear as a pillar of the governing classes, as did Wellington, for example. Indeed, Nelson stressed that his captains were a "band of brothers," implying social equality in the service of the country. Although the historically informed skeptic might note that Nelson's initial appointment involved patronage, clearly his rapid subsequent advancement rested on his remarkable talent. He could be portrayed as an earnest, self-made man. Add romance, a tinge of scandal, irreverence toward conventional authority, and a heroic death while ensuring the safety of British shores for generations, and the image was complete. The memory of Trafalgar also provided psychological reassurance, for the victory of British arms, unassisted, over an opposing coalition was a comforting precedent when it appeared that Britain was again menaced without having reliable allies.

Participation in, or even observation of, ritual observances emphasized those factors that drew Englishmen together, that what they shared as a heritage was ultimately more significant than class, religious, or ethnic di-

visions. The ceremonies also suggested that Englishmen bore collective responsibility for not squandering the priceless gift of naval supremacy. Some league
members, such as Herbert Wrigley Wilson, even feared that these celebrations
might prove too effective by providing an illusory sense of self-confidence.
"There is always danger in pluming ourselves upon our successes," warned
Wilson in 1896, as he pondered the relevance of the Trafalgar anniversary. "We
are too ready to suppose that circumstances will repeat themselves, and too
prone to imagine that because we have often won against heavy odds we can
always do so."[50] Likewise, Fred T. Jane, of naval annual fame, was bitterly
distressed that the league had become too "clogged with Nelson" and that its
glorification of Trafalgar, apart from antagonizing the French, detracted from
any serious consideration of contemporary naval problems.[51]

By the late 1890s, then, it seemed to the league's executive committee that
the most fruitful approach involved the combination of the food supply issue
and Nelsonian/Trafalgar celebrations. Local pressure had persuaded the committee to shelve ideas of reforming the Admiralty, *pace* Wilkinson and Jane,
and, in the absence of that initial focus or of a coherent political strategy,
policies that evoked any positive popular response were gratifying. The tandem
of sentiment and stomach, whereby the patriotic invocation of naval history
was paired with the "knife and fork" food issue, was calculated to broaden the
league's appeal. It assumed that each issue would complement the other, and
the projected pairing was certainly not unusual. "Imperialism and social reform" is the way historians have characterized a number of largely (though not
exclusively) right-wing efforts to revive Britain, whether this involved economic rejuvenation, inculcation of military-like habits of obedience and authority, or, as in the case of the Navy League, "straining at the screwjack which
is steadily raising British patriotism and British national spirit."[52] It is important to realize, however, that the particular foci of various such schemes
changed over the two decades preceding the First World War; it is equally
crucial to discover whether these schemes were confined to a coterie of energetic publicists and politicians or if they achieved a wider resonance among the
public.

Anatomy of the Navalist Movement

Considerable initiative was exercised by Navy League branches. Two of the
most consistently active were those established in Bristol (1895) and Liverpool
(1896). Little of what these two branches undertook was in response to dictation from London, and there were frequent conflicts between center and
periphery in regard to local self-determination. On most issues the branches
themselves carried the day, including the critical topic, money. According to
the Navy League's constitution, local branches were to remit fifty percent of
the income they collected to the central London office, to be disbursed as
London saw fit. In return, at least in theory, the branches would receive services of equal value, such as trained speakers or quantities of literature. Both

the Bristol and the Liverpool branches consistently refused to remit the required amounts, contending that local use of local resources was more effective and efficient. The central office periodically acquiesced while maintaining that each concession was not to be construed as a precedent.[53]

Both branches inaugurated ambitious local educational programs. They each urged the appropriate authorities to introduce naval history into their curricula and to incorporate Trafalgar Day observance in their school calendars. And both branches were particularly proud of their sponsorship of essay contests for schoolchildren on naval topics. In Liverpool, "many thousands of boys and girls" entered the annual competition, and winners were rewarded with prizes and certificates bestowed by the lord mayor on behalf of the branch at city hall.[54] Prizes for the older students included biographies of Nelson and editions of Mahan. The Bristol branch reported that "work in the schools has been vigorously pushed forward." In 1901, for example, 2,590 boys (apparently only boys were eligible) from 58 schools competed, and the best essayists received their prizes at Mansion House, Bristol, on, of course, Trafalgar Day.[55] Likewise, the local branch consistently met with the Bristol School Board to ensure adoption of its recommended textbooks (which often were written by league members expressly for school use). They encountered opposition from individual board members who objected to the "teaching of war" rather than peace, but successfully pressed their case for the importance of naval history.[56] Also recommended was the Navy League map, which, provided it was hung in the classroom, would serve as a daily reminder of the length of Britain's trade routes and the breadth of its imperial possessions.

The Liverpool branch went further still, in a direction that revealed local concern over the position of the working class as clearly as that evidenced in the House of Commons by Seton-Karr or Yerburgh. The centerpiece of the Liverpool branch's program was the Lancashire Sea Training Home for Poor Boys, which finally opened its doors in 1903. Its purpose was twofold: to reduce the number of foreign seamen in either the Royal Navy or Merchant Marine by providing trained British alternates and to provide working-class children who might otherwise go astray with skills and attitudes serviceable to an imperial power. The home was only open "to lads of good character who have never been convicted before a magistrate and are the sons of poor parents."[57] It was an expensive proposition, and the "liberal support of local merchants and ship-owners" to the extent of some £17,000 was necessary to establish and maintain the home in its first 4 years.[58] Within that period, that is, by 1907, nearly 300 boys graduated and found positions at sea. Their instruction in seamanship and naval history, however, had been supplemented with a regimen designed to suppress any tendencies toward juvenile delinquency. Participation in sports, in the home's musical band, and in religious services was compulsory. Thrift was strongly encouraged, as were other attributes of good character. Indeed, the Liverpool branch's success in this endeavor was extolled in the *Navy League Journal* with a revelatory series of "before and after" photographs that purportedly demonstrated the remarkable improvement in the boys' posture, cleanliness, and attitudes since entering the Lancashire Home.[59]

Both Bristol and Liverpool had a rich nautical heritage and a core of business and commercial enterprises that depended at least in part upon the sea. The Bristol branch's executive committee included Sir George Edwards, a fourtime mayor, chairman of two Bristol Conservative associations, and also chairman of Edwards, Ringer & Co., a tobacco and snuff manufacturer. Also reliant upon imports were Charles Wills of Imperial Tobacco Company; Alfred Deades, chairman of Anchor Tin Mines; and George Perrin, a timber merchant and president of the Bristol Chamber of Commerce.[60] Liverpool's committee had an even more pronounced nautical flavor, drawing as it did upon the cream of the city's mercantile and shipping community. Included were the current and several past presidents of the Liverpool Chamber of Commerce, the chairmen of the Liverpool Steamship Owners Association and the Liverpool Sailing Shipowners Association, and the chairmen of several shipping lines, including Sir Alfred Jones of the preeminent Elder, Dempster & Co. Insurance and banking were also well-represented, and the local executive committee was filled out with a local Unionist MP and with the editor of the city's Unionist newspaper, the *Liverpool Daily Post*.[61] Clearly here was a source of the funds accumulated to support the Lancashire Sea Training Home, but the opportunity, at least in cities inclined to utilize their links with the sea, had been seized only through a combination of provincial pride and undeterred local initiative.

Although the Navy League frequently cited the Bristol and Liverpool branches as examples of its own productive local effort, neither branch was entirely representative. As a whole, the league grew very slowly at first and more rapidly only in the late 1890s. From barely 1,000 members in 1896, it expanded to about 12,000 by mid-1901.[62] The foundation of local branches followed the same general pattern, as from frail beginnings the Navy League consolidated its position by the turn of the century. Again local initiative was instrumental in the formation of individual branches, in contrast to a decade later when the emergence of new branches was often tied to circuit tours by paid organizers dispatched from London. For example, both the Bradford and the Leeds branches owed their existence to the determination of a few individuals in the areas concerned. In May 1896, W. W. Marks, clerk of the peace for Bedford County, contacted the Navy League and explained that he had compiled the names and addresses of those people he thought would respond favorably to an appeal for a local league branch. Within 3 weeks the league was also contacted by the secretary of the Bedford Conservative Association, again with regard to the possibilities of a Bedford branch.[63] With the essential preliminary work already well underway, all that was required was the imprimatur of the league itself. Two personal visits from London by the league's secretary sufficed, and in August 1896 the Bedford branch was officially inaugurated. Similarly, in June 1898, W. B. Boyd-Carpenter, a son of the Bishop of Ripon, wrote to the league offering his services as secretary of a Navy League branch in Leeds for which he would undertake to enlist the necessary members (the league's constitution stipulated a minimum of ten members for any branch). The executive applauded Boyd-Carpenter's industry, but regretted that the league's precarious financial position precluded its being able to offer him a salary. If the committee expected this disconcerting communication to arrest the development of a Leeds branch, it underestimated its man. Undaunted, Boyd-Carpenter pressed on and succeeded in soliciting fourteen subscriptions by July 1898. During the following month the Leeds branch was founded, with Boyd-Carpenter (apparently still unpaid) serving as secretary.[64]

Nonetheless, fourteen members for a city the size of Leeds was hardly a compelling figure, and it had taken 3 years from the formation of the Navy League as a national organization to reach this figure. There remained, even by the turn of the century, startling omissions in the league's branch structure: no branches in Manchester until 1902 or in Newcastle until 1904. The first branches to be established, with the exception of that in Bristol, were located in areas having little reason to be involved with the fleet, namely, London's Hyde Park, Bath, Brighton, Windsor/Eton, and Cambridge. There was, however, a common pattern, either residential, recreational, or educational, of England's upper class. Moreover, in each there were strong Conservative connections, each constituency having regularly returned Conservatives or Liberal Unionists since 1886.[65] In his report for 1901, the league's secretary delicately alluded to the most persistent problem when, after first citing the efforts of Liverpool and Bristol, he noted that "it is to be regretted that all our branches do not display equal energy."[66] The fortunes of the Bath branch illustrated his point all too well. It had been one of the league's very first, having been founded in January 1896. Just 2 years later, however, the local secretary warned the executive committee that the membership of the Bath branch "had fallen off very considerably," and that autumn he suggested that "the inhabitants of Bath appear to have lost all interest in the Navy League." In response to his distressing reports, the committee declined to take any action. Finally, in January 1899, the exasperated local secretary resigned, claiming that the branch had "practically fallen to pieces."[67] Thereafter the Bath branch remained dormant until it revived during the electoral turmoil of 1910.

On the eve of the Boer War the Navy League numbered thirty-four branches, 9 of which were overseas. Although the league valued the naval issue as a means of promoting closer imperial ties, and despite the pains it took to emphasize the empire's dependence upon sea power, the imperial branches rarely lived up to the league's expectations. Canadian and Australian branches were lukewarm, the executive's "endeavoring to urge the Auckland branch to more activity" serving to summarize efforts there. There was "scant evidence of life" in South African branches (Capetown, Durban), which, in 1901, the league, with some plausibility, attributed to the war there.[68] Efforts in India were particularly disappointing, and even during the First World War the league would prove ineffective in either organizing branches there or introducing naval themes into Indian curricula.[69] New Zealanders proved to be the most responsive to the league's appeal. Aided by zealous headmasters, many of the New Zealanders enrolled in the league were schoolchildren. Within Britain itself, an overwhelming majority of local branches were confined to England. A few branches emerged in Scotland, largely in urban areas such as Edinburgh or Glasgow; on the whole, the Celtic fringe remained impervious to the charms of navalism. The average size of the English branches, apart from that in Liverpool, fell within a relatively consistent range. In 1899, nearly 5 years after the league's foundation and by which time it had enjoyed ample opportunity to propagate its message, its branches were secure but unimpressive. There were four branches within London, of which the Third (Kentish Town, NW) numbered 121 and the Fourth (Belgravia, Mayfair), 101. Torquay counted 53 members; Cambridge, 34; Worcester, 151; but Birmingham, only 52.[70]

Judged on this basis, the Navy League by 1900 had compiled a mediocre record. An apostle of empire, the league had achieved little with its overseas branches. Dedicated to providing navalists with a firm, nationwide organizational structure, the league evinced a patchy pattern of branches at best. Committed to focusing and coordinating navalist sentiment, the league had grudgingly to concede that its most conspicuous successes were the result of local initiative rather than centralized direction from London. Nor could the navalist movement legitimately claim to have reached every sector of the population. The numbers involved (even the 12,000 total membership by 1901) are perhaps proof enough. The league's shaky financial situation was another indication. From its inception and throughout its early development, the Navy League barely escaped bankruptcy. Its preliminary appeal for subscriptions had raised only £243, which was barely sufficient to cover founding costs.[71] When 10,000 leaflets were ordered in February 1895, the league stipulated that they be printed on "cheaper paper."[72] The prominent newspaper proprietor, Alfred Harmsworth, proposed to ease the league's financial difficulties by offering £100 with the provision that nine other donors match his figure. The league, however, wished to conceal its precarious financial position and "resolved to restrict to private means for the present the means of making known Mr. Harmsworth's offer."[73] Nine matching donors were not found, and the league's balance on hand slipped to £36. When the league held its first annual meeting in January 1896, the executive committee admitted that income for that year totalled a paltry £1,086. Thereafter improvement was both modest and uneven, with total income reaching £2,417 in 1898 and £2,682 by 1901.[74]

But there is additional evidence to suggest that the Navy League, by 1900, still had failed to reach an adequate cross section of the population. The social basis of the navalist movement remained narrower than its exponents predicted or even privately contemplated. Speaking to Navy League members in early 1896, the treasurer outlined with commendable brevity and candor the prevailing view of their association as "a body of cranks" and "a neglectable quantity."[75] In its early years the Navy League drew its core of members from a limited social range. Local secretaries fell primarily into three groups: retired naval officers, headmasters, and solicitors (less frequently, barristers, too). The former, by reason of their prior service and current leisure, were logical candidates for positions of responsibility within local branches. Similarly, given the league's focus upon educational work and the fears for the moral and material welfare of the working class, which also spurred its efforts, the presence of schoolmasters was encouraged. Finally, solicitors commonly served as secretaries in voluntary organizations or as temporary political agents before the appointment of permanent professional agents. These social groups also were well-represented on local executive committees, though committees tended often to include people whose connection with the league was rather perfunctory. One MP whose membership was courted was assured that he would be "unburdened with any work" and that, regardless of his participation, it was hoped he would permit the use of his name. Accordingly, committees included landowners who, frequently as justices of the peace, would never have accepted so menial a position as secretary. Businessmen, professionals, publicists, and the military–clerical complex filled out the local committees.[76]

The league maintained a series of membership classifications that emphasized the social gradations among its adherents. Of course, some distinctions had to be made in that the daily operation of local branches required some to commit their time as officers. But other distinctions were less functional; a contribution of £5 annually, for example, entitled one to a vice-presidency, and a lump sum of £25 secured that position for life. Yet a vice-presidency carried no additional privileges or responsibilities beyond that of regular membership, the sole compensation lying in the fact that vice-presidents were more likely to be listed in annual reports or other official league publications. Roughly seventy people had availed themselves of this opportunity by 1898. The other principal distinction was that between members and associates. For 1 guinea annually (rather than the pedestrian pound sterling), or for a 10 guinea contribution for life membership, one was entitled to the full benefits of regular membership, principally the rights to vote at annual meetings and to receive literature, primarily the monthly journal. Those who desired the literature but eschewed voting privileges could become associates for an annual subscription fee of 5 shillings. Finally, although in its earlier years the league chose not to emphasize this particular alternative, those who wished to demonstrate their adherence to the Navy League's objectives were eligible to join without privileges of any sort for a smaller sum (not stipulated, but a minimum of 1 shilling was usually recommended). The majority chose to commit themselves as either associates or minimal subscribers, with only some fifteen percent opting for regular membership.[77]

Nor was the league entirely democratic in terms of gender, but, given its clientele and the prevailing norms, this should occasion little surprise. League officers claimed to welcome the participation of women, as in an appeal by the Earl of Drogheda at the league's first annual meeting. In a Lancashire constituency with a "very large Radical majority . . . a lady took it in hand, and in the course of a year or two managed to establish branches of the Primrose League, and the result was that at the next election a Conservative was returned." The lesson the earl drew for his audience was "that the aid of the ladies is very much to be sought and we shall be very delighted indeed to have their assistance, particularly in working up the branches of the Navy League."[78] Drogheda's political sympathies were as obvious as his condescending tone, and his particular example, the Primrose League, emphasized entertainment, conviviality, and the patronage of the socially superior.[79] The women's range of contacts might be useful in attracting potential members, but they were denied any role on the London-based executive committee in administering the Navy League. Ample scope for their activities, the argument went, existed in the nurture of patriotism within the family and in the extension of assistance to the less fortunate. The league inaugurated a "Women's Page" in the *Navy League Journal*, which described the care of elderly sailors in navy rest homes. Married women were expected to attend league functions with their husbands or were canvassed for support in recruiting their husbands into the league, but without any intention that these efforts should precede a more independent role.

Within local branches the course of events rarely conformed to the expectations of or instructions from London. In several cases, women were instrumental in the daily administration of branch affairs; in 1898 four of twenty-five secretaries of home branches were female.[80] As such, they were far more intimately involved in significant branch activities than were many other officers whose roles were cosmetic or perfunctory. All four women were single. The league publicly recognized the efforts of Miss Woodruffe, secretary of the Fourth London branch, "for her energetic work in connection with the branch generally," but it singled out for special attention her role in organizing a ball to raise money for the Sailors' Home at Chatham.[81] This focus accorded more harmoniously with traditional expectations than would, for example, a female secretary who studied the details of military ordnance or the distribution of the fleet. A number of branches involved girls as well as boys in their educational work, including the essay contests, but this practice was not universal. In contrast to the more open policies of the Maidstone and Liverpool branches, the Bristol branch confined its contest to boys. League women were all too frequently valued for benevolent or philanthropic work, for which their allegedly innate domesticity had particularly suited them. And, while some tasks or some branches proceeded cooperatively, without reference to distinctions of gender, it cannot be pretended that this was the norm.

The Discordance of Political Action

By the turn of the century, the league's policies were in transition, partly in response to initiatives from below. Nevertheless, dispelling the preconceptions that continued to surround the Navy League's work would be difficult. The *Daily Telegraph* spoke for many sympathetic but distressed observers when it suggested that the league should "keep its shriekers in hand and give more work to its teachers."[82] Moreover, several of the league's ventures, however well-intentioned, were interpreted as having been directed against the Admiralty. For example, the Navy League justified its offer of prize money to ships judged the most accurate in gunnery trials as being a legitimate means of encouraging improvements in this critical aspect of naval efficiency.[83] But the Admiralty considered such offers an unwarranted infringement upon its jurisdiction; it suspected that the league might seek publication of the rankings in defiance of prevailing Admiralty policy and thus attempt to focus unwelcome publicity on crews that had not performed well. Undeterred by the adverse reaction its initial offer in 1898 had provoked, the Navy League returned to the topic again late in 1901. The league's secretary, W. C. Crutchley, sought to forestall possible criticism by stressing to the Admiralty his organization's best intentions:

> The executive committee of the Navy League respectfully ask permission to offer the sum of 50 guineas for the purpose of providing a prize for that ship . . . most efficient in its gunnery duties. . . . I am directed respectfully to express the hope that the Lords Commissioners of the Admiralty will believe that however misguided, injudicious or violent the efforts of the Navy League in the past may have been considered to have been, the action of the League has been dictated by considerations of patriotism alone.[84]

Nonetheless, the overture, however obsequiously phrased, was premature in that it followed too swiftly the harsh criticism of the Mediterranean fleet by Arnold White to carry much conviction. The Admiralty refused, although to soften the blow it conceded that "the attitude adopted by the Navy League on questions of naval policy has been advantageous to the navy" and that the league itself "was influenced in its action by patriotic motives."[85] Given the precedents, it is understandable that the Admiralty suspected the league's shriekers might be preparing to shriek again.

Simultaneous efforts to improve the league's image, therefore, were only partially successful. It was at some pains to stress its educational concerns, to persuade skeptics that the infusion of headmasters and teachers within its ranks would produce more moderate policies and that the focus of its efforts would broaden from Whitehall or Westminster into the classroom. Curricula and textbooks emerged as new topics of debate within the league, and members set out to contact the appropriate authorities or to publish the necessary materials. After all, the lessons of sea power were, in the Navy League's estimation, no less essential to the shaping of responsible Englishmen than were traditional subjects. Although such instruction was not made compulsory, as the league advocated, by 1902 lectures on the Royal Navy were no longer uncommon in the classrooms of sympathetic instructors.[86]

Despite evidence of progress, however, educational work could function only as a supplement to, rather than a substitute for, the Navy League's primary concern. The naval estimates were debated and voted in Parliament, so the Navy League could not forego intervening in politics, even if this reopened the divisions of 1895. Efforts to translate the naval issue into a comprehensive and successful electoral strategy resurfaced in 1898 when the executive committee met to draft a general policy on the subject. No resolution was reached, and the committee could only agree to postpone indefinitely any decision.[87] The following year the committee debated and finally approved the mobilization of "all efforts" in Northampton to defeat its Radical member, Henry Labouchere.[88] This decision was an isolated case, not a prelude to greater action. The inactivity is all the more surprising in light of Britain's foreign situation: the Fashoda crisis and the first German naval law in 1898 and the outbreak of the Boer War in 1899 each focused attention on Britain's capacity to meet new military threats. The league's committee discussed the provision of supplies and transportation of troops to South Africa, but not until May 1900 did it again grapple with the issue of political action.

In three cases the league's committee—for there is no evidence that this issue was explicitly discussed with the general membership as a whole—agreed to support candidates (two Unionists, including future league president Robert Yerburgh, and a retired naval officer, Captain Lambton, standing as a Liberal). The assistance was modest, limited in this instance to moral support and some £10 or £20 toward campaign expenses.[89] Beyond that the Navy League still would not go, and, on 1 October 1900, the first day of polling in the general election, it decided that "it was inadvisable to interfere further in the election unsolicited."[90] In part the Navy League was reluctant to proceed in political agitation because it was unsure what formal naval policy to attribute to the Liberal party as a whole, given the debates within the opposition. Liberal attitudes to the Boer War were divided, but the split between Liberal Imperialists and pro-Boers involved several issues, including doubts about the legitimacy and utility of the war and about the conclusion of peace once a military decision was inevitable. There was no precise or even obvious relationship between positions on these issues and that of British naval policy. But, more generally, the Navy League's leadership continued to display a profound ambivalence toward electioneering. It simultaneously expressed concern that politicians fulfill their public trust by maintaining British naval supremacy (with the obvious implication that those who failed to do so, as measured by the league's standards, be denied the opportunity to endanger the country), yet delayed implementing that policy for fear that such a move would divide its membership and impugn its credibility.

Finally, in early 1902, these inconsistencies were exposed to public scrutiny. Many league members felt a particular fondness toward Admiral Lord Charles Beresford, a flamboyant and prominent naval officer who was known to be particularly sympathetic to the fledgling association. In 1898, for example, the league had reprinted a glowing endorsement from a Yorkshireman that "the name of Admiral Lord Charles Beresford is sufficient warrant that, if he be returned, no efforts will be wanting to make our homes and our commerce secure."[91] The fact that the author claimed to be a Radical bore eloquent testimony, in the league's view, to the sincerity of his convictions. It had been Beresford above all who had advocated greater public attention to the needs of the Royal Navy.[92] The Navy League itself faced increasing internal criticism for its complacency toward Parliament, which, in the harsh words of one observer, "found ample time to discuss dogs, midwives, and poor laws, but the strength of the navy and the existence of the Empire [were] of no concern to it."[93]

Beresford seemed to be the solution to the league's dilemma. Clearly, if elected, he would speak on naval issues with particular experience and professional expertise, in sharp contrast to the Navy League itself, whose credibility was still not universally acknowledged. Beresford was possessed of commendable vigor, again unlike the league, which appeared somewhat staid or even stagnant. Perhaps he might even prove less objectionable to British Radicals, who could be counted upon to reject the big navy advocacy of civilians, but might accept the professional judgement of Beresford. The Navy League's executive committee envisioned Beresford, or convinced itself that he could be portrayed, as an independent member dedicated only to the security of Britain and to the greater glory of her fleet and empire. As its chairman explained at one league meeting, "Lord Charles Beresford, although the Tory member for York, and probably a very good Tory member, is first and foremost a member for the Navy. (Hear, hear.) Lord Charles Beresford has perhaps done more than any other man in England, irrespective of politics, to get our naval defensive forces in a comparatively good position."[94]

As a naval officer back on active duty, Beresford was barred from standing for Parliament, but in January 1902 he was about to haul down his flag and indicate his renewed eligibility as a candidate. The timing seemed ideal, for a vacancy occurred in the north London constituency of Hampstead. Known as a secure Tory seat, Hampstead had already witnessed several uncontested elections; from the league's point of view there was no reason to suspect any departure from that tradition, given Beresford's stature as a public figure and his previous service in Parliament. On 13 January 1902, the Navy League's executive committee unanimously agreed to play an active role in the Hampstead by-election, invited the cooperation of all members as canvassers or financial contributors, and authorized the sum of £50 with "more if need be" toward Beresford's expenses.[95] The Navy League was proceeding on the assumption that Beresford would readily be adopted by Hampstead's Unionists. Indeed, league president Robert Yerburgh (himself a Unionist MP) conveyed an official resolution supporting Beresford to the Hampstead Conservative Association and also approached the Conservative Chief Agent, Captain Middleton, to secure an agent for Beresford for the campaign.

Despite these precautions, the Hampstead by-election soon proved a fiasco. Local Liberal Unionists had already met on 10 January at which time a majority favored Beresford. Three days later, the Conservative Association formally met to discuss the election. A second potential Unionist candidate had come forward, Thomas Milvain, on the recommendation of Conservative Central Office. "The meeting was of a very protracted and animated character," reported the local press, "there being a strong body of members present in favor of adopting Lord Charles Beresford as the Conservative and Unionist candidate, as against Mr. Thomas Milvain, K. C., a stranger to Hampstead who, rightly or wrongly, is regarded in many quarters as having been thrust upon the constituency by the official Conservative organizers in London."[96] Resentment at dictation from London was exacerbated by the fragmentation within local Unionist ranks. Beresford had represented Plymouth as a Liberal

Unionist, which evidently disqualified him in the eyes of Hampstead Conservatives who preferred to maintain party distinctions. The Conservative association voted by a two-thirds majority to adopt Milvain. The Liberal Unionists then met to reconsider their previous endorsement of Beresford and debated a resolution to support Milvain because "Hampstead is a constituency in which the right of nominating the party candidate belongs primarily to the Conservatives." This motion passed by only one vote (cast by the chairman) and a counterresolution urging Liberal Unionists to abstain from the by-election was defeated again by the identical narrowest of margins. Beresford subsequently withdrew and with that decision exposed the futility of the league's scheme. Yerburgh extracted from Captain Middleton the admission that the Conservative organization would welcome the return of Beresford to Parliament at the "earliest possible moment"; he pronounced himself satisfied that the league's goal had thus been fulfilled.[97]

Nonetheless, Yerburgh's transparent effort to cloak events that flatly contradicted the league's recent actions was doomed to failure. After all, the candidates had just begun to fight. The local Liberals had adopted G. F. Rowe, a local stockbroker, but more importantly an advocate of "efficiency" and "a member of the Navy League of some years' standing."[98] Presumably with Beresford having withdrawn, the Navy League would throw its support behind its own member, Rowe. The local Conservatives sought to discredit Rowe as a pro-Boer and a toady of Campbell-Bannerman. Yerburgh and other members opted to support Milvain, and at Milvain's major meeting Yerburgh specifically disclaimed any Navy League support for Milvain's opponent.[99] To nobody's surprise, in view of Hampstead's political complexion, Milvain was returned for the constituency with 3,843 votes compared with 2,118 for Rowe.

Announcement of the poll did not put the matter to rest. Rowe subsequently complained that Navy League officials had violated their pledge of nonpartisanship by actually supporting the candidacy of Milvain, who certainly had not been standing on "non-party lines or as a pronounced advocate of the league's policy."[100] What had outraged Rowe was the fact that, despite his own membership in the Navy League, fellow members had chosen to support his opponent, whose commitment to naval supremacy very probably was inferior to his own. Whether they did so officially on behalf of the Navy League or in a private capacity (as Yerburgh claimed in defense) was, in Rowe's opinion, irrelevant, for their participation would be interpreted as a logical consequence of the support the league had originally promised Beresford.

In short, no matter how one approached the Hampstead election, there was little for the league to take comfort in. The Conservative organization had repudiated the league's propositions and secured the adoption of its chosen candidate, Milvain. While the party might insist that only Unionists displayed the firm resolve necessary to maintain Britain's naval supremacy, in this case it was evident that other claims were accorded priority. Local candidates' views on the naval question were subordinated to other considerations. Similarly, the local Unionists were not swayed by navalist arguments; partisan loyalty continued to take precedence over any supposed navalist priorities. Those Navy

League members who presumed that the naval issue might serve as a patriotic umbrella under which to unite supporters of different parties saw their hopes dashed. For navalism was insufficient to reconcile even Unionist factionalism within a single, small, solidly Tory constituency, let alone within the nation at large. Indeed, some observers drew from Hampstead the conclusion that navalists should abandon any pretensions of political neutrality and face the realities of the situation. One member, Charles Stribling, ridiculed the phrase "strictly non-party" and argued "that it served no useful purpose, whatever, but quite otherwise. All who take interest or action in the political life of this Empire know this league cannot be conducted on such lines with success," he continued, and, as if to emphasize this point, he predicted that "we cannot hope to approach the German Navy League in numbers until the words 'strictly non-party' are expunged from our declaration."[101] Stribling claimed that "many others were displeased at the action of the Navy League," and indeed it was difficult to deny that the league's own president had flagrantly violated the league's "non-party" creed by choosing a nondescript Unionist over a Liberal navalist. In the 7 years since the league's formation, it had helped to organize and articulate navalist sentiment, but the efficiency, clarity, and direction of its efforts remained in doubt.

2

National Inefficiency:
Diagnosis and Prescription

If the year 1815 had occasioned celebration and self-satisfaction, 1902 did not inspire comparable elation. In both years the British finally brought military conflicts to a successful conclusion, but the difficulty experienced in eventually defeating two small Boer republics seemed all the more disturbing for the future when compared with the triumphs of the past. The death of Queen Victoria in 1901, just a few weeks after the advent of the new century, appeared to symbolize the end of a distinct and memorable era in British history. So the question that journalist J. L. Garvin would pose to his readers in 1905 was already a familiar one. "Will the Empire which is celebrating one centenary of Trafalgar," he wondered, "survive for the next?"[1] Garvin was inclined to be pessimistic, and he was by no means alone in his assessment. Throughout the country voices were raised in consideration of the new "condition of England" question, a debate no longer confined to the social impact of industrialization, but one that considered in the broadest terms the country's position as a great power.

As a result, the nationalist agitation entered a new phase in 1902. In particular, the naval issue relinquished center stage, to be replaced by the state of the nation's military and economic health as the principal topics of concern. Both the economy's deceleration and susceptibility to foreign competition and the army's embarrassing reverses in the Boer War lent credence to the view that England was an "inefficient" nation. Often couched in elaborate biological metaphors, this diagnosis indicated that settled, aging England was not meeting the challenge posed by younger, more vigorous nations, above all Germany.[2] Prescriptions to eradicate inefficiency, while they varied widely, nonetheless shared the assumption that traditions and cherished, time-honored practices were in large part responsible for England's current arthritic condition.

Military Necessity and National Service

Understandably, much attention was focused on the army's traditional reliance on voluntary enlistment. For centuries, a volunteer army had been extolled as

38

the best guarantee of civil liberties; an army of conscripts, on the other hand, aroused the long-standing antipathy toward standing armies and smacked of continental-style militarism. The fiascos of the Boer War, however, suggested that a volunteer force might ultimately threaten rather than guarantee the preservation of English liberty because of its inferior military capability. Yet the inviolability of voluntarism in preference to coercion was a principle so firmly established that to dispute it was tantamount to heresy. Given the enormity of such a task, then, the heretics sought institutional expression by forming the National Service League in February 1902. In so doing, they consciously looked to the Navy League as their model. J. G. B. Stopford, for example, in advocating the need for some sort of "Army League," explained that "the success of the Navy League in bringing home to the mind of the nation the overwhelming importance of adequately protecting our coasts and our vast commercial fleet . . . is, doubtless, the cause of looking to a league to endeavor to place our land forces on an equally safe footing."[3]And, as National Service League spokesman Colonel Pilkington argued, "the Navy League had done a great deal for the efficiency of the navy, and public opinion made the authorities do what they would not otherwise have done, and it seemed to him [Pilkington] that the National Service League might do something in the same way for the defences at home."[4]

There certainly was a similarity of purpose. The National Service League sought to direct the public's attention to the inadequacy of a particular service to meet the requirements of a major war. The Boer War had demonstrated how difficult it was to field a large, properly trained army in a crisis. Too few experienced professionals were available; men volunteered in sufficient numbers, but a staggering sum were found unfit on grounds of poor health. The suspicions of local recruiting authorities (in Manchester the proportion of men rejected on medical grounds ran as high as 40 percent) were hardly dispelled by the sobering statistics in the 1904 report of the Committee on Physical Deterioration.[5] Moreover, those men who could enlist then required the necessary physical and mental training to enable them to function effectively in combat. The continental powers, by relying on conscription, had a substantial pool of previously trained men who could rapidly be mobilized, while an ill-prepared England struggled in vain to catch up with a band of amateurs. But the National Service League was prepared to push its case further. After all, it might be contended that the aim of British diplomacy was to avoid those commitments that would embroil them in a major continental war and that a large professional army was therefore irrelevant to the pursuit or protection of British interests. The Royal Navy, on this reading, was the crucial instrument of British policy and thus sea power the proper focus of governmental expenditure and military preparation.

The National Service League would have none of this, arguing that the real danger lay close to home. Rejecting the notion that the fleet could guarantee Britain's security from invasion, the league contended that English citizens must face the possibility of having to repel an invading army (probably, though not necessarily, German) as it stormed ashore the English beaches. It took as its *urtext* George F. Shee's *The Briton's First Duty*, published in 1901, which argued that adequate military training was each male's civic responsibility. Suitable training could only be achieved through conscription, though the euphemism *national service* was substituted in recognition of the difficult struggle that the league faced in seeking to overturn deep-seated popular preconceptions. The spotlight of the nationalist agitation had shifted, despite the continued opposition of the "blue water school," which maintained that the fleet unaided would be capable of repelling any invasion.[6] Indeed, if anything, the national service issue proved divisive for those who had slowly, painfully begun to articulate a navalist position. It would be incorrect, however, to suggest a decisive fracture in the nationalist bloc between supporters of the Navy League and those of the National Service League. Some Navy Leaguers were sympathetic to the proposals of the new organization and hoped to enact both a major naval building program and conscription as the surest way to security. Within a month, in March 1902, the Navy League contacted Shee, and there were subsequent efforts to avoid friction between the two organizations.[7]

Nonetheless, there were important points of dispute. First, the prospect existed that a dual-pronged agitation, so to speak, might degenerate into a bitter interservice rivalry for limited funds and thus that every additional pound sterling allocated to the army might produce a corresponding reduction in the naval estimates. If concessions were granted to both services, then other areas of governmental expenditure might be imperiled unless fresh sources of revenue could be found. Increased taxation would be an obvious source of such revenue, but might alienate the prosperous strata of society in which the navalists had found an important base of support. Second, there was cause for concern as to how the British public would accept the National Service League's message. While the Navy League's stress on naval supremacy seemed in accordance with the nation's heritage and traditions, it could not be disguised that conscription conspicuously lacked a similar basis in the recent British past. Indeed, like free trade and soggy vegetables, voluntary enlistment was prized as one of those features that distinguished the English from their less fortunate continental neighbors. In fact, some Navy Leaguers had advocated naval expansion as a means of avoiding conscription; they feared that public debate on military issues might blur the distinction they had drawn and thus lump them with the conscriptionists as a group of militarist lunatics deserving the public's opprobrium. What little credibility the navalists had so painstakingly achieved would be squandered.

These difficulties were not resolved by the National Service League's concessions to public opinion. Rather than openly admit that it advocated conscription, the league preferred to stress the necessity of some form of "universal training," "compulsory service," or "national service." The National Service League was constantly on the defensive, having to explain how universal training would not disrupt the economy or promote despised "Prussianism." League officials even felt compelled to travel to Switzerland to publicize Swiss "national service," which clearly had neither threatened Swiss democracy nor generated Swiss militarism. Like its predecessor, the National Service League grew slowly, numbering only 1,725 members by October 1904.[8] With the Navy League it also shared the label of "scaremonger," which its claims to act as "an instrument of peace" did little to dispel. Nor could the National Service League look to the Unionist party for much in the way of support. While there was some sympathy within the party for the league's position, only a rash politician would have staked his career on compulsory service. For its initial 3 years, then, the league lacked a celebrity to speak with conviction and authority on its behalf.

Confronted by the dilemma of securing popular support for an unpopular platform, and caught between a hostile party (the Liberals) and a hesitant and suspicious one (the Unionists), the advocates of national service rehearsed many of the same debates and decisions that the naval issue had precipitated. They stressed their nonpartisan stance. In the *National Service League Journal*'s inaugural issue, for example, an enthusiastic greeting by Lord Beresford was followed by an appeal that began with the ominous question, "Are you a Conservative?" Those readers who answered in the affirmative were assured that the advocacy of national service would bring "security."[9] Yet the league had good things in store for those of differing partisan loyalties: Liberals were promised social amelioration; Radicals, an equitably distributed burden of defense; and Socialists, a practical form of cooperative socialism. Just as heightened concentration on the naval issue would, in the view of the Navy League, produce benefits beyond the assurance of national security, so too national service was touted for its social and moral effects. The rigors of outdoor training in the English countryside would soon invigorate the constitution of even the most pallid denizen of the nation's working-class districts. Here, in particular, the league was responding to the revelations of persistent malnutrition and prevalent disease, a view that dovetailed neatly with the Navy League's emphasis on the precariousness of Britain's food supply. Indeed, the editor of the *Navy League Journal* had expressed very similar sentiments several years earlier when he argued that England's national character had softened. He had attributed this lamentable deterioration in part to "the long reign of peace and the essentially unmilitary character of the people."[10]

Character as well as physique would be toughened; the National Service League preached a form of patriotic self-reliance that harked back to the sturdy English yeoman or the Crecy longbowmen. Nonetheless, independence had its limits, for national service was envisioned as a means of organizing a coherent, collective force for home defense with a recognizable hierarchy of command. In its list of projected readers, the league included clergymen, to whom it suggested that the league promoted "self-control and obedience." This echoed Prussian sentiments of the army as the "school of the nation," in that military service, even if experienced in the informal settings of rifle clubs or home defense units, left an indelible mark upon the participants. Submission to higher authority as an ingrained, reflexive response was a lesson civilians, presumably intoxicated with free discussion, might find difficult to learn. But it was one that was essential to military discipline. Once learned, the habit of deference would persist when the trainee returned to civilian life. To Conservative politicians this prospect appeared wholly admirable. As character improved, inefficiency waned. As submissiveness to constituted authority increased, threats to the domestic status quo diminished. National service, in other words, could serve a dual purpose: improve Britain's capacity to resist its external enemies and arrest the spread of internal enemies, namely, progressive or, especially, socialist movements. While the league's propaganda might preach the democratic aspects of national service in the universal participation and camaraderie this would foster and might label this as a form of cooperative socialism, the advocates of compulsory training envisioned anything but truly democratic values.

Economic Necessity and Tariffs

Whatever the domestic ramifications, it is unlikely that the National Service League would have been founded without appreciation of the growing threat posed by Germany. The mercurial Kaiser's clearly stated preference for a Boer victory and his commitment to a major program of German naval expansion were more than sufficient to arouse anxiety. When H. O. Arnold-Forster reported on his visit to the German ports of Kiel and Wilhelmshaven in August 1902, he concluded that "against England alone is such a weapon as the modern German navy necessary; against England, unless all available evidence and all probability combine to mislead, that weapon is being prepared."[11] Selborne, the First Lord of the Admiralty, agreed, confiding to the cabinet that "the new German navy is being carefully built up from the point of view of a war with us."[12] It could not be intended for a war against France or Russia, he instructed his colleagues, because that type of conflict could "only be decided by armies and on land, and the great naval expansion on which Germany has embarked involves a deliberate diminution of the military strength which Germany might otherwise have attained in relation to France and Russia." But the German threat was not purely a military one, or, more precisely, the military challenge rested upon the spectacular recent achievement of German industry, which contrasted so sharply with a lackluster British performance.

The Royal Commission constituted to investigate the Depression in Trade and Industry (1886) was a preliminary but clear manifestation of growing unease about the British economy, as indeed was the Fair Trade League as well. Increasingly, attention was directed toward Germany, whether as an example of "efficiency" to be copied by inefficient Britons or as the source of the nation's economic difficulties to be despised for having unfairly disrupted British trade. A series of articles in the *Times*, collected by Arthur Williamson as *British Industries and Foreign Competition* (1894), pointed the finger squarely at Germany. More important, however, and comparable to Mahan's work in its significance in drawing together various strands of debate and focusing public attention, was the publication in 1896 of *Made in Germany* by E. E. Williams.[13] Prompted by the Merchandise Marks Act of 1887, which had required all foreign products to be marked with their country of origin,

Williams advised his readers to "roam the house over and the fateful mark will greet you at every turn."[14] Whether one peered under the piano or rifled through the cutlery, they were sure to be stamped "Made In Germany." England's industrial glory, he warned, "is departing and England does not know it." After surveying various sectors of British industry and comparing them unfavorably with their German counterparts, Williams summarized his recommendations in a chapter entitled simply, "What We Must Do To Be Saved." "A consideration of the facts," he explained, "forces the conviction that England's Free Trade policy, existing side by side with protection in Germany, has been responsible in no small degree for the strides which Germany has made at England's expense."[15] The "inevitable conclusion," in Williams' view, was that "our fiscal policy requires to be reviewed if not recast." Specifically, he urged commercial federation of the empire, secured by imperial preference, and insisted that "Fair Trade is within the range of practical politics."[16]

In anticipating the natural triumph of Fair Trade in 1896, however, Williams was unduly optimistic. Just 3 years earlier the Imperial Federation League had collapsed because many of its members had insisted on deferring any economic reforms until closer military cooperation within the empire could be arranged. Some who espoused commercial federation did so only to disguise their blatant protectionism in the more fashionable form of imperialism. Moreover, when in 1895 the Fair Trade League had dissolved, the Conservative party did not seek to resurrect it for fear of alienating the Liberal Unionists, who finally had agreed to accept office within a Unionist administration.[17] Salisbury's magisterial leadership and delicate success in defusing controversial issues boded ill for potential dissidents. Thus in early 1902 the grounds for nationalist agitation were still not fully developed. The Hampstead fiasco and the National Service League's undramatic foundation both suggested that the naval and conscription issues would neither arouse enormous public support nor budge the Conservative leadership from its olympian position. Yet within a few months the situation would be transformed.

In April 1902, Sir Michael Hicks-Beach, the chancellor of the exchequer, reimposed a registration duty on imported corn. He defended this action as a wartime expedient necessary to raise revenue, insisted that it would only be temporary, and denied that it signalled a return to protectionism. Several months later, in July, Salisbury retired, and with the change of administration Hicks-Beach was replaced by C. T. Ritchie, who was known to be uncompromising in defense of free trade principles. It was not long, indeed, before Ritchie was at odds with his cabinet colleague Colonial Secretary Joseph Chamberlain. The Canadian government had hinted that perhaps the registration duty might be retained and made the basis of a preferential remission in Canada's favor. While the Canadian "request" was never explicit, Chamberlain seized upon it as proof of widespread sentiment within the empire in favor of imperial preference. He raised the matter of reciprocal preference with Canada in the cabinet in October 1902. Then, believing he had convinced his colleagues to support continuation of the registration duty although the Boer War had ended, Chamberlain departed for a 3 month tour of South Africa. In Chamberlain's absence, however, Ritchie worked to reverse the cabinet's sympathies by alluding to the tenuousness of the Canadian reaction and citing powerful arguments drafted by the Treasury. Ritchie eventually persuaded his colleagues that the British public would reject the duty in peacetime as a politically disastrous food tax and an impediment to British foreign trade. When Chamberlain returned, therefore, in March 1903, he found Ritchie prepared, apparently with the cabinet's blessing, to introduce a determinedly free trade budget.[18]

There has been much speculation, by both contemporaries and subsequent historians, about Chamberlain's motives for adopting the protectionist cause he had so vociferously repudiated in the past. After all, no more vocal opponent of fair trade had existed in the 1880s than the former mayor of Birmingham. Some observers suspected that Chamberlain's tariff reform campaign was an attempt to divert attention from his responsibility for disasters in South Africa, especially the fiasco of the Jameson Raid in which Chamberlain's complicity appeared likely.[19] Another interpretation was predicated on Chamberlain's ambition, superficially disguised, for it was commonly presumed that Chamberlain had been scheming for the premiership. Indeed, he had been incapacitated in a cab accident when Balfour succeeded Salisbury, a misfortune that some surmised Chamberlain regarded as having denied him his long-deserved post as prime minister. Thus tariff reform might be designed to overthrow Balfour before he had the opportunity to secure his own position. Not long after Chamberlain's return, for example, Lord George Hamilton commented that "the subtraction of Salisbury, Goschen and Beach from the Cabinet has upset the old balance of opinion, and Chamberlain is undoubtedly far stronger now." With remarkable prescience, he predicted that "Chamberlain is so fond of attempting a big coup that I never should be surprised if some proposition of a startling character were made."[20] Hamilton might also have mentioned the recent retirement of Captain Middleton, long-time chief of the party organization, whose departure might expose the constituencies to Chamberlain's predatory influence. A third alternative was suggested on the basis of what appeared to be an extraordinarily fluid period in party politics. Chamberlain's own party loyalty was clearly suspect—and no wonder, given his secession from the Liberal party and his commitment to the formal organizational independence of Liberal Unionism. Perhaps Chamberlain was not angling to supplant Balfour so much as to inaugurate a new centrist party. Such a possibility, unlikely in retrospect, seemed somewhat less farfetched in light of the dissension within the Liberal party that swirled around Lord Rosebery and the Liberal Imperialists.[21]

The prospect also might have appeared less outrageous if considered within the perspective of the nationalist agitation of the last decade. A persistent theme of that agitation had been the desirability of transcending established partisan rivalries and constructing a new consensus based upon certain essential national and patriotic issues. There had been much debate, however, whether such an attempt would dissolve party conflict or crystallize it further. In short, might the Unionists strengthen their position by monopolizing English nationalist appeals? Certainly their Liberal opponents were divided over the Boer War, and that fact that Liberal critics of the war (the so-called pro-Boers) were roundly criticized by fellow Liberals (the Liberal Imperialists) suggested that under further pressure party allegiances might waver. There was no likelihood of Liberal Imperialist defections to the Unionist party, but perhaps the imperial issue could be utilized to disrupt existing political groupings.

Few observers doubted that imperial themes were critical to Chamberlain's espousal of tariff reform. Those who sought to defend Chamberlain from his detractors and to discover a thread of consistency in his erratic career were apt to stress this commitment to the maintenance and unity of the empire. It was the strength of this belief that might link 1886 and 1903 and explain his extraordinarily destructive impact upon both major parties. Furthermore, as mayor of Birmingham he had not been inflexibly wedded to laissez-faire policies, and in 1902–1903, then, he was temperamentally inclined to measures of greater state intervention.[22] On this reading, preference, and thereby imperial unity, motivated Chamberlain, rather than mere protection for which Chamberlain explicitly contended "he would not even take off his coat."[23] His trip to South Africa was not coincidental, because he returned doubly convinced of the need to reintegrate the empire and confident that he had rediscovered the means to do so. Efforts to safeguard the empire with a German alliance had collapsed, only to be followed by a new German tariff in 1902. Frustrated abroad, and in the cabinet as well, Chamberlain logically turned to his loyal following in Birmingham, whom he addressed in a momentous speech on 15 May 1903.

Chamberlain's speech is regularly cited as the essential spark that ignited the tariff reform movement, an assessment that reflects both his stature as a politician and the controversial content ascribed to his text that May afternoon. One enthusiast hailed his speech as a challenge "as direct and provocative as the theses which Luther nailed to the Church door at Wittenberg."[24] In fact, Chamberlain assured his audience that his intention was only to initiate a discussion of Britain's fiscal system rather than to provide a fully developed alternative policy. He went little further, really, than the Fair Traders of the 1880s. The question, therefore, is why a speech that rehearsed relatively familiar arguments should have achieved such notoriety. A conventional answer is that Chamberlain's imprimatur was sufficient. It is certainly true that he provided a readily indentifiable focus for fiscal disputation, but his degree of intellectual engagement and creative rigor was hardly analogous to the role of Luther in the Protestant Reformation. Tariff reform was not reducible to "Chamberlainism," and the Birmingham autocrat did not develop and articulate a set of central texts to be digested and disseminated by awed and adoring disciples. Despite his undoubted talents, Chamberlain's speech would not have attracted such attention unless it were situated within an evolving debate given meaning, shape, and direction by the nationalist agitation. As his son Austen later recalled, "the immense echo of my father's speech in May 1903 is inexplicable unless it is appreciated that the train was already laid."[25]

On the very day of the Birmingham speech, Henry Chaplin, a Unionist MP whose sobriquet "the squire" conveyed his self-styled role as spokesman for the agricultural interest, led a deputation to Westminster to protest the removal of the corn registration duty. Prior to his defection from the Liberals, Chamberlain frequently had singled out the landed interest for harsh criticism ("they toil not, neither do they spin"). There was no assurance, therefore, that Chamberlain's enthusiasm for tariffs was not simply tailored to the needs of the Birmingham business community at the expense of the landlords he had once pilloried. Nor was the business community spurred to action solely by the clarion call of 15 May 1903. In March 1902, E. E. Williams, the author of *Made in Germany* and a journalist for the *Financial News*, had been requested by his editor, H. H. Marks, to assist in the formation of a protectionist organization. He agreed, despite the fact that there already had been several abortive attempts to do so previously. Twenty-four leading manufacturers met in April 1902 to discuss the foundation of a Fiscal Reform Association, but, despite considerable sympathy as evidenced by the collection of some 2,500 signatures for a manifesto, nothing specific materialized.[26] Changing tack, Marks later approached the industrialist George Byng to arrange a meeting at the Commons of sympathetic members to be chaired by the speaker, James Lowther. They assembled on 14 May 1903 to form the Protection League; according to Williams, "not a soul present had an inkling that the very next day Mr. Chamberlain was going to light his torch at Birmingham."[27] Although it seems Williams doth protest too much, the fiscal issue had reemerged prior to Chamberlain's speech, in fact had been a matter of discussion for the past year. Tariff reformers did not require a lead from Highbury before they discovered their convictions, and, if anything, the infant Protection League was initially skeptical of Chamberlain until he amplified his position in the Commons 2 weeks after the Birmingham speech.[28] Once Chamberlain had declared his position, even if he had not explained it, a process of semantic improvisation began to bowdlerize the new organization. The Protection League soon became the Imperial Tariff League, located in Pall Mall offices obligingly provided by Marks. Yet, in the face of friction between Marks and the veteran protectionist from Sheffield, Sir Howard Vincent, further cosmetic changes were necessary, and, on 21 July 1903, the Tariff Reform League finally emerged.[29] A note of urgency had intruded, for the rival Free Food League had beaten the new Tariff Reform League to the post by 8 days. In its current guise, any specific link with protectionism was dismissed, while the label "reform" was appropriated to suggest the league's progressive intentions.

The inaugural meeting, held, like that of the Navy League, in London's Westminster Palace Hotel, provided few clues about the new organization's intentions. Remaining preliminary arrangements were undertaken at Stafford House, the elegant London residence of the Duke of Sutherland, who served as the league's first president. He would have little to do with the actual administration, and the more significant positions were those of chairman, filled by *Daily Express* proprietor C. Arthur Pearson, and secretary, accepted by a lawyer, J. Ratcliffe Cousins. Noticeably absent was Joseph Chamberlain, despite what the press described as a "large attendance." The league's stated goal was "the defense and development of the industrial interests of the British Empire," an elastic definition that nonetheless seemed to relegate agricultural interests to a secondary role. Tariff reform would, in Sir Herbert Maxwell's summary for the audience, "add the bond of material interest to the already existing bond of sentiment which united the mother countries and the colonies."[30] A revision of Britain's fiscal system would allegedly solve two pressing problems. First, as British manufacturers secured improved terms of trade through the threat of protective retaliation, the domestic economic climate would improve. Second, the preferential remission of duties on colonial trade would stimulate commerce within the empire and thus promote durable bonds with Britain. The result would be a sort of "Colonial *Zollverein*," a customs union that would, as it had in the case of Prussia, stimulate economic growth, patriotic sentiment, and military power.[31] An ambitious agenda, then, at least as articulated in the exuberance of the founding meeting, and one that aroused expectations that the Tariff Reform League might yet achieve the successful synthesis that had eluded the Fair Trade and Imperial Federation movements of the 1880s and 1890s.

Chamberlain publicly extended his best wishes to the new league, but privately he remained cautious, proof again that the Tariff Reform League was not his personal creation. He confided to Jesse Collings that "I cannot depend entirely upon it, and I must have my own organisation, entirely under my control, which will deal with points that others may omit. That is the reason for the Birmingham Tariff Committee."[32] The latter, soon renamed the Imperial Tariff Committee, maintained offices in Birmingham staffed by Chamberlain's Liberal Unionist cronies.[33] Chamberlain served as president, in contrast to his studious avoidance of the same position in the league. He continued to brush aside requests for assistance or advice concerning the Tariff Reform League. Even an economist of stature such as W. A. S. Hewins, from whose professional advice Chamberlain might well have profited, was dismissed by the Birmingham politician with the curt response that "it is impossible for me, with the pressure upon me, to take any part in the organisation which is to help popularise the impending discussion."[34]

The "impending discussion," as Chamberlain dryly put it, would proceed on several levels. Clearly the attitude of the cabinet and the prime minister would be decisive insofar as tariff reformers might expect the assistance of the party. That would in turn affect the related problem of whether tariff reform was to be promoted as a Unionist or an independent policy, whether it should be disseminated through the official party machinery or, alternately, be confined to the distinct branches of the Tariff Reform League. Finally, Chamberlain's stress on the need to "popularise" tariff reform raised the question of its popular resonance. Would, for example, fiscal reform appeal to sectional interests, or could it be adapted to mobilize a broader audience? The proponents of the naval issue had sought an answer to the dilemmas of popular conservatism by stressing the precariousness of the nation's food supply and by implying that everyone benefitted from the navy's protection, even if the shipping and armaments industries' profits were the more visible. Yet protectionism was widely identified in the popular consciousness with greed, privilege, and sectional gain. Tariff reformers were thus faced with the burden of demonstrating that, contrary to widespread expectation, their policy could sustain a major nationalist agitation. None of these levels of discussion was independent, of course; it was the interplay between them that contributed to tariff reform's erratic momentum.

Within the cabinet, no resolution of the issue occurred until September 1903, and even then it was less that the matter was resolved than that the divisions of opinion were revealed with greater clarity. The politicians themselves had an imprecise notion of the economics at stake, a situation aggravated by Chamberlain's failure to enunciate the specifics of his new commitment to tariffs. Balfour correctly sensed the seriousness of the challenge Chamberlain represented, and thus he was reluctant either to endorse his colonial secretary's controversial propositions or to repudiate them in favor of an uncompromising defense of free trade. He instinctively sought the middle ground, fearing that to commit himself too firmly would spell the effective end of his leadership of the party and shatter the party itself as had happened in 1846. Above all, Balfour devoted the full measure of his skill, tact, and duplicity to avoid repeating the disastrous precedent (as he perceived it) of Sir Robert Peel's repeal of the Corn Laws, which had excluded the divided Conservatives from power for decades. His refusal, therefore, to depart from an intermediate position placed greater pressure on Chamberlain, whose advocacy of tariff reform might be considered a violation of the cabinet's convention of collective responsibility. By 18 September 1903, Chamberlain was persuaded that his new "unauthorized program" would be better served if he resigned from the cabinet, a course also adopted by a trio of his colleagues—C. T. Ritchie, Lord Balfour of Burleigh, and Lord George Hamilton—who felt their staunch free trade convictions were compromised by Balfour's delicate intermediate position.[35] The defections were not halted by Balfour's effort at public justification in a speech to the annual meeting of the National Union of Conservative Associations in Sheffield on 1 October. His position could best be described as nonprotective retaliation, by which he suggested the possibility of moderate, temporary duties intended to promote freer trade. Retaliation would enlighten Britain's protectionist trading partners by forcing them to suffer the consequences of their ill-considered actions. He expressed sympathy toward the tariff reformers' goal of imperial preference but refused to accept that their chosen course, which included food duties, lay within the realm of "practical politics."

To prove effective, Balfour's delicate balancing act necessitated the demonstration that the alternate positions were either impractical or incompatible with the traditions of the Unionist party. If his audiences suspected that tariffs would lose votes or that they would innovate dangerously rather than conserve, the inertia of indecision would preserve his position and, so he hoped, the party. Tariff reformers would have to give serious consideration to the second of these propositions, namely, the accommodation of a tariff reform platform within the conservative tradition, but any effort to do so was partly predicated on the popular response to the fiscal issue. After the lull during the summer of 1903 was dispelled by the cabinet contortions in the fall, the tariff reformers redoubled their efforts. Five days after Balfour's Sheffield speech, Chamberlain himself in Glasgow inaugurated a major series of speeches designed to clarify his position and to generate a surge of momentum that Balfour and Conservative Central Office would find irresistible.[36]

Political Necessity in the Constituencies

Chamberlain's well-publicized tour coincided with, and itself stimulated, an upsurge of political activity on the local level. Anticipating the inevitable dissension, the ardent protectionist Sir Howard Vincent adopted the unusual course of publishing an open letter in July 1903 to all Conservative agents. "The present situation is undoubtedly a difficult one," he admitted. Recognizing that most agents would have strong prior convictions on the fiscal issue, he reminded them of the unique opportunities they enjoyed to "mix with the masses of the electorate [or to address them] in small gatherings" and therefore to "know what subjects are popular with them."[37] Vincent conceded that the local member of Parliament or prominent supporters might well be "lukewarm or even hostile," but sought to turn that possibility to his account, arguing that

> It will, however, generally be found that the more decided a Parliamentary candidate or representative is, the more decided will be his majority and his hold on the constituency. What voters, and working men especially, abhor is an undecided man. Strong opinions produce, of course, bitter hostility. But even opponents respect a determined attitude and a fixed purpose, while they are invaluable in arousing enthusiasm.[38]

Vincent assured the party agents that both the National Union and the Primrose League intended to preserve an impartial attitude, but he had structured his argument in such a way that it encapsulated several of the themes tariff reformers would subsequently develop. Although he pleaded with agents to "avoid committing their Party to a hostile attitude to the new proposals until they have been thoroughly examined in all their bearings," Vincent's contemptuous dismissal of a "wait and see" attitude carried the clear implications that hesitant Free Traders, and probably Balfour too, lacked the decisive resolve of the tariff reformers. He urged the "education of the electorate" and explained the sources from which agents might receive protectionist literature.

Vincent's assessment, entitled simply "the situation," may be interpreted as an effort to persuade skeptics that tariff reform could be practical and that they should not, therefore, reflexively dismiss it in deference to the prevailing ascendancy of free trade. He recognized the weight of potential opposition. The group most susceptible to dissension was Chamberlain's own Liberal Unionist party, which had since 1886 existed as a curious amalgam of Whigs and Radicals whose distaste for each other was sufficiently overshadowed by their opposition to Irish home rule to perpetuate a tenuous cooperation. The Whiggish section of Liberal Unionism, however, could not be ignored, for it included politicians of weight and stature within the country and the cabinet. Above all, they looked to the Duke of Devonshire, whose lineage and service were presumed to have produced political wisdom. Chamberlain's problem was that the duke was a firm free trader, "content to leave his financial conscience in the hands of Mr. Gladstone," and contemptuous of protectionist arguments as "all a muddle."[39] He was suspicious of "pushful Joe," who seemed to spout economic claptrap, who aroused class antagonism, and whose methods seemed directed at reducing the influence of the aristocratic circles that the duke himself exemplified. Devonshire had resigned after Balfour's Sheffield speech in distress over the prime minister's evident doubts about free trade and his questionable conduct during the cabinet crisis in mid-September. With both Chamberlain and Devonshire no longer restrained by the responsibilities of office, the conflict between tariff reformers and Unionist free traders quickly escalated. Chamberlain sought to distribute tariff reform propaganda through the official Liberal Unionist party organization, a policy that the duke stoutly opposed, but unsuccessfully. Goaded by this defeat and by Chamberlain's impressive autumn tour, Devonshire responded on 12 December 1903 by publishing an open letter advising Unionist voters not to support any candidate advocating tariff reform.[40] His letter was timed for maximum effect, since two by-elections were scheduled for 15 December at Dulwich and Lewisham. It was widely presumed that these elections would offer the first real public verdict on the progress of tariff reform as it had developed since the policy addresses of early October. Devonshire's letter stressed that the defense of free trade should take precedence, if necessary, over party loyalty; the implication was that Liberalism was a lesser evil than protectionism.

A Liberal windfall, however, was not immediately forthcoming. The results of the two by-elections exceeded the hopes of even the most ardent tariff reformer. The Unionists took both seats, despite the fact that the tariff reform candidate for Dulwich, Rutherford Harris, had an appalling record. He had been unseated from Monmouth Burghs for illegal electoral practices and censured for his part in the Jameson Raid.[41] If a candidate of such questionable accomplishments could win a seat in the face of determined opposition from members of his camp, who could imagine what the tariff reformers might accomplish? Minds were certainly excited at Victoria Street, headquarters of the Tariff Reform League, where Cousins, the secretary, boldly proclaimed that the league "is by resolution determined to oppose the return of all free fooders whether Unionist or Radical, and we shall use the whole of our organization for this object."[42]

Accordingly, the Tariff Reform League intensified its activity in the constituencies. It was not long before Unionist agents responded to the intrusions. As one explained:

> I write a few lines for the information of brother Agents who have not yet come into personal contact with the Tariff Reform League. In the first place,

let me explain that I have the honour to serve an Association which might be, but is not, over-burdened with funds. There is in the constituency a Liberal Unionist Association, which taps one wealthy section to the extent of a few hundred, and a County Conservative Association which does the same. So when the Tariff Reform League sent an agent here I naturally enquired whether, if they started a local branch, they were going to solicit funds. I was solemnly assured by the representative that this was not the intention, as they had all they required. To cut a long story short, Agent No. 1 has gone, and in his place a Permanent Agent has been appointed with instructions to collect sufficient funds to pay local expenses. What good the Tariff Reform League is going to do here for the money I fail to see, especially as my candidate is not a "Whole Hogger." Personally, I am debating in my mind whether I had better not anticipate events by starting a Free Trade Unionist Association. As the Tariff Reform League advance agents generally call on Conservative Agents on their arrival in a strange constituency, I thought by giving your readers my own experience, they may use their own judgement in the matter.[43]

Such local friction contributed to a series of embarrassing by-election reverses that the league absorbed in the first few months of 1904 and that swiftly dispelled the euphoria of the previous December. The Tariff Reform League responded by renewing its pledge to defeat Unionist Free Traders. Successful opposition to a few of the more prominent ones would serve to warn vacillating candidates (those who suspected that recent by-elections indicated the prudence of a middle course) that their failure to embrace tariff reform would lead to defeat.

In many ways the principal villain of the 1903 Cabinet Crisis, from the league's perspective, had been C. T. Ritchie. As chancellor of the exchequer, he had been responsible for convincing the cabinet in Chamberlain's absence to abolish the temporary registration duty on corn rather than retain it as the first measure toward a comprehensive system of imperial preference. In October 1903 a Tariff Reform League branch was established in Ritchie's constituency, Croydon, with maximum fanfare, including addresses by league heavyweights Edward Goulding and Henry Chaplin. Fifteen meetings were held on the ward level within the next 2 months, and twenty members of the local Unionist association's executive committee were persuaded to join the new branch. Furthermore, "a thorough canvass of the Division was undertaken and a house to house distribution of literature made." The total amount of literature thus distributed, including material handed out at various local meetings, amounted to 500,000 leaflets.[44] Fourteen articles highly critical of free trade and of Ritchie's position were authored by the league's literary department and obligingly published in the town's Unionist weekly, the *Croydon Guardian*. Having created an environment favorable to tariff reform, the league secured the repudiation of Ritchie by his local association and the substitution of a candidate who would stand firm on tariffs. Resolutions were laid before the Croydon association in July 1904 that any candidate representing the association must accept a program of fiscal reform and imperial preference. The resolutions were justified on the grounds that both items were elements of

Unionist party policy. As the league's report on Croydon recounted, "by a systematic organization a full attendance of tariff reformers was secured at the Unionist Association meeting, and these resolutions were carried."[45] Later that month the 66-year-old Ritchie reluctantly announced that he would not stand at the next election.

Another constituency earmarked for action was Durham, held since 1898 by Arthur Elliot. He had served as financial secretary to the Treasury and had resigned his position in September 1903 in the wake of the exodus of Ritchie, Balfour of Burleigh, and Hamilton from the cabinet. His staunch adherence to free trade provoked dissatisfaction among local Chamberlainites, and in January 1904 a Durham branch of the Tariff Reform League was founded. Two local tariff reform MPs, Sir George Doughty and Sir Henry Seton-Karr, helped the league to orchestrate a campaign against Elliot and to promote John W. Hills, a Chamberlainite solicitor, as his possible replacement. Hills could point to his Eton and Balliol education and to a captaincy in the Bedford-shire Yeomanry, but his record clearly paled before that of Elliot. League pressure against Elliot was difficult to resist, however, and, after Chamberlain himself intervened personally by endorsing Hills, the Durham Constitutional Association repudiated Elliot and adopted Hills in January 1905. Elliot would be forced to stand as an independent Unionist with Liberal support.[46]

A similar pattern prevailed in Greenwich, which had returned one of the most talented and vocal of the Unionist Free Traders, Lord Hugh Cecil. A Tariff Reform League branch was formed in Greenwich to coordinate anti-Cecilian activity and to intimidate the local Conservative association. In July 1904 the local league branch felt strong enough to denounce Cecil and to demand a new candidate; although the Conservative association was as yet unwilling to repudiate him, it did nonetheless in October raise some doubts about Cecil's reelection. In January 1905 the Tariff Reform League organized a major meeting in opposition to Cecil, and, 2 weeks later, on 7 February, his association formally requested that Cecil not stand for reelection for Green-wich.[47] Only thirty or forty of the local association's members were still willing to support him. Cecil, however, was made of sterner stuff. He was Balfour's cousin; but, nepotism aside, it was universally agreed among impartial ob-servers that his talent would be a tremendous loss the party could ill afford. Ten days later, Conservative Chief Whip Acland-Hood sprang to Cecil's defense and urged the Greenwich Conservatives to readopt him. Chamberlain, who hoped the Tariff Reform League would "give special attention to Greenwich," countered with a letter criticizing Cecil and proposing I. Hamilton Benn as a more suitable candidate, given that his advocacy of tariff reform was not in dispute. As in Durham, the tariff reform candidate was officially adopted, and Cecil chose to run as an independent Unionist in a three-cornered contest.[48]

Despite these local achievements, throughout 1904 tariff reform continued to face obstacles. Writing in midyear to explain "why by-elections are lost," a veteran party agent noted that many local Conservative associations were reluctant to educate the electorate on tariff reform, despite that fact that, in his view, it was "unquestionably the winning card in any constituency where proper steps are taken."[49] Chamberlain bitterly complained that he had fought "almost alone" on the fiscal issue.[50] In December 1904, Balfour received reports that Chamberlain was in "a rather badly hurt frame of mind" and that "he alluded bitterly to Hood and Wells and said they worked against him everywhere."[51] The same month Chamberlain proposed to Acland-Hood that he appoint an official representative from the Conservative Central Office to sit on the Tariff Reform League's executive committee. Selborne foresaw "difficulties in the proposal," but believed it to be a "bone fide one to satisfy Hood that the Tariff Reform League is running straight as regards his members."[52] Balfour, ever alert to the ambiguities and difficulties of any situation, decided it was impossible "to have an official representative on the Tariff Reform Committee without incurring some responsibility for the operations of that impulsive organization."[53]

Impulsive, perhaps, and sometimes inefficient as well. Joseph Chamberlain agreed with league enthusiast Lord Ridley's suggestion in November 1904 for an executive committee meeting "at which the present situation might be frankly discussed. I am well aware," he informed Ridley, "that it is not entirely satisfactory."[54] Inevitably, responsibility rested with the chairman of the executive committee, C. Arthur Pearson, who fatally undermined his position when he published an unauthorized tariff program in the *Standard* during January and February 1905. Pearson "wants to have a policy of his own which will not go exactly as I do, or on my lines," Chamberlain remarked to Hewins, and which, he added, "may therefore commend itself to the weak-kneed among his supporters."[55] Insubordination was thus compounded by vacillation. Within a week Chamberlain had decided. Pearson must go. "I am much disappointed at Pearson's action and do not understand it," he first explained to Hewins, before drawing the logical conclusion.

> It will not do, however, that the political cause which we have at heart should be in any way prejudiced in order to suit the exigencies of a newspaper, and while we have no right to press Mr. Pearson to do anything against his own interest we must I think ask him to separate his fortunes from ours so that each may stand on their own.[56]

Shortly thereafter Pearson officially resigned as chairman, ostensibly in response to the increasing pressure of work and to his failing eyesight.[57] To replace Pearson, Chamberlain invited Lord Ridley, already prominent in the Northern Tariff Reform Federation (a regional grouping of league branches), which had just successfully secured the repudiation of Arthur Elliot by the Unionist association in Durham. The terms of Chamberlain's offer were designed to remedy the abuses he associated with Pearson's lax tenure as chairman: he proposed to initiate and to attend weekly committee meetings (at least during the parliamentary session) and insisted upon "a chairman with leisure who can make himself fully acquainted with the work that is going on and arrange and conduct the business for the weekly meetings."[58]

There was no guarantee that greater efficiency, however, would yield corresponding results, especially in constituencies that habitually voted Conservative. In the London borough of East Marylebone, for example, the league sought to dislodge the sitting Unionist Free Trader Lord Robert Cecil (Lord Hugh's brother). The local Tariff Reform League branch demanded in mid-December that Cecil pledge himself to favor a tariff intended to strengthen Britain's position in the negotiation of commercial treaties (namely, retaliation), to accept a general tariff on foreign manufactured goods, and to support Chamberlain's policy of colonial preference. As expected, Cecil refused to accept dictation from the league; the combination of Balfour's support, his own stature within the party, and, above all, the failure of the league to persuade any credible candidate to oppose Lord Robert Cecil, enabled him to override, temporarily, at least, any local opposition.[59] Not far to the south, in Norwood, the league attempted to unseat G. Stewart Bowles, though it chose to proceed through both the local Unionist association and the corresponding Tariff Reform League branch. The Norwood Conservative Association met late in October 1905 to consider Bowles' fiscal views and formulated a resolution to be conveyed to their candidate for his endorsement:

> That this meeting records its conviction that a readjustment of taxation on a broader basis will ameliorate the present condition of trade and lessen the number of unemployed; believing also, that the adoption of a system of colonial preference is essential for the purpose of widening the area of food production within the limits of the Empire, as well as for safeguarding our Colonial Trade, pledges itself to support only such parliamentary candidate who, clearly and without reservation, declares himself to be in favor of fiscal reform. . . .[60]

Bowles was willing to support the possibility of occasional retaliation and to initiate negotiations toward closer economic relations within the empire, which he understood to constitute the platform of Balfour himself. He construed the resolution, however, as an expression of Chamberlain's more drastic policy, including food taxes and a general protective tariff, both propositions that he utterly rejected as beyond the party platform or electoral realization. "If you wish," he informed the association, "I shall be most happy to join with you in writing to Mr. Balfour to ask him which of us has most correctly interpreted his meaning."[61] Tariff reformers refused to budge, and Bowles was warned that his "interpretation of the pronouncements of the Prime Minister is one the Executive Committee cannot possibly accept." Bowles, for his part, persisted in the opinion that he, not his opponents, better understood the party's policy. "The difference between us is thus quite definite," he responded, and, repeating his view that Balfour had commited himself neither to the "preferential taxation of food" nor to "a general protective tariff", he advised the committee that nothing further could be accomplished "until this plain question of fact has been settled." After another month of debate, the Norwood Tariff Reform League finally labeled Bowles "a decided opponent of the erection in this country of any general protective tariff" and denied him their assistance in the forthcoming election. Despite its chastising tone, this reproach was little more than an admission of Bowles' tactical success in cloaking himself in the ambiguity of party policy, which in turn hampered (and in Norwood precluded) efforts to run an opposing tariff reform candidate.[62]

Whatever tariff reform had accomplished by the end of 1905, it clearly had prompted unusual dissension within the Conservative and Liberal Unionist parties. Tariff reformers were prepared to lay at least a measure of the blame directly at the feet of their party leader, Arthur Balfour. The Conservative agent for Scotland warned of the "belief in many minds that the Prime Minister has not stated with sufficient clearness of definition his policy about tariff reform."[63] Indeed, Balfour deliberately cultivated ambiguity as the only means to preserve even a semblance of party unity, despite the volume of criticism his tactical dexterity provoked. He was condemned for seeking refuge in philosophy and golf, and his treatise in defense of philosophic doubt was pilloried as evidence of an effeminate character that contrasted with Chamberlain's "manly," straightforward stand on the issue. It had been the differing interpretations that could be placed upon Balfour's policy that prolonged the debate between Bowles and the Norwood whole-hoggers. An unambiguous lead from Balfour, tariff reformers asserted, would minimize divisions and popularize policy. Yet Balfour's studied evasiveness was ultimately the result, and not the cause, of tariff reform's divisiveness.

Fiscal Fictions and Factions

Reasons for tariff reform's controversial nature lay elsewhere. Fiscal reform was presumed to have a direct bearing on Britain's position as a world power. When two Navy League MPs had raised the issue of food supply and the nation's survival in 1897, Henry Seton-Karr had concluded his speech by urging commercial federation of the empire and contending that "free trade was a question, not of principle, but of expediency."[64] This was a theme to which protectionists warmed. James Lowther seized the opportunity to instruct his colleagues in the House that "our present fiscal system could not go on providing us with unlimited revenue. Therefore, those who deliberately excluded from the possibilities of the near future a return on a large scale to a system of indirect taxation were cutting themselves off from the only source of revenue that would be available in a time of real pressure in this country."[65] Britain was now, in the view of tariff reformers, susceptible to "real pressure."

Tariff reform, then, involved an analysis of the sources of Britain's weakness that inevitably colored the nature of the solutions it anticipated. Like the navalists, tariff reformers feared that their country's ability to compete in the world had suffered in relation to the growth (in particular) of German power. It had been the vulnerability of commerce in war that Seton-Karr and Yerburgh had broached in 1897, but the issue quickly shaded into the nation's economic health. One of Chamberlain's most decisive contributions lay in the fact that he reemphasized the imperial aspects of the problem, namely, that Britain's empire appeared to exhibit dangerous signs of fragmentation at precisely the point when European rivals were extending their own colonial possessions. He would not rest content, therefore, with transient measures of retaliation designed to elicit more equitable commercial relations with Britain's trading partners. The increased prosperity that such adjustments might bring to British manufacturers was desirable, but not in itself sufficient. In this regard, then, nationalist agitation had moved beyond the concerns of many Fair Traders of the 1880s for whom the prospect of this limited improvement was satisfactory enough.

Increasingly the issue became one of resources and British power. Only by relying on the additional resources of its empire could Britain compensate for its deficiencies, in population or in agricultural production, for example. Colonial markets, if secured largely (or perhaps exclusively) for British goods, would stimulate domestic industry and, of equal or greater importance, sharpen consciousness of a great shared tradition. There was an unmistakable racial tone to aspects of tariff reform predicated on the belief in Anglo-Saxon destiny and capacity that constituted an immense moral and military reservoir awaiting only the capable politician determined to tap it.[66] If the problem of Britain's changing position was diagnosed in this manner, then clearly the solution must involve the colonies to a significant degree. This was the attraction of colonial preference—a reciprocal remission of duties between mother country and colonies.[67] Assuming that trade would seek the path of least resistance, it would naturally gravitate in the desired direction rather than struggle in vain against obstacles to commerce erected by European rivals. One can understand why retaliation, as espoused by Balfour, was deemed inadequate, for imperial preference would function best if tariffs in other potential markets were substantially higher so as to emphasize the comparative advantage of intraempire trade. Yet Balfour's policy seemed designed to extract terms of trade from continental Europe that would rival those being contemplated for the empire and would remove any material inducement to strengthen existing "bonds of sentiment." Retaliation would ensure continued profits for Britain's rivals, in contrast to a policy of imperial preference, which would exclude the foreigner and weld the empire into a self-sustaining, self-contained economic and military unit (truly a "Colonial *Zollverein*").

Therefore, reintegrating South Africa after the Boer War and responding to the Canadian "offer" of preference were for Chamberlain an irresistible combination, one that galvanized him to stake his political career to a movement already in the process of reemerging.[68] But Chamberlain's imperial aspirations dictated that preference rather than mere protection was the ingredient essential to tariff reform, and, for any system of colonial preference of substance, duties on agricultural products would have to be considered. This was especially true in light of the fact that many colonies were reluctant to see their modest local industries overwhelmed by massive imports of British manufactured goods. Duties on imported grain or other foodstuffs, (un)popularly known as "food taxes," even if believed to be indispensable toward imperial integration, were universally acknowledged as an unpopular addition to the cost of living. Food taxes inevitably raised the specter of the Corn Laws, and, indeed, the term *Hungry Forties* was popularized after 1903 to remind tariff reformers of the precedents of their actions.[69] Even Chamberlain recognized that the moderate duties he proposed, on wheat "not to exceed 2s. a quarter" and "a smaller tax of about five per cent on foreign meat and dairy produce," would increase the average working-class budget.[70] Whole-hoggers hoped to counter popular apprehensions in two ways: first, they would be willing to reduce current duties on tea, sugar, cocoa, and coffee as a means of compensating for rising prices; and, second, they portrayed any increases as "small and transient sacrifices" that paled before the significance of their ultimate goal of greater imperial unity.[71]

Food taxes were, it was widely presumed, electorally disastrous. They soon were symbolized, in both print and illustrations, by the shrunken protectionist "little loaf" of bread that contrasted so sharply, and unfavorably, with the enormous and appetizing "big free trade loaf." Balfour had been well aware during the 1897 debate that "the broad political fact" was "that for various historical reasons, partly arising out of the enormously high price of bread which prevailed during the late war, partly out of the great controversy ending in the abolition of the Corn Laws, the masses of this country view with ineradicable prejudice the notion of any return to anything at all resembling the old Protective duties that used to be levied."[72] Or, as he tried to explain to Chamberlain himself, "the prejudice against a small tax on food is not the fad of a few imperfectly informed theorists: it is a deep-rooted prejudice affecting the large mass of voters."[73] Four months after his Birmingham speech, Chamberlain conceded that "the big loaf cry is a very hard one to overcome. The superstition in regard to it is extraordinary in this country." Unrepentant, however, he foresaw "no reason to modify [his] principles," maintaining that "preference and reciprocity are in my brain absolutely necessary if the country is to hold its own."[74]

The Tariff Reform League remained committed to the "whole hog" Chamberlainite policy, namely, food taxes coupled with imperial preference, despite the incredulity of many observers who found it difficult to understand why anyone would persist in a policy that aroused such pronounced popular opposition. Clearly *tariff reform* as a euphemism for *protection* was no more successful than *national service* for *conscription*, but ardent tariff reformers had no wish to conceal their intentions. Some whole-hoggers may have harbored skepticism about food taxes, but deferred, believing that fiscal reform would only succeed with the support of someone like Joseph Chamberlain. If preference was the price to be paid for achieving protection, then so be it, for the struggle for protection alone might prove even more elusive if Chamberlain were alienated. Support for food taxes and preference was also a method of cloaking protectionism (thought sordid and avaricious) in the idealistic guise of imperial concern. Preference and imperial unity might lend a certain sense of sacrifice and nobility of purpose to the movement. In a reversal of roles, Chamberlain could pose as the man of principle, forsaking his career and rational political calculation for what he believed to be right, while opponents who clung to outmoded notions of free trade could be denigrated as timid but self-centered men who obstructed the preservation or recovery of British greatness.

Moreover, genuine imperialist sentiment was a further motivation. An appreciation of the potential of the empire and pride in its acquisition were not confined to tariff reformers. Proponents of the naval issue based much of their case on the breadth of Britain's commitments overseas and often devised ways in which the colonies might assist the mother country in the discharge of those responsibilities. Schemes for military cooperation and the expansion of Canadian or Australian naval forces were proposed, and in a similar vein the Navy League stressed its own contribution in consolidating the empire through its broad network of branches, which throughout the varied possessions stimulated a common commitment to Anglo-Saxon right and might. Whether celebrated in "muscular Christianity" and the monarchy (especially Queen Victoria as the empress of India) or on cigarette cards and biscuit tins, imperial symbols and themes were a pervasive feature of prewar British society.[75] There was no reason to doubt the sincerity of Chamberlain's commitment to the retention of the empire nor, in its initial stages, the central role of imperial considerations in the development of tariff reform. If preference seemed the price protectionists might be required to pay for the realization of their goals, so the food taxes specifically might prove the unlikely, unpopular, but unavoidable means to imperial unity.

Divisions emerged, however, not simply between tariff reformers and free traders, but across the whole spectrum of the Unionist party. Balfour sought to shelter all but the most extreme members from either faction under the umbrella of his centrist disposition. Six years before Birmingham, he had already ventured that "the apostles of Free Trade have too much elevated themselves into a sect professing a peculiar orthodoxy, and basing themselves upon certain perfectly sound abstract arguments, they have been too apt to found upon these abstract arguments rules of public policy which they sometimes assume are true to all nations, races and times."[76] Three weeks later, Balfour was called upon to respond to a protectionist measure in the House, whereupon he acknowledged that "most unquestionably two or three generations ago England stood in solitary grandeur, so to speak, as the great manufacturing country, and now it sees other countries following its steps." He would "not deny that in some respects and from some points of view this new condition of things is of the nature of a national danger . . . but do not let the House take the view," he countered, "that it is a pure and absolute loss, as my hon. Friend [Howard Vincent] supposes, either that other countries should manufacture or that we should import."[77] Balfour was a master of words, though he appeared to believe that linguistic dexterity and the delicate qualifications he employed so often were a substitute for consensus. Even in 1897, however, the outlines of Balfour's attitude were taking shape. Free trade was not unassailable dogma, but might in certain but undefined circumstances be subjected to revision. Opposition to such revision stemmed from "prejudice," a defect under which Balfour himself, in his clarity and rationality of mind, would not labor. Nonetheless, the willingness to contemplate fiscal reform that these attitudes seemed to suggest was tempered by Balfour's conviction that antiprotectionist prejudices were "ineradicable" and that any interruption of Britain's current commercial arrangements was not necessarily beneficial. His policy as set forth in the party's campaign guide for 1904 reflected his search for a *via media*:

> As in its design it has no purpose other than that of obtaining freer markets for British goods, so in its application it has nothing to do with the protection of weak industries, or with the formation of reciprocal arrangements with the colonies. It lies entirely aside, therefore, from a policy of Protection on the one hand and from Mr. Chamberlain's scheme on the other.[78]

Estimates of Balfour's success varied. One Unionist Free Trader, his soul "exercised by the tactics of these Tariff Reform Leaguers," complained that they were "going about all over the country saying AJB's policy is but the first step" toward Chamberlain's and "that in substance they are the same."[79] The strength of the various factions was open to interpretation and depended on the flexibility of the debate and stringency in definition.[80] It was most unlikely that the free trade wing of the party would support substantial measures of fiscal reform, but, although it contained several of the more distinguished Unionist spokesmen, the center of gravity within the party lay with the Balfourite faction. If, as it appears, most were sympathetic to the imposition of some protectionist duties, why were they unable to compose their differences with the whole-hogger wing? The Chamberlainites' refusal to reconsider food taxes clearly was a major obstacle to reconciliation, but, perhaps more fundamentally, disagreement extended to the very nature of the party itself. As with the naval issue, nationalist agitation brought to the fore the issue of the permeability of partisan barriers. In particular, this meant determining what should be done with nationalists who were not Unionists, or even Unionists who were deemed not to be sufficiently nationalist. On the tariff issue these dilemmas were posed with a particularly chilling starkness. Tariff reformers seemed to have scant regard for the proprieties of party or tolerance for amiable disagreement, and on occasion the Liberals appeared willing to adopt the same line. "The opposition have made the battle one of Free Trade vs. Protection," wrote Balfour's private secretary to his dear chief in early 1904, "and they have labelled your timid followers with the latter designation."[81] Many Unionist moderates, he suspected, were "as afraid of the name of Chamberlain as the French children were of the name of Marlborough."

Mere mention of Chamberlain's name was usually enough to provoke a stream of invective from the Cecils. Lord Hugh feared "Protection will do for us what Home Rule has done for the others. Joe, in spite of all his immense popularity and influence, cannot carry his plan without the help of the old, quiet, peace-loving Conservatives."[82] His ally Ritchie reminded Balfour that "Chamberlain's views have for many years been frankly protectionist" and then condemned his former cabinet colleague from Birmingham. "What in my opinion is not permissible," Ritchie argued, "is that a leading member of a Cabinet should be at liberty to institute a campaign in the country on a vitally important question on which his colleagues were not agreed. This was what Chamberlain insisted upon doing and this was what in the end broke up the Cabinet."[83] By early 1905, it was alarmingly clear to Lord Robert Cecil where the tariff reformers were leading the party—to disaster—and it was imperative that the party leadership recognize the gravity of the situation. He minced few words with his prime ministerial cousin:

> there is an organized attempt by the Tariff Reform League to drive all Free Traders out of the Unionist party in the House of Commons and . . . Chamberlain as vice-president of the League approves this attempt. If this attempt cannot be arrested reprisals by the Free Traders will inevitably follow; to be succeeded by further Tariff Reform aggression until the Unionist party is irretrievably overthrown.[84]

What alarmed so many Unionists, then, was the apparent dogmatism of the tariff reform movement. Sandars, Balfour's secretary, warned him in October 1905 that Chamberlain's attitude, "if he persists in it, will be disastrous to your wing of the Party."[85] The Liberal Unionist Council he dismissed as "a hothouse of protection" that selected candidates solely on the merits of their loyalty to protectionism.[86] Acland-Hood spoke from experience when he summarized Chamberlain's assault on the party machinery. "He has been trying all along to break into our Central office," Hood informed Sandars. "He tried first of all to seduce the cook (me), then he tried it on the kitchen maid (Wells) and . . . finally with the Lady of the House (AJB)."[87] Lord Robert Cecil doubted that the prime minister had "a glimmering of what has been going on in the constituencies" or that he understood that the "Tariff Reform League had stirred up opposition at Greenwich."[88] Lord James of Hereford, a Unionist Free Trader, echoed all of these charges:

> Powerful organizations supported by the majority of Unionist newspapers are employing huge sums of money and exercising untiring energy for the purpose of destroying Free Trade. In every contested election since May 1903 the question of Protection against Free Trade has been the absorbing question before the electorate. . . . Mr. Balfour can scarcely be aware of the insidious agitation now being carried on in favour of Protection. Does he know that unceasing efforts are being made to capture Unionist organizations? Does he know that success had attended those efforts? Liberal Unionism with all its perfect machinery has—subject to some secessions—been entirely captured. Is he aware that in a Home Counties constituency a most eligible Unionist candidate has been rejected by the Conservative organization because he is a supporter of Mr. Balfour and not of Mr. Chamberlain? But certainly he must note that an organized attack is being made up on the constitution of the Central Office, the object being to put a Tariff Reformer in chief command.[89]

Balfour was not unaware, although he phrased his displeasure over the Tariff Reform League's actions with characteristic subtlety. He would "be sorry to see the work of awakening the country to the need for fiscal reform left entirely in the hands of those in whose minds interest in this great question is sometimes apt to exclude the full recognition of the many other vital questions of which the Unionist party is the guardian."[90] Elegant phrases, however, could not conceal the widening fissures within that party. Ardent tariff reformers insisted that priority be accorded their policy because the urgency of the situation demanded the immediate implementation of their remedy. Policy was paramount and the Unionist party of significance insofar as it provided the best instrument for achieving tariff reform. Traditional concerns of the Conservative party, such as defense of the constitution, the monarchy, and the Anglican Church, were distinctly secondary, and to those less enthusiastic about tariffs it appeared that tariff reformers might willingly sacrifice the party in the process. Chamberlain's association with tariff reform only aggravated such fears, for his career hardly suggested consistent party loyalty. To Balfour, ever aware of his historic burden as party leader, tariff reformers had everything the wrong way round. Specific policies were ultimately less important than the survival of the Conservative party itself as the necessary bulwark against rapid change. Nationalist agitation had not developed to the point where the party could be dismissed as irrelevant, but astute observers could not ignore that Chamberlain's tariff reform initiative was launched in the wake of Liberal dissension and speculation about the possibilities of a centrist party. Lord Hugh Cecil shrewdly anticipated the split between many tariff reformers and the "old, quiet, peace-loving Conservatives" for whom party loyalty and stability were paramount. Balfour was not blind to these considerations, as Lord Robert Cecil feared; rather, like Lord Nelson at Copenhagen, he preferred to turn a blind eye when it suited his position to do so. Yet he could not afford to ignore the tariff reformers' preoccupation with imperial preference to the probable detriment of party strength, nor could he fail to notice their continued insistence that they possessed a unique capacity to remedy the nation's economic ills and attract working-class support.

Anatomy of the Tariff Movement

Several decades earlier the fair trade movement had attracted some, but not universal, support from the business community, and it had failed to overturn prevailing sentiment in favor of free trade. When the tariff reform movement reemerged as a significant political force in 1903, its agenda required the demonstration that fiscal reform was "practical politics." To do so involved providing a justifiable intellectual basis for tariffs and proving that they represented the best way of attracting business and working-class support. Efforts to give institutional expression to these concerns resulted in the formation during 1904 of the Tariff Commission and the Trade Union Tariff Reform Association.

Newspaper magnate Alfred Harmsworth had broached the idea of some form of investigative commission in October 1903, and Chamberlain was receptive toward the idea and discussed possible preliminary arrangements with Pearson over the next 2 months.[91] They envisioned the prospective commission to be a source of information, an arsenal of facts and figures with which to prime the Tariff Reform League for its struggle in the constituencies. Moreover, the commission was intended to demonstrate the widespread support for tariffs that was alleged to exist in the British business community. It was difficult to reconcile the commission's pretensions to independence with its obvious connection to the Tariff Reform League, and critics were quick to denounce it as "a protectionist organization" that lacked even a semblance of impartiality.[92] But, when outlining the role for his proposed commission in December 1903, Chamberlain stressed that it would function as "a non-political Commission of experts to consider the conditions of our trade and the remedies which are to be found for it." It would comprise "leading representatives of every principal industry," "invite witnesses from every trade," and eventually frame a "scientific tariff."[93] While not official, Chamberlain's unofficial body might be confused with Royal Commissions by the unenlightened; it was clearly intended to set to work with a dispatch uncharacteristic of either Royal Commissions or parliamentary committees. Such rapidity was, supposedly, to be complemented by prudence, in that the Tariff Commission's deliberation were to be guided not by political considerations, but by the practical experience and sound fiscal responsibility of the business men of whom it would be composed. In part, this argument reflected the current vogue for "efficiency," which demanded rational scientific decisions based upon expertise. Simultaneously, it suggested to those who feared such scientific calculations as too impersonal that fiscal reform would be rooted in the needs of average individuals and not confined to abstract speculations. But, above all, as the progression of goals revealed, the commission would demonstrate substantial support for tariffs, which might belie Liberal politicians' assertions about the continuing hold of Cobdenite principles. The commission's proceedings would demonstrate that free trade reigned only insofar as alternate proposals had been denied representation, a situation that no doubt could be attributed to the self-interest of cosmopolitan gentlemen who prospered from free trade at the nation's expense.

It was essential, therefore, that the commission endorse some form of tariff protection. Chamberlain himself served as president, Pearson of the Tariff Reform League as vice-chairman, and W. A. S. Hewins, a pro-tariff economist, as secretary. Potential members were screened in advance, as, understandably, "Mr. Chamberlain is particularly anxious not to write to anyone unless it is quite certain that they are favorable to his policy."[94] Likewise, Hewins dismissed two possible members as "Radicals and no use for our policy."[95] To found the Commission, Pearson arranged a dinner at the Hyde Park Hotel with "the very best of menus" and the "choicest of wines," and, in an expansive mood recalling Emerson's dictum that men are Conservatives after dinner, some £7,000 was raised and an additional £20,000 pledged to cover expenses for the next several years.[96] The fifty-nine member commission first met officially on 15 January 1904, examining witnesses from selected trades or industries and soliciting responses to questionnaires distributed to a broader range of firms. In all, it held 140 sessions, examined some 400 witnesses, and considered the replies of approximately 15,000 firms.[97] Accordingly, the tariff reform movement went well beyond the navalists' occasional conferences on the food supply issue and informal surveys of the armaments and shipbuilding industries. The Tariff Commission could reasonably claim to have investigated an impressive range of industries and to have brought the issue of tariffs to prominence on a more permanent basis. But, as with efforts to mobilize trade union support, legitimate doubts persisted in regard to their representativeness and effectiveness.

From the outset tariff reformers had grappled with the issue of attracting working-class support for their program. To a degree this was unavoidable, given the working-class presence within the electorate. But the concern ran deeper than this. There had been a reservoir of "patriotic labor," working men who in deference to their social superiors voted for Conservative candidates. More recently, however, the working class had begun to demonstrate unwelcome signs of independence, such as the emergence of the Independent Labour party in 1893, followed by formation of the Labour Representation Committee in 1900. Whether working-class voters were indeed independent or were largely shackled to the Liberal party by the provisions of the Gladstone–MacDonald pact was irrelevant in one sense, for either way these voters were lost to the opposition. As class became the primary issue in political mobilization, the Conservative party's loss of working-class support seemed destined to accelerate to the point where the party would be reduced to a permanent minority. Contemporary developments appeared likely only to aggravate that tendency: imperialism to which workers appeared either indifferent or hostile, syndicalism to which some might be receptive, economic fluctuations that might be supposed to provoke labor unrest. If power was essential to keep the Germans away, prosperity was necessary to keep the workers at bay. This welter of concerns may appear rather crude, but it underlines the sense of urgency that prompted efforts to reach British working men. It explains why Sir Howard Vincent urged fellow Tories to learn what subjects were popular with the working class and to comprehend how the current industrial situation affected them.[98]

Tariff reform was displayed as evidence that Conservatives were finally willing to reconsider trade questions as they affected working men. The basic thrust of the tariff message was disarmingly simple: that any increases in the cost of living would be more than offset by the greater prosperity of the economy as a whole. Relief from unemployment or underemployment would be swift and dramatic, and even workers who were regularly employed might see wages rise as their firms prospered under newly adjusted "fairer" terms of trade. If tariff reform was to be touted as a legitimate solvent of class conflict, however, some evidence would have to be found that it appealed to workers already organized and regularly employed. In practice this meant trade unionists who, by virtue of the residential and property qualifications for the franchise, were among the most likely workers to vote. Moreover, because it was widely assumed that trade unionists would be in the vanguard of the opposition to Chamberlain's proposals, any hint of union sympathy for tariffs would be most valuable.

It is this particular thrust that explains the attention paid to the otherwise unprepossessing Trade Union Tariff Reform Association (formed on 5 April 1904). Its members participated as individuals rather than as delegates from particular unions, which did little to refute disparaging remarks concerning its unrepresentativeness. The association's chairman was F. Hastings Medhurst, a consulting engineer and director of the Electrical Department and Finance Corp. Ltd., a man whom Hewins dismissed as being ill-informed about both tariff reform and working men. Medhurst himself was the principal financial sponsor of the association, which, despite claims of independence, survived only with regular, direct financial assistance from the Tariff Reform League. Only fifty-eight individuals attended the first annual meeting in May 1905; they were drawn disproportionately from the Northeast, the Midlands, Scotland, and London and reflected modest interest on the part of the building, engineering, and glass-manufacturing unions. From a mere 14 branches in 1905 the association expanded to 41 in 1906 and 54 the following year. It did not, however, produce its own literature (relying on material provided by the league) and could hardly claim by the general election of 1906 to have accomplished much in the way of mobilizing protectionist sentiment among the English working class.[99]

When in December 1905 Balfour's Unionist government resigned, weary of strife and satisfied by passage of several critical bills, it provided a natural opportunity to take stock of the tariff reform movement and, in particular, to assess the breadth of its support. The Tariff Reform League had grown rapidly during its initial year to 220 branches and, although that growth slowed appreciably in the following year, it nonetheless numbered a very respectable 250 branches by July 1905.[100] The league's rapid expansion owed something to spontaneous eruptions of local tariff sentiment, but common procedure was for league officials to identify a sympathetic local figure of some prominence and work through him. In the small Sussex town of Lewes, for example, a meeting was advertised in December 1903 "for all those in favour of Tariff Reform, preference to our colonists over the foreigner, and the protection of Home Industries, and for the formation of a branch of the Tariff Reform League for Lewes and District."[101] Captain John Shiffner, a major local landowner who was to chair the session at the best hotel in town (the White Hart), prudently canvassed several of his acquaintances for their support prior to the meeting and secured the future branch's president and vice-presidents. Shiffner took particular care to ascertain the views of the division's member for Parliament, Sir Henry Aubrey-Fletcher, a Conservative who had held the seat since 1885 and had been returned unopposed at the previous two elections. In this particular instance, Aubrey-Fletcher endeavored to stay clear of the matter, electing to decline the opportunity to support the branch but undertaking no measures to oppose it. By June 1905, under Shiffner's guidance, the Lewes branch had enrolled 104 members.[102]

Unfortunately, the Tariff Reform League preserved a degree of secrecy about its exact membership, distribution of branches, and financial resources, all in contrast to the reasonably informative approach of the Navy League.

From the Tariff Reform League's inception, wild rumors circulated that attributed vastly exaggerated capabilities and accomplishments to the league, and it is understandable that tariff reformers might have hesitated to dispel them. The league's journal, *Monthly Notes on Tariff Reform*, goes some way to compensate for the absence of informative annual reports. Judging from the notices it published, the league's initial strength lay in the Midlands, metropolitan London, and, to a lesser extent, in the Southeast. All were areas of firm Unionist support. Brighton counted 119 members in 1904 and 1,404 a year later (although 1,300 of these were enrolled as associates), while the nearby Kent County Federation comprised 34 branches and no fewer than 920 vice-presidents! Active branches within the London area included West St. Pancras (500 adherents in 1905), Norwood (344), Hampstead (150), and Kensington (which added 383 additional members during 1906).[103] Rural areas were by no means uniformly receptive to the tariff reform gospel. The Sussex County branch ailed despite the best efforts of Lord Leconfield, another prominent landowner, to "make the country ring with tariff reform." Despite his activity, a 1905 branch executive meeting concluded that its finances "were found to be in a most unsatisfactory state and the idea of wider programme had to be abandoned. Practically no response was received to either of my [Leconfield's] appeals to the county and we are face to face with the question whether the branch can be continued or not."[104]

And yet the Sussex County branch languished in close proximity to the successful Brighton branch. Is one to assume that branches whose efforts went unrecorded in the *Monthly Notes* were essentially idle or that their lack of publicity was imposed by journalists anxious to avoid regaling the public with tedious and repetitious accounts of mundane activities? The first prospect would appear more likely, but in either case it is advisable to rely upon firmer evidence when possible. One of the better sets of surviving records is that for the Northern Tariff Reform Federation, an umbrella organization that incorporated local league branches, the whole being divided into separate divisions covering the counties of Durham and Northumberland. While the records do not reveal the characteristics of the complete membership, they do afford a glimpse at the local movement's core of support: the vice-presidents, who collectively formed a majority of the federation's subscribers. To a degree the Durham and Northumberland divisions reflected the distinctive economic coloration of the region, particularly in the prominence of representatives from the coal and iron industries (see Table 1).

Yet other aspects of this group are also significant. The members tended to be experienced, but hardly elderly, the median age of 49 years suggesting that they were securely established and at the age when some then feel able to turn toward politics.[105] Furthermore, the group included a number of men associated with shipping, shipbuilding, and marine engineering, despite the commonly held view that the shipping interest was determinedly "free trade" from the conviction that tariffs would prejudicially affect the volume of British trade. Tariff reformers were able to enlist a number of the region's more prominent businessmen and industrialists: Sir Andrew Noble (Armstrong

Table 1. Northern Tariff Reform Federation Vice-Presidents[a]

Occupation[b]	Northumberland		Durham	
	Number	Percent	Number	Percent
Iron manufacturer	5	16.7	7	16.3
Shipowner	4	13.4	6	14.0
Shipbuilder	2	6.7	4	9.4
Colliery owner/director	2	6.7	11	25.6
Turbine manufacturer/marine engineer	1	3.3	3	7.0
Engineer/electrical engineer	2	6.7	3	7.0
Chemical manufacturer	1	3.3		
Grease manufacturer	1	3.3		
Rope maker	1	3.3	1	2.3
Paper maker			1	2.3
Cement maker	1	3.3		
Aluminum manufacturer			1	2.3
Home furnishings/contractor	2	6.7		
Timber merchant			1	2.3
Provisions merchant			1	2.3
Wines and spirits/brewer	2	6.7	1	2.3
Banker/insurance	1	3.3	1	2.3
Solicitor	1	3.3		
Land agent	2	6.7		
Surgeon	1	3.3	1	2.3
Architect	1	3.3		
Minister			1	2.3
Total	30	100.0	43	100.0

[a]Compiled from lists of vice-presidents (1905) in the Ridley MSS (Northumberland Record Office), ZRI 25/99; *Directory of Directors* (1905); *Stock Exchange Yearbook* (1901, 1905); J. Jamieson, *Durham* (1906); Jamieson, *Northumberland* (1905); *Northumberland Leaders Social and Political* (1909).

[b]Inevitably, there is some overlap of occupation, a colliery owner being a shipowner as well, for example. I have tried to indicate the primary occupation.

Whitworth), Charles Parsons (Parsons Turbine), Sir Thomas Wrightson (iron-master), and H. Pike Pease (the Unionist member of an otherwise Liberal family of ironmasters).

Could the tariff reform movement's support, therefore, be condensed to a handful of prominent and visibly ailing industries? Whatever the woes of sectors of British industry, shipbuilding and marine engineering remained competitive in the world market. A list compiled early in 1905 of individuals who subscribed or donated a minimum of £50 to the Tariff Reform League exhibited a reasonable spread. In addition to steel magnates such as Alfred Hickman or electrical engineers like George Byng, the league attracted support from brewers (Courage & Co. Ltd.), stockbrokers, insurance firms, and a variety of mercantile interests ranging from tobacco (Wills Ltd. of Bristol) to diamond mining (Alfred Beit; see Table 2).

Nonetheless, some contemporary observers dismissed many of these individuals who subscribed to tariff reform as being isolated examples and thus

Table 2. Initial Subscribers to the Tariff Reform League of £50 or More[a]

Occupation	Number	Percent
Merchants	5	13.1
Publisher/printer	4	10.5
Electrical engineers	4	10.5
Iron/steel director	3	7.9
Miner	3	7.9
Colliery owner/director	3	7.9
Shipping	2	5.3
Insurance	2	5.3
Brewers	2	5.3
Department store owners	2	5.3
Stockbrokers	2	5.3
Railway director	2	5.3
Chemical manufacturer	1	2.6
Tobacco merchant	1	2.6
Solicitor	1	2.6
Estate agent	1	2.6
Total	38	100.0

[a]List of 11 March 1905, Ridley MSS, ZRI 25/99.

unrepresentative of the movement's rather narrower but presumably firmer core of support. Subsequent historians have often adopted a similar view, as in the case of Bernard Semmel in his important study of *Imperialism and Social Reform*. Semmel, quite legitimately, contends that the membership of the Tariff Commission might provide a convenient sample through which to investigate the nature of the economic interests that supported tariffs.[106] Before considering Semmel's argument, however, there are several important qualifications to be borne in mind. First, the Tariff Commission and Tariff Reform League were separate organizations. Despite their obvious congruence and despite frequent public confusion of the two, they aspired to separate functions and distinct budgets and sources of income. Second, the Tariff Commission was designed to conduct its business with maximum publicity, and members by their attendance at sessions or imprimatur on final reports would be visibly identified with tariffs. It is likely that other individuals sympathized with tariff reform but hesitated to demonstrate their commitment in quite so public a way. One should exercise a degree of caution, therefore, before assuming that economic interests were represented in the Tariff Commission in a proportion identical to that in the Tariff Reform League as a whole (as Semmel appears to do). Finally, there is the fact that the Commission was formed during the early stages of the tariff controversy (1904) and cannot be taken to indicate the composition of the movement over the entire span (a decade) when the fiscal issue was under debate.

With these caveats in mind, the Commission's membership can nonetheless yield important information on the economic basis of the tariff movement.

Semmel's analysis is based on two suppositions: that industries with a significant export market will favor free trade, while those relying on the domestic
market but faced with foreign competition will opt for tariffs, and that industries within the Midlands would demonstrate an especially marked inclination
toward tariff reform, no doubt mesmerized by the magnetic presence radiating
from Chamberlain's fiefdom in Birmingham. Accordingly, after a brief survey
of the commissioners, Semmel concludes that "iron and steel, tin, building
materials, glass and chemicals, all Midlands products hard hit by German and
American competition . . . constituted the heart of the Commission and of the
League itself."[107]

Yet it appears that Semmel's preconceptions governed his selection, given
that the examples he cites account for only ten of the commission's fifty-nine
members. Furthermore, as A. J. Marrison has demonstrated, many commissioners had interests in more than one industry and often had combined
interests that would be incompatible if one rigorously applied the criteria of
export/free trade versus domestic/protectionist.[108] Sir Charles Tennant, to
take but one example, was a prominent representative from the supposedly
beleaguered (and therefore presumably protectionist) chemical industry, yet he
also maintained interests in mining and banking, each persistently labeled as
staunchly free trade. The point is that it is misleading to argue that specific
industries were united on opposite sides of the tariff divide or to imply that
economic interest was the sole motivating factor.

Further evidence of divided interests can be drawn from commissioners
whom Semmel neglects. These include three representatives from agriculture
and seven involved in a related interest (food processing); their presence serves
as a reminder that tariff reform was not purely an industrial matter. After all, it
had been the agricultural community that had been the longest-standing pro-
ponent of protection, originally in opposition to many manufacturing interests, and indeed throughout the 1880s landowners had lent their support to fair
trade. When the landed interest considered Chamberlain's proposals after
1903, they had several new aspects to digest that militated against immediate,
reflexive support. Chamberlain's earlier harsh denunciations of landowners
still rankled; he had begun his career in the family screw business and by his
experience and Unitarian faith might have been inclined to greater sympathy
for fellow businessmen than the Anglican landed aristocrats whom he clearly
despised. Moreover, as tariff reform developed, at least as it was portrayed by
some of Chamberlain's zealous supporters, it seemed to herald a broader sense
of political participation at the expense of Britain's landed elites. Finally, the
priorities outlined by Chamberlain in the autumn of 1903 suggested that his
determination to bind the empire through imperial preference would promote
the importation of colonial wheat, perhaps without due regard to the desires of
the English agricultural community. The difficulties to which Leconfield alluded, then, in the progress of tariff reform within agricultural Sussex become
more explicable. Moreover, within the agricultural interest, those producing
arable crops were suffering the aftershocks of depressed prices, yet livestock
producers were benefitting to the degree that feed prices dropped. Counter-

balancing this, however, was the undeniable fact that many landowners were wedded to the Conservative party, and they would respond to a firm signal on tariffs from the party leadership. However distasteful some, perhaps most, landowners might find Chamberlain personally or his Birmingham men of push and go, there was still the vein of traditional agricultural protectionism ready to be tapped.

The Tariff Reform League's rhetoric, however, seemed tailored to disguise associations with the traditional landed interest and to emphasize a bold new attitude necessary to implement any significant improvements in the country's economic position. The language of tariff reform was the language of business, though not always that of staid boardrooms so much as that of practical, "hands on" business expertise. In a sense tariff reformers drew upon the vocabulary of Manchester liberalism, while updating it in the fashionable guise of efficiency. Samuel Storey, for example, himself a former Liberal MP who had become chairman of the Northern Tariff Reform Federation, condemned the lack of a comprehensive national trade policy and predicted that just "as an organized football team will beat a scratch team . . . [so] in this industrial battle the organized states will beat the unorganized state of Great Britain."[109] It was, he continued, "a business problem to be discussed on business lines." Herbert Pike Pease, on the floor of the Commons, dismissed a Liberal critic who had the temerity to scorn a tariff policy as someone who "cannot have had anything to do with business during the course of his career."[110] Even the cautious Lord Lansdowne described Chamberlain's policy as an effort "to put the affairs of the Empire upon a more business footing than has hitherto been the case."[111]

Of course, these claims often provoked the now familiar response that the league's political vocabulary was simply the language of sectional self-interest. If the tariff reform movement is set within its proper context, it becomes apparent that this was not exclusively the case. Tariff reform was one aspect of the developing concerns of the nationalist agitation. One of its motivations was to secure profit and privilege by a diversionary strategy aimed at persuading workers that protectionism could assure economic security and prosperity in a way that Socialism could not. The influence of domestic politics was unmistakable here. Yet foreign realities were no less influential. The frequency with which the German analogy was invoked (the Colonial *Zollverein* or Bismarck's tariff policies) illustrates this particular attraction. After all, Germany boasted the largest and best-organized Socialist party in Europe, hardly the image tariff reformers had in mind. What they singled out for attention was Germany's emergence as a dynamic industrial giant and a significant world power. Without taking measures to equip Britain to survive in an ever more competitive world, it was foolish to think only of ways to ensure that its affluent citizens continued to prosper.

Still, the pull of self-interest cannot be dismissed easily. Much attention has been focused on the Unionist members of Parliament, who constituted a clearly defined and manageable sample. The divisions within this group over the fiscal issue can then be analyzed for evidence of an economic dimension. Several aspects are suggestive, even if their ultimate significance is not always clear. As Neal Blewett has demonstrated, tariff reformers were far more likely to be drawn from manufacturing or commercial circles than were the Balfourites, who tended to represent the more traditional center of gravity within the party, namely, the landed interest and the military and civil services.[112] But free fooders also tended to be drawn from commercial and financial interests, although from sectors and regions conventionally associated with the benefits of free trade (banking, "the City," Lancashire). One could certainly point to a number of prominent tariff reformers from diverse backgrounds—Bonar Law (iron), Edward Goulding (son of an Irish fertilizer manufacturer), Hewins (his father an iron merchant), Page Croft (son of a brewer), even Chamberlain himself, whose fortune was derived from the family screw firm. Yet in many instances such sons received an education that removed some of the taint, as it might be regarded, of business origins, and they might find themselves working for tariff reform alongside men such as Viscount Ridley, whose Northumberland estates exceeded 10,000 acres.

But perhaps the more important point is the degree to which the debate swirled beyond the boundaries of individual self-aggrandizement. The cleavages between protectionists, preferentialists, and free traders could not be reduced simply to a matter of occupational status. The fiscal issue as a critical aspect of nationalist agitation encompassed attitudes to empire, party, class, and nation, and a position on one issue was not an infallible guide to an individual's view on the others. The debates that raged were bitter and divisive, but they were nonetheless conducted in an atmosphere in which the Unionist party still clung to power. So long as the party retained its parliamentary majority, there was at least the possibility, as it appeared to many of the agitators, that the measures critical to the nation's survival might still be contemplated. If that assurance were gone, the debate would grow even more acrimonious.

3

In the Wake of Disaster

When the Balfour government resigned in December 1905, it did so in the hope that the Liberal party under Campbell-Bannerman might find the experience of office as wearisome and divisive as it recently had proven for the Unionists. After all, Liberalism resembled an umbrella of sectional interests (or "faddists," as they might less charitably be described), which might disintegrate into squabbling factions, each insisting that their particular needs should be addressed first. Campbell-Bannerman's shrewd leadership and prompt call for a general election rapidly dispelled any such hopes, but it was already abundantly clear to most Unionists that their string of electoral successes was about to end. Even Joseph Chamberlain, who had spent more than 2 years extolling the virtues of tariff reform, recognized that the Unionists would be defeated.

Few people, however, expected the verdict registered in January 1906. The result was a spectacular defeat for the Unionists, tariff reformers and free traders alike. The Unionist opposition was reduced to a meager 157 members in stark contrast to some 400 on the Liberal benches. A disaster of that magnitude inevitably prompted a coroner's inquest, with the prominent question being whether tariff reform had administered the fatal blow. One astute journalist observed that never "in the history of electioneering had a party to fight so many and such heterogeneous confederates as did the Unionists at the late election."[1] Permanent disabilities—such as the inevitable unpopularity of governments seeking reelection (and the Unionists had held power since 1895)—were compounded by a lethal mixture of particular circumstances. Among these were "Chinese slavery" (the use of Chinese labor in South Africa after the Boer War), the 1902 Education Act and the Licensing Act, which had galvanized Nonconformists into even more fervent support of Liberal candidates, and the 1903 Gladstone–MacDonald pact, which had minimized friction between Liberals and the Labour Representation Committee. In short, there was *prima facie* evidence to suggest that tariff reform could not be blamed as the sole cause of the Liberal landslide. It was equally difficult to discern a clear verdict from the fortunes of prominent tariff reformers. Joseph Chamberlain's reelection for Birmingham was, in the words of Sir Herbert Maxwell (himself inclined to a sympathetic view), "no more a vote for tariff reform . . . than for the improved cultivation of orchids."[2] If Sir Howard Vincent, Sir Gilbert Parker, and Herbert Pike Pease won at Sheffield, Gravesend, and Darlington with Tariff Reform League assistance, their compatriots Sir Alfred Hickman and Sir Alexander Henderson (the league's treasurer) were defeated for West Wolverhampton and West Staffordshire.

Even the fiscal convictions of the Unionist rump did not admit of a positive answer. Shortly after the election, the *Times* classified more than two-thirds of those Unionists returned to Parliament as tariff reformers (109 of 157).[3] Historians, more sensitive to the subleties of the issue, have revised the figure downward to approximately one-half, with smaller clusters of Balfourites and free fooders.[4] But two points were nonetheless clear: first, because tariff reformers constituted a strong proportion of the party, Balfour would have to take additional steps to accommodate them; and, second, Unionists as a whole would have to come to terms with a Liberal administration whose progressive intentions were bolstered by its remarkable majority. Because the Unionist party had become accustomed to the exercise of power, having governed for 17 of the past 20 years, this second point was all the more difficult to accept. The problems identified by the nationalist agitation urgently required solutions that even the Unionist party had balked at. What, then, could be expected from a Liberal majority?

Fisher and the Fissuring of the Navalists

Indeed, with the return of a Liberal government, it was not long before the naval issue emerged again as a topic of cross-bench concern. Unlike 1893, however, a new ingredient had been added with the appointment in 1904 of Sir John Fisher as First Sea Lord. Fisher was a brilliant but peculiarly abrasive man, who had little patience with incompetence or opposition, even if founded upon a legitimate difference of opinion. He was convinced that the Navy urgently required a thoroughgoing program of reform and redistribution, and he determined to carry it through regardless of the "fossils" or vested interests he might antagonize in the process. Britain was "weak everywhere and strong nowhere," the Admiral contended in correspondence liberally seasoned with expletives and injunctions to personal loyalty.[5] To meet what he believed would be the unprecedented demands of a future war, he scrapped older vessels he considered obsolete, reorganized the process of officer training, redeployed many ships toward home waters (even creating an entirely new "home fleet"), and introduced a series of capital ships whose design revolutionized naval architecture. The first of these ships, *H. M. S. Dreadnought*, combined firepower and speed to a degree that no existing ship could match, and thus its name was appropriated as a generic appellation for this powerful new class of battleships.[6]

Each of these measures contradicted aspects of traditional Admiralty policy, and it was not long before the Admiral encountered rough waters. Older vessels were believed by many experts to be indispensable in "showing the flag" and thus of real diplomatic value even if their military capability was limited. Likewise, the Mediterranean fleet was considered critical to imperial security (indeed, the 1893 scare had arisen over a perceived threat to British interests in precisely this area), and any reduction in its strength, even if to augment home forces, was viewed with profound suspicion. And the *Dreadnought* itself, by inaugurating a new naval race in these superior ships, rendered at a stroke Britain's long-standing supremacy in numbers inconsequential, for existing pre-Dreadnoughts would be virtually worthless against German ships modelled on Fisher's masterpiece. The naval race in progress with Germany since 1898 now assumed a qualitative as well as a quantitative character. Furthermore, Fisher's personal role in securing these reforms, and his pronounced tendency to regard any criticism as a distinct personal affront, encouraged not a few observers in their belief that a despotic regime was emerging at the Admiralty, one directed by a tyrant whose megalomaniacal instincts were at odds with all that was cherished in the Senior Service. Finally, the First Sea Lord's policies resulted in a reduction in the naval estimates, an accomplishment that, late in 1904, by forestalling a possible budgetary crisis, only strengthened the already firm support Fisher enjoyed from Unionist party leader Arthur Balfour.

But with Balfour in 1906 consigned to the opposition benches, and the German Reichstag apparently willing to continue appropriating massive funds for Tirpitz's naval building program, Fisher's position was growing more exposed. It became more isolated still in July 1906 when it was revealed that the First Sea Lord had agreed with the Liberal ministry to reduce the scope of Dreadnought building programs as envisioned earlier. To Fisher, given Britain's jump on the Germans, there were sound financial reasons and acceptable military ones to do so. To his growing band of critics, however, especially those clustered toward the right of the political spectrum, Fisher's decision nearly smacked of treason, for he had been championed as a bulwark against unwarranted efforts at naval economy. He now appeared to have relinquished this role and thus robbed the Unionists of a critical ally in their struggle to maintain a supreme navy. Increasingly, his close personal relationship with Balfour came under scrutiny, and to ardent tariff reformers such as Leo Maxse it seemed suspiciously as though Fisher had imbibed of the party leader's watered-down brew and was trying to preserve free trade by avoiding the financial crisis all tariff reformers knew must inevitably befall any revenue-starved free trade government. "We are demobilizing our seagoing squadrons for the sake of free imports," charged Maxse in his *National Review* as he probed for a chink in Fisher's armor.[7]

Within the Navy League, too, opposition to the "Fisher revolution" began to mount. The first tiny fissures in what would later develop into a massive internal rift were apparent at a meeting of the league's executive committee on 29 October 1906 when two members urged the league to confront both the Admiralty (namely, Fisher) and the Liberal government over their apparent neglect of the nation's defenses. More specifically, they proposed that the Navy League address an official letter to local chambers of commerce advocating meetings and public demonstrations to pressure the government to reverse its pattern of declining naval expenditure. The principal force behind these recommendations was Harold F. Wyatt, who had for nearly 2 years between 1902 and 1904 toured the Empire to stimulate navalist interest. "With what eloquence and energy Mr. Wyatt prosecuted his mission is known to all our readers," the *Navy League Journal* had observed approvingly in 1905.[8] "His success has been practically attested by the formation of twenty-one branches abroad." In his criticism of Fisher, Wyatt soon attracted the firm support of his executive colleague Lionel Horton-Smith, a barrister with a taste for the Scottish heritage. Over the following year, the two would be inseparably linked in their campaign to persuade the Navy League officially to repudiate the naval policy allegedly formulated by Fisher and ratified by Campbell-Bannerman. Wyatt and Horton-Smith's original recommendation was shelved, as was their suggestion a week later of a mass meeting at the Albert Hall to protest the evasion of the two power standard. Shortly thereafter, the chairman of the executive committee met with Fisher, though precisely with what results was not revealed. Wyatt and Horton-Smith were, nonetheless, advised not to push matters any further.[9]

The new year brought no immediate resolution to the issue. In late January 1907, an embattled Fisher elicited from Balfour a further promise of support, and the Unionist party leader strove to separate the issue of Fisher's naval reforms from the question of adequate shipbuilding (for which the Liberal government must assume responsibility), both of which Fisher's critics tried to conflate and lay at his feet. Balfour's authority within his own party was by no means unchallenged, and the growing dissension within the Navy League provided one convenient focus for both Unionist critics and the Admiral's assorted existing opponents who sought "a new hearing for their old complaints."[10] In February the league unsuccessfully attempted to stifle Wyatt and Horton-Smith, and its secretary was compelled to issue a circular to all league speakers requiring them to reemphasize that the Navy League was nonpartisan and not bent on criticizing Admiralty policy.[11] An impasse was finally reached in April when Wyatt and Horton-Smith threatened to resign from the committee if the league failed to endorse the now publicly circulating demand that work be begun on three dreadnoughts projected but whose construction had been delayed by Fisher and the Liberals. The league's leadership refused, and the two dissidents countered by stating their intention to bring forth an amendment critical of the executive's policy at the forthcoming annual meeting scheduled for 15 May 1907.[12]

For the next 2 months, the cleavage within the Navy League was revealed to all who cared to follow it in the daily press and the political reviews. Retracing the course of dissension reveals a number of the dilemmas confronted by nationalist agitators, for the events of May–July 1907 were not a simple, clearcut confrontation between "navalists" and "pacifists," but a deeper, more complex set of disagreements among individuals all pledged to support the predominance of the Royal Navy. Wyatt and Horton-Smith continued to be subjected to strong pressure to desist from a path that, it was feared, might shatter the Navy League permanently. Some members sought to wash their hands of the whole affair; Sir Frederick Pollock, for example, recorded his "protest against the constant questions raised about matters outside the proper work of the Navy League." He further stated that "Mr. Horton-Smith appears to imagine that all the Governments of Europe are engaged in watching the action of our committee."[13] But the cynics appear to have been outweighed by those who genuinely believed that the naval issue had reached a critical point.

Certainly that was the thrust of Wyatt and Horton-Smith's amendment as presented at the annual meeting. It scrupulously avoided any specific mention of Fisher or any condemnation of past league policy; rather, it deplored "the diminution in our naval strength involved in the reduction of the naval estimates from £36,800,000 for the year 1904–5 to £30,400,000 for the year 1907–8" and cited seven specific instances of impaired naval strength resulting from these reductions. And, finally, it urged that "the Navy League throughout the United Kingdom should do its utmost by every kind of legitimate agitation to rouse British citizens to a sense of the danger involved in these economies."[14] The executive committee's response was dictated in part by the strength of its own position. Wyatt and Horton-Smith's criticisms had only recently come to light, and, given the perennially sparse attendance at annual meetings, it was unlikely that they would have the opportunity to mobilize a large faction in opposition to committee policy. The weight of inertia thus lay on the committee's side, as did, for the moment, the fact that Wyatt and Horton-Smith's amendment was seemingly confined to anti-Fisher concerns without necessarily linking them to the issue of Liberal party policy. In other words, in the early stages of the controversy, the dissidents had tried to establish their respectable credentials by avoiding overtly partisan attacks and by stressing their intention to remain within the confines of previous league policy. Indeed, Wyatt had admitted as much when citing "the league, in whose interests and for the sake of whose duty I am bringing forth this Amendment."[15] By structuring the argument in this way, the potential terrain for debate was thereby limited, largely to the committee's benefit.

Committee members did not hesitate to exploit favorable opportunities. "It is impossible, in such a discussion as we are engaged upon this afternoon, to keep out of mention the name of the great protagonist, around whom the fight wages—namely, Admiral Sir John Fisher (applause)."[16] After alluding to Fisher's hypnotic touch (an obvious parallel with the "Nelson touch"), the speaker affirmed that the First Sea Lord had "given such signal service to the country" and had stimulated "eager interest, remarkable competence, and extraordinary keenness among officers and men." The committee defended its position by reminding the audience that "a body which exists for the service of the Navy of the country must be in touch and in sympathy with the Navy, and if we are out of sympathy with the Navy . . . we are more likely to do harm than good. . . . We feel that an attack upon the Navy and upon the administration of the Navy by a body of landsmen is certain to fail. (Hear, hear.)" If the issue, therefore, was to be Fisher's reforms or the alleged incapacity of the Admiralty to provide for an adequate fleet, these were professional matters in which the Navy League, by definition largely civilian, should not dare to tread. There were a variety of possible responses to this line of argument, one of which was that the league contained a number of prominent retired naval officers or well-informed military correspondents whose judgment on the situation was worth considering. But by forcing voting members to choose between what was represented as an anti-Fisher vendetta and a responsible if reverential committee, indecision or caution would tell in the committee's favor. The league's president, Robert Yerburgh, exercised his prerogative to limit debate; he later claimed not to have noticed outraged members who were denied the opportunity to speak, to which they responded by likening his convenient failure of eyesight to that of Nelson at Copenhagen, albeit to less noble ends. When the amendment was put to a vote, it was defeated by a majority of seventeen, and the committee's policy was thus temporarily sustained.[17]

The two dissidents were left with no recourse but to petition for an "extraordinary general meeting" at which they might yet alter the course of league efforts. Wyatt and Horton-Smith advocated "attack by the pyrotechnics of the platform and letters to the Press," in contrast to the Navy League's "less picturesque . . . more practical, steady spade work of education."[18] Or so the Navy League suggested. Wyatt and Horton-Smith's indictment of the executive committee accepted this characterization, but sought to turn it to their account:

> Briefly, our case is that the committee of the league has violated its constitution and reversed its objects by advocating, championing, and defending naval reductions, which the league was founded to resist. We say that the committee persist in imputing to reasons of strategy measures obviously prompted by reasons of finance. We maintain further that . . . in proclaiming they regard educational work as the paramount object of the league, the committee again altogether deny and defy the league's constitution.[19]

The severity of the situation was underlined by the preparations and precautions taken by both sides. Wyatt and Horton-Smith sought to publicize their case despite the opposition or indifference of many London papers.[20] They maintained close communication with the league's Third London branch, in part through Wyatt's sister, Grace, who served within it. Wyatt also attempted to secure a complete list of league members in order to canvass more thoroughly for support. He failed at the Companies Registration Office, Somerset House, because the league had not been required to file a list, and his subsequent efforts to extract one from the league's secretary, W. C. Crutchley, encountered several delays.[21] For its part, the committee threatened to resign if Wyatt and Horton-Smith's policy was approved at the extraordinary meeting now set for 19 July 1907, and on 1 July took the additional precaution of distributing proxies to league members eligible to vote with the accompanying notation that Wyatt and Horton-Smith sought to "paralyze and wreck" the league.[22] The two dissidents again attempted to secure their own list of league members, but not until 8 days later (on 9 July) were Wyatt and Horton-Smith able to contact individual Navy League members in the hope that many might withdraw their proxies and resubmit them in their favor.[23]

The fervor with which the battlelines had been drawn extended to the meeting of 19 July itself. Harold Wyatt repeated his previous assertions that the Admirality had been derelict in its professional duty by sponsoring reductions in the naval estimates that, he insisted, corresponded to an alarming reduction in effective naval strength. This lamentable situation was then aggravated by grievous errors of strategy and distribution. To this point, the discussion had proceeded along now familiar lines. Yet the Navy League's executive committee had, among its other preparations in the wake of the annual meeting, taken the opportunity to alter the position it sought to defend. This new terrain was embodied in an amendment submitted at the extraordinary meeting for the membership's approval. It endorsed "the action of the executive committee of the league in refusing to initiate a public agitation upon matters of controversial detail," but pledged to "take immediate action" if necessary to maintain the two power standard. More significantly, it also expressed "serious apprehension" that the Channel fleet was not at present maintained "in constant readiness for instant service."[24] These slight, but important, modifications in policy placed an additional burden on the dissidents to demonstrate that the Navy League was supine when it came to public action and that their own criticisms concerned crucial larger issues rather than mere controversial points of detail.

Wyatt and Horton-Smith were up to the challenge, however, and chose fresh emphases in a manner calculated to bring the Navy League crisis more directly within the developing concerns of the nationalist agitation. It was not sufficient, Wyatt contended, simply to blame Sir John Fisher, for the real responsibility lay not with the "servant," but the "master," "the power behind him," namely, the Liberal cabinet. The recent changes in the Royal Navy, it therefore followed, stemmed not from reasoned professional calculation but, as Wyatt stressed, from "the force of party spirit, the force of the whole Government, of a Government which has been returned to power not seriously believing in the possibility of war. (Cheers.)"[25] "There is no getting away from this"; he continued that

during the last general election there was an enormous outbreak of anti-military feeling. I know it from the personal experience I had in the constituency for which I was standing, and I know that my experiences were duplicated and triplicated all over the country. I do not think it can be disputed that a large number of the present majority in the House of Commons are actuated by an intense hatred of armaments. As sensible men, must not we take that enormous fact into consideration when we are dealing with and thinking over the naval policy for which the Government is responsible? Are we children to live for ever in the land of make-believe? Are we to go on in this place of dreams, or in this house of pretence? Are we to go on for ever preaching that the Cabinet has no power, no voice in regard to naval regulations, but that the permanent officials of the Admiralty are the sole people? It may be that a man like Sir John Fisher is able to exercise great

influence—I do not say one way or the other—but it still remains the fact that
the real power behind him is the Government. (Hear, hear.) But if the present
Government had been returned to power pledged to effect an increase of
armaments, as they were pledged to a decrease of armaments, I say, does any
sane being suppose that we should have had these naval reductions?[26]

Much of the debate at the previous meeting had read like a recapitulation
of those in the league's initial year that had swirled around Spenser Wilkinson.
It was understandable that the executive committee and many members were
loath to ignore the "lessons" of 1895–1896, namely, that the Navy League
should abstain from professional naval matters, that the Admiralty and strategy were "off limits," and that educational work was less controversial and
more successful. Wyatt and Horton-Smith's challenge seemed to reopen those
old wounds, but, by infusing the issue with the problem of party politics, it did
far more. Wyatt argued that the league had the wrong end in mind, for it was
the Liberals, not the Admiralty, who were to blame, and that the league had, in
its mistaken assessment, adopted the wrong means, namely, educational work
rather than public agitation. Rather than seizing the opportunity to denounce
the naval reductions, the Navy League had cowered behind protestations of
nonpartisanship and deference to professional opinion, and, in so doing,
appeared to condone the various threats to the fleet it had been founded to
resist. It had "exchanged the role of watchdog of the public for that of the
spaniel of Whitehall" and was, Wyatt charged, "stifling public opinion."[27]
As committee members squirmed and members of the audience interrupted
with expressions of support or disapproval, the debate grew increasingly
heated. The committee could take little comfort in the fact that Wyatt expressly denied the possibility of charging any of its members "with any conduct
unworthy of British citizens" (thus raising precisely that notion in listeners'
minds), only to hear him conclude by labeling the league, "during the last few
months, a national curse instead of a national blessing."[28] But the explosion
was detonated when F. T. Jane, the occasionally wayward navalist who had
already tangled with the committee over its appropriation of the image of
Nelson, rose to rebut a rather rambling presentation by the chairman of the
Liverpool branch, Sir John Gray Hill. Despite Hill's legal training, he had
failed to respond to the new direction of Wyatt's charges and had instead
confined himself to restating the traditional position of the Navy League as it
had evolved in the mid-1890s. Hill emphasized that the league was "not like an
opposition to the Admiralty. (Yes, we are.) Are we prepared to take the place of
the Admiralty if the Admiralty goes out?" he asked his fellow members. "I
know Lord John Russell thought he could command the fleet," the Liverpool
chairman continued, "and perhaps Mr. Wyatt and Mr. Smith can do it. I
cannot, and I do not pretend to. And you, ladies and gentlemen, for the most
part, are no more competent than I am to judge upon a highly expert question."[29] He reminded the audience that the committee "consists of English
gentlemen trying to do their duty, and they are not to be assailed as if they were
criminals in a Continental court of law." Finally, the tart rejoinder from the

audience that "we are very much interested in the real question, and we are not in the least interested in Sir John Gray Hill (Cheers)" provoked a slight acceleration in the Liverpool chairman's otherwise labored style.

By the time he finally sat down, three points were tolerably clear.[30] First, Hill had justifiably pointed out that "the efficiency of a Navy, British or any other, can be much more seriously affected, either for good or for evil, by changes in administration or organisation or training than by probable reduction of pecuniary expenditure." In short, there was no specific, inviolable correlation between expenditure and efficiency. Second, Hill laid great store on the "moderation and restraint that is to be expected from an association of Englishmen formed for the public good," and he contrasted this with a politicized and thereby discredited German Navy League. Third, and following naturally from the previous point, the current effort to press the naval issue might shatter the Navy League beyond repair, imperilling not only any potential political effectiveness, but the philanthropic and pedagogic institutions it had nurtured. Here Hill spoke at length about the considerable achievements of the Liverpool branch itself.

In response, Jane came to the point with brutal directness. The amendment endorsing the executive committee's policy he dismissed as "little better than a white lie" and "absolute rubbish." The plain fact of the matter was that the Liberal government had "cut the Navy down because of a few dirty little Radical and Socialist supporters. (Order, order.)"[31] Even a member who described himself as "a strong Conservative" objected to Jane's language, but, undaunted, Jane added that "every man, whatever he may call himself—(uproar)—who cuts down the Navy is to be regarded as a public enemy, and should be treated as such." He ridiculed arguments that "if this thing and that thing is not done, the Navy League at Liverpool will go to pieces," charged the committee with "going well on the way to imitate the Pro-Boers," and, intoxicated by the uproar, demanded of them, "Is this league founded for Nelson or is it not?" "There is no hostility to Admiral Fisher," Jane concluded; "the hostility is to those who keep him short of money."[32]

The direction in which the dissidents sought to channel the naval issue was now abundantly clear. Fisher was relegated to a symptom rather than an underlying cause of the fleet's alleged ill-preparedness. The naval issue was no longer envisioned as a means of drawing Englishmen together; rather, its function was to be divisive and aggressive. It would separate unpatriotic Liberals—for this is what willful neglect of the nation's security amounted to—from patriotic Conservatives. A handful of nonpartisan Imperialists might muddy the issue, but the battle lines could be drawn and the enemy clearly identified. Bazaars or bound volumes of Nelson's life, such as the Liverpool branch might treasure, were really irrelevant when compared with the urgent task of public agitation focused on the removal of the Liberal government from power, which constituted the only effective safeguard of naval supremacy. Thus Horton-Smith, dismayed at the obstinate refusal of the executive committee to view matters from his perspective, scoffed that one "would almost think the Navy League existed for the Liverpool branch" and reiterated

that "Sir Henry Campbell-Bannerman threw overboard" the two power standard. "Is Sir John Fisher going to tell me, or is anybody going to tell me, that a
Navy which costs six million less than the Navy did three years ago, is as good
a Navy as the Navy of three years ago?"[33] Of course, there were impertinent
replies to his rhetorical question, but it was a thought-provoking case, impas-
sionately argued. Little wonder, then, so intensely were the issues debated, that
Wyatt concluded by recommending that "the best thing would be to take all the
Navy League pamphlets and journals and make a gigantic bonfire of them."[34]

There were, however, in the eyes of the committee and its sympathizers,
compelling reasons not to accept the dissidents' contentions and to refrain
from inaugurating an agitation "upon matters of controversial detail." One of
the league's very first members claimed that the committee originally had
functioned "as a body of patriots who dearly loved and cared for our country
and its security" who, "whichever party was in power, never gave it a
thought."[35] He deplored efforts to infuse the naval issue with the aura of
partisan politics, as did one of the league's founders, W. L. Ainslie (who had
written in the spirit of "average Englishmen"). Ainslie denied that the Navy
League favored tne Liberal government, countering that seventeen of the
twenty committee members were Conservatives. He then insisted that "although I have been all these years on the executive committee, I really did not
know the party politics of one man in five who were on the executive. (Hear,
hear.)" Indeed, Ainslie reaffirmed his commitment to keeping party politics
out of naval discussions, and he predicted that any public agitation on that
point would inevitably call forth "an equally strong counter agitation" from the
Liberal benches. As to the merits of the dissidents' specific points, there were
the lessons of the past whose import was only too clear to men like Ainslie who
sought a generous, even conciliatory, nationalist synthesis of Englishmen of all
party stripes. "Now from the very first time this league was started," Ainslie
reminded the audience, "it has always been a principle of action on the part of
the Executive not to endeavour to agitate unless we had strong professional
opinion to back us; and times without number the best professional opinion
which has been urged in support of proposals put forward at the executive
committee by Mr. Horton-Smith and Mr. Wyatt has been their own. It is an
authority we did not recognize," Ainslie remarked, and, he added, "it is an
authority which is no good to us for public purposes."[36]

This theme of insufficient professional opinion favoring agitation was
seized upon by Yerburgh, and eagerly so, because it provided a more conventionally satisfying riposte to the dissidents than any professed distaste for
partisan action (which would have worn rather thin given Yerburgh's role in the
Hampstead by-election). Personal animosity, professional jealousy, and legitimately differing assessments all contributed to a lack of unanimity on the part
of the Royal Navy in regard to Fisher's reforms. In addition to the lack of a
clear lead from the Admiralty, Yerburgh stressed the country's generally improved diplomatic situation, particularly the alliance with Japan, the demoli-
tion of much of the Russian fleet by the Japanese, and the new understandings
with France. In a relatively favorable climate, and "at a time when the people

of the country are so overburdened with taxes," it would be detrimental to campaign for a massive increase in naval spending.[37] Colonel John Gretton, one of Yerburgh's Unionist colleagues in the House, concurred that "when you take up a question of great policy, it should be on broad lines [not on matters of controversial detail] upon which you are absolutely certain that you are well founded, and upon which you know you will carry a great weight of naval opinion to support you. It is no good quoting this one naval officer or that one naval officer. (Hear, hear.)" To Gretton, the logical conclusion was inescapable: "You will not carry the country on any lines of that sort."[38]

Many of the speakers who supported the executive committee were prepared to consider wisespread political agitation, not inflexibly wedded to a purely educational approach as some critics suggested. But they rejected Wyatt and Horton-Smith's insistence that such agitation be undertaken immediately. W. Hayes Fisher, for example, was itching to give the naval issue a try as a political one that would reach a mass audience, but he counseled patience for the most opportune moment. He was, he assured an audience still buzzing about Jane's remarks, "ready to vote money for the Navy, ready to go down to a Democratic constituency to tell it that its Navy ought to be its first care, and that it cannot and ought not to begrudge money for the Navy."[39] Yet, as a self-styled "commonsense Englishman" and an "agitator of some experience," he stressed the insufficiency of any material to sustain a naval agitation.

Herbert Nield, secure in his Unionist constituency, argued along similar lines. Proud of his role as a Unionist opponent "condemned to sit opposite the most incompetent Government that was ever got together, and to listen to the diatribes of the Little England party,"[40] Nield evidently harbored no reservations about turning the naval issue to partisan account. He claimed "no interest except to throw discredit upon those who purport to govern the country at the present time" and freely admitted that he would seem temperamentally suited to support Wyatt and Horton-Smith rather than the Navy League's executive committee in whose defense he now spoke. Nield based his position, however, on an appreciation of political realities:

> It is no use your going to the public of this country—and the election which was announced today is one of the surest indications of it—and attempting at the present moment, without the most ample of grounds, of trying to create an agitation against our present rulers upon naval matters. The answer of the Colne Valley election is that they will have none of that.

Instead, Nield urged the league to close ranks and reserve its "platform fervour" for "the time when the real storm of indignation must be aroused throughout the country."[41] Otherwise, he predicted, crying "wolf" once too often would have the most drastic repercussions.

Divisions within the navalist movement, as revealed by the dissension in the Navy League, and the utility of the naval issue as a touchstone of nationalist agitation were both murky and complex subjects. That dissatisfaction within the Navy League itself was not confined to a handful of zealots bent on its destruction (as the executive committee had tried to imply) was indicated by the votes cast at the conclusion of the extraordinary meeting. A majority of those who attended voted in support of Wyatt and Horton-Smith (the exact count being 87–73), but the committee's position was ultimately sustained by proxies that ran heavily in its favor (897–559). Nonetheless, 646 dissenting votes of 1,616 (40 percent) could not be disguised. A significant split had occurred. To those who envisioned navalism as an integrative force, it was of little importance which government was in power, for the best guide in naval matters was the Admiralty, and it was sufficient that ordinary civilians be educated to appreciate the benefits of a strong navy, but not encouraged to evict a particular party from power. The number of navalists who by 1907 subscribed to this position seemed to have shrunk.

A more common attitude, especially as expressed by many Unionist politicians within the Navy League, was not to absolve the Liberals of any untoward determination to prune the fleet or even to deny that partisan agitation on the naval issue was unprincipled, as the previous group had argued, but rather to suggest that any major effort was premature. These Conservatives recognized the potential value of the naval issue as a political weapon, but insisted that two criteria had to be fulfilled for it to be employed with maximum effect. They preferred to be perceived as supporting the legitimate and unanimously held claims of the Admiralty, which were being denied by an irresponsible Liberal government. It was far more difficult to agitate effectively against both the Liberals and the Admiralty as the dissidents were prepared to do. And there had to be more convincing proof of a clear and imminent threat to British security. To a good many observers, the German threat seemed fairly clear, but not necessarily imminent. Indeed, it was both Wyatt and Horton-Smith who pleaded most insistently that inaction would send the wrong signal overseas. Wyatt himself stressed the most dire implications:

> Remember in Germany there is a vast organisation, the German Navy League numbering over a million members, all for activity and urging a forward policy. Do you think that their eyes have not been turned on this dispute here? Do not you think the news of this controversy has already travelled far? The issue to be decided is more important than that of the resignation of the Committee. The real point is that the verdict given here today will be taken abroad in Germany as being typical of public opinion of this country, and if the verdict should be in favour of naval reduction, says that the NAVY LEAGUE approved a reduction in the Navy Estimates of six million; that would be indeed a message of hope and encouragement to the German Navy League. They would increase their activities; they would say "England is falling behind; even their League is ceasing to advocate for the Navy." The result will be an enormous increase of the German programme. (Cheers.) I ask you for God's sake and for Britain's sake not to send that message to Germany today. Do not tell the Germans that the heart of England is beginning to fail. Send them a different message. Show them there are still men and women who are bent upon having a naval increase, and bent upon resisting a naval decrease, and they in Germany would see that by that message you desire that the path of Britain should be upwards and not downwards amongst the nations of the world. (Cheers.)[42]

The controversy was also significant for its intimations of where Wyatt and Horton-Smith's agitation might lead if pushed to its logical conclusion. Expressed with characteristic vigor by Leo Maxse, it proceeded from strong partisan attachments (Maxse admitted to being a "strong and violent party man upon most questions") but emphasized the essential duplicity of all politicians on defense issues and the consequent need to appeal directly to the people as the only means of ensuring that they did their expected duty. "Either front bench, when in power, whatever may be their vigorous protests in Opposition, always try to sneak a battleship or to steal a pound from the Navy whenever they think the public is not looking."[43] These complaints were reminiscent of those voiced at the Navy League's foundation. But they went further in that they suggested that certain individuals, once devoutly partisan, might seek a direct appeal to the people and deny that the parties exercised any legitimate role in the execution of defense policy. The intention would be to circumvent the party system, not to supplement it.

The second ingredient was the effort by each side to appropriate national identity and to identify its argument with allegedly corresponding facets of the national culture. Those speakers who defended the committee's position stressed the inherent tolerance or reasonableness of English political behavior and the absence of partisan malice. This was in line with the Englishman's essential "commonsense," by which was conveyed an innate caution, suspicion of the sorts of quick solutions promoted by Wyatt and Horton-Smith, and even—shades of Cecil here—a conservative approach to the issue of political agitation. Contrasts were drawn, not specifically with Germany so much as with the Continent in general. Meanwhile, the dissidents' language tended to evoke the responsibilities of empire, and the conduct it implied was characteristic or "worthy" of British citizens was not moderation, but rather a steadfast adherence to original principles. It was the courage of their convictions, their fidelity to the league's initial goals, that prompted the dissidents to take appropriate action when confronted by changing circumstances.

In the months following the vote of 19 July, there were efforts to bring the factions together again, and even F. T. Jane offered his unlikely services to accomplish this. Such attempts were fruitless, because, as it appeared to the committee, "the views held by the dissentient members are so divergent, a reconciliation is impossible under the present circumstances."[44] On the local level as well the cleavage was becoming all too apparent. The secretary of the Third London branch (Kentish Town and Northwest London) approached the executive about the correct response to the presence of Wyatt and Horton-Smith within his branch; the executive responded with a warning that they were "understood to be endeavouring to injure the league."[45] Simultaneously, Wyatt and Horton-Smith were lining up support for a new, "navier" league to conduct the public agitation on the naval issue that the Navy League had eschewed. The decisive test of strength appears to have come within the Third London branch at a special meeting on 11 January 1908 at which a majority of that branch's members decided to secede to Wyatt and Horton-Smith's proposed new organization.[46] Two weeks later, on 27 January 1908, the Imperial

Maritime League was formally founded, with the two dissidents serving as its joint secretaries. The dissension within navalist ranks was now institutionalized.

Professional opinion was divided as to the relative merits of the two leagues. Beresford and his supporters gravitated toward the Imperial Maritime League, given its anti-Fisher orientation, as did a number of journalists (Blumenfeld of the *Daily Express*, Gwynne and Cope Cornford of the *Standard*), and a sprinkling of former Navy League branch officers (Lord Ampthill, W. B. Boyd-Carpenter, F. T. Jane, Rudyard Kipling, and Charles Stribling).[47] Battalions of critics, however, massed on the other side. Lord Esher, for one, wasted little time in condemning the new association, and his harsh letter in the *Times* of 6 February 1908 reminded readers that the Imperial Maritime League's vendetta against Fisher would ultimately benefit Germany. Admiral Sir John Hopkins applauded Esher's "double-shotted broadside," and, although he expected little from the new league, he thought Esher prudent "to open fire before it deludes others who don't know."[48] H. O. Arnold-Forster, a former parliamentary secretary and an acknowledged authority on military affairs, criticized both sides in the controversy, believing that "the incompetence of the leaders on the one side was fairly balanced by the violence and want of judgement shown on the other."[49]

Indeed, the Navy League was in no mood to compromise with its new competitor. Its executive committee immediately began to discuss ways of reconstructing the league and to attend to complaints about the nonattendance of many executive members. In November 1907 it prepared instructions for branches to improve their membership and finances, and the following January it reacted to the report of a visit by Wyatt and Horton-Smith to the London suburb of Clapham by directing that a Clapham branch of the Navy League be founded without delay.[50] The day after the Imperial Maritime League had been officially founded, Navy League executive members contacted a solicitor about legal action against the new organization, but upon his recommendation dropped the idea. Two weeks later, the Navy League's stalwart lecturer, Lt. Knox, was dispatched with committee member Alan Burgoyne to the House of Commons to detach from the Imperial Maritime League any MPs who might already have pledged their support to Wyatt and Horton-Smith.[51]

More significantly, the league began to revise its assumptions about political intervention. A comprehensive nationwide program of agitation remained problematic, but direct partisan support of candidates seemed more acceptable. In mid-February 1908 the executive resolved to "gibbet" all antinavy candidates with the sole proviso that such action would be undertaken insofar as funds permitted.[52] This firmer resolve was displayed at the Peckham by-election the following month. The Unionist candidate affirmed his support of the fleet in accordance with the league's definitions; his Liberal opponent, who declined to do so, was then condemned for his alleged neglect of the nation's security. Examples multiplied in the following months: Unionist MPs proliferated on the Navy League's executive committee, general action was authorized in the constituencies of all "Little Navy" members (in other words, not confined to seats with contested by-elections), and the Navy League began to utilize its Unionist connections to thwart local efforts by the Imperial Maritime League.[53] The latter had sought to arrange a major meeting in Ealing, perhaps with a view to embarrassing its sitting member, Herbert Nield, a strong advocate of the Navy League. The Imperial Maritime League insisted that "all attempts to raise the Radical government by non-party action have failed," that "the 'non-party' attitude is imperiling the very existence of England as an independent state," and that "the present effort of the Imperial Maritime League is to rouse the Unionist Party to take action in defence of the British Navy." As Wyatt explained:

> We had naturally invited, and were beginning actually to receive, the cooperation of the Unionist Association at Ealing in this effort to direct public attention to the state of naval defence. Now to our unspeakable amazement, we have received a letter from the official secretary of the Unionist organization in the locality, to the effect that he and his association are deterred from giving further aid by the resentment and the opposition of the Navy League's members. These appear to desire, with a furious malignity, that the patriotic gathering fixed for November 12th should not be held.[54]

By the end of 1908, then, the ability of the naval issue to sustain nationalist agitation presented some curious features. From the mid-1890s, there had been divergent views about the means of ensuring naval security and the likely consequences for a Liberal party that seemed to be partially, but not universally, committed to maintaining the fleet at levels that might be precariously low. But by 1908, many more navalists were willing to contemplate partisan action to elect nationalist Unionists and defeat unreliable Liberals. Certainly both the Imperial Maritime League's stated platform and the Navy League's series of decisions in the spring of 1908 contrasted with the indecision of 1900 or the confusion of 1902. Yet convergent policies also produced greater discord, for many navalists seemed bent in 1907–1908 on a peculiarly self-destructive course in which their energies were directed primarily against each other rather than against the enemies of national security they claimed to have exposed in such profusion. Fisher's controversial policies and personality were important here, but ultimately counted for less than the critical fact of a Liberal administration in power. It was the pressure from a progressive government that ultimately forced a reassessment of perennial Conservative claims truly to represent the national interest. And this was to be as true with regard to domestic and economic questions as with foreign or military issues.

Enforcing Fiscal Orthodoxy

Nowhere was the greater urgency of patriotic commitment among Unionists that the Campbell-Bannerman government was felt to have necessitated more evident than in regard to the issue of tariff reform. Balfour's ability to resist tariff reform pressure had been eroded, though not destroyed, by the predominance of tariff reformers in the parliamentary party after January 1906, and it was therefore clear that he would have to come to an arrangement on the issue with Joseph Chamberlain. If not, Balfour's very leadership of the party might be in jeopardy, especially if Chamberlain seized the opportunity provided by Balfour's temporary absence from the Commons (the former prime minister was himself among those candidates defeated and had not yet found a safe by-election seat on which to return). The Birmingham leader specifically denied this possibility in a long letter to Viscount Ridley of 6 February 1906 intended for publication. After a flurry of activity, the two politicians reached a compromise on 14 February, sealed by an exchange of letters subsequently known as the Valentine compact. Balfour accepted that fiscal reform must remain "the first constructive work of the Unionist party" and conceded that establishment of a moderate general tariff and imposition of a small duty on foreign grain were "not in principle objectionable."[55] Although liberally sprinkled with caveats and disclaimers to which Balfour would return, the Valentine letters were interpreted as evidence that the Unionist party would now march to a tariff reform beat.

Yet any optimism that tariffs could be the most visible and effective weapon in a well-stocked nationalist armory was unfounded. Balfour preferred to concentrate on the educational question, and a temporary economic upturn seemed to contradict tariff reformers' persistent claims of a causal link between free trade and economic distress. Furthermore, on 13 July, Chamberlain, no longer able to maintain the gruelling pace of the past 3 years, suffered a stroke. He remained partially paralyzed thereafter, and for 1906 the paralysis extended to the Tariff Reform League as well. In the aftermath of electoral disaster, inefficient organization was always a convenient excuse, and dismayed league members were to offer no exception. One visitor protested at the "chaotic state" of league headquarters, and Ridley admitted that "the Tariff Reform League must be reformed."[56] "I have endured tortures with the present people there," he complained to Chamberlain shortly after the election. Personnel changes were made, including in the critical post of secretary in which the energetic T. W. A. Bagley replaced Ratcliffe Cousins.[57] Reforms in the Unionist party machine were also demanded, especially to permit increased access from below so as to reflect growing tariff reform sentiment in the country. While the whole-hoggers succeeded in capturing the National Union, they were unsuccessful in efforts to restructure or pressure the party's Central Office, which continued to take its cue from Balfour.

By the winter of 1906–1907, tariff reformers were growing restive. Leo Maxse, whose bitter assault on Central Office in July 1906 had not endeared him to Balfourites, complained of "the comparative inactivity of Tariff Reformers, which *ex hypothesi* is largely due to the unfriendly, not to say treacherous, attitude of Balfour and Co., who are doing all they can do to damp down and destroy our movement."[58] This inactivity posed a dilemma for activists no less troubling than that which many navalists were facing at the same point. Clearly any notion of tariff reform as a nonpartisan policy to attract nationally minded Liberals could be dismissed outright. If tariff reform were to be enacted, it could only be through the advocacy of the Unionist party. But this requirement raised two further critical problems: how should efforts to provoke a public agitation on the issue proceed if the party leadership resisted on the grounds that to do so would be premature; and what degree of latitude would be permitted to party members whose credentials were otherwise impeccable but who refused to lend their support? In other words, should strictly partisan or nationalist agitational considerations be given priority? The two problems were related, and, when one was resolved, it would inevitably affect the other: a stronger lead from the leadership would narrow the room for maneuver by Unionist free fooders, and increasing unanimity on the fiscal issue at the local level might persuade the leader to follow.

Accordingly, in 1907, the Tariff Reform League began to redouble its efforts. Given the veneer of party unity lent by the Valentine compact, dissident actions were attributed to the supposed secret "inquisitorial arm" of the Tariff Reform League, the "Confederacy."[59] The Confederacy was not a separate, distinct organization, although league members sought to maintain that fiction when it suited their purposes, but an informal group of ardent, younger tariff reformers who intended to intimidate Unionist free traders into withdrawal or conversion. Elaborate threats often concealed its modest size, yet standing behind it were the considerable resources of the Tariff Reform League itself. It functioned most successfully as a means for devolving responsibility for aggressive tariff reform action and, in particular, for enforcing stringent definitions of doctrinal purity on the fiscal issue. Sandars reported that "Percival Hughes now came to me with the complaint that everywhere the Liberal Unionists—posing as Liberal Unionists but in reality being Tariff Reform Leaguers—are, with the encouragement of Austen and Co., trying to squeeze out or capture our local conservative associations."[60] In reply, Balfour noted the logic of this strategy, for the principle of local autonomy was an ideal shelter for tariff reform persuasion or intimidation:

> From their point of view they are perfectly right, since the very essence of our Party organisation is that the local associations are (within their own sphere) supreme, and the task of capture ought not to be very difficult seeing that a majority of the Party, and I suspect the great majority of its local office bearers, are Protectionists at heart.[61]

Sandars also detailed examples that the league was "inducing many of our best local committeemen to leave our local associations and to join or work for the Tariff Reform League branches."[62] Simultaneously, a Primrose League official complained to Balfour that tariff reformers were recruiting workers away from the Primrose League and justifying their predations with the claim that fiscal reform reflected the true Unionist cause.[63]

This growing weight of evidence Balfour could not ignore, and, indeed, he had not been unreceptive to the idea of fiscal reform if a way could be found of sanitizing it so as to preserve party unity. In October 1907, Balfour admitted that "a great change has manifested itself within the last year" with the result that the party was "so deeply committed" to tariff reform that "it is inconceivable that they should ever take office without making it their main business to carry it through."[64] He had been genuinely impressed by preferentialist sentiment at the Colonial Conference earlier in the year, and he also had been exploring the issue with W. A. S. Hewins, admitting that he found it "very agreeable talking to a fiscal reformer who really knows something about his case."[65] Much is made of the impact of Balfour's eventual public profession of tariff reform in November 1907, but clearly the resurgence of tariff sentiment preceded rather than followed his decision; his conversion symbolized the attractions of tariff reform, not the other way around.

Appropriately enough, Balfour's commitment was given in Birmingham, in a speech to the annual meeting of the National Union on 14 November 1907. He outlined four major benefits of fiscal reform, and in the course of explaining them illustrated the evolution of the fiscal issue since 1903: the retaliatory power of tariffs, the necessity of colonial preference, the ability to safeguard domestic productive industries, and the desirability of broadening the basis of taxation.[66] Balfour had warmed to the first of these themes early on, for it was susceptible of interpretation as a policy of either free trade or fair trade. A league pamphlet entitled "The Policy of Tariff Reform" depicted an English fighter in the ring whose gloves were chained together with manacles labeled "Free Imports." The clear implication was that economic uncompetitiveness could be attributed to unfair advantages currently enjoyed by the nation's foreign competitors, and if tariff reform did not restore free trade (and there is little evidence that most tariff reformers anticipated this), it nonetheless offered the prospect of a swift remedy. By shifting the blame to other countries, an emphasis on retaliation obviated the need to reexamine British institutions and practices that otherwise might be presumed defective. It is hardly surprising, then, that this alternative recommended itself to the less adventurous who clustered around the Balfourite center of the Unionist party, or that it was deemed insufficient by those who sought precisely a thorough overhaul of the nation's institutions and practices to "update" them for changed conditions.

Colonial preference, however, involved a more sophisticated appreciation of national vulnerability, which, along with the established unpopularity of food taxes with which it was associated, accounted for its controversial nature. The league cited preference as the

> greatest of the four problems of Tariff Reform [that] must be approached and solved from two distinct though closely related points of view. . . . We have to regard it from the standpoint of our own insular interests, our interests as a small manufacturing island in the northern seas with a large and growing population for whom permanent employment is the essential condition of continued subsistence. And we have also to regard it from the imperial standpoint, as it concerns the social, industrial, and political development of those great Colonies and Dependencies which together make up this British Empire of which we also form a part, and without which the United Kingdom would quickly sink to the level of a third- or fifth-rate European power.[67]

The great difficulty had always been to domesticate this imperialist vision, to adapt it to working-class interests as a "knife and fork" issue without becoming trapped in the mire of "food taxes." Efforts to stress that any price rises would be transitory or compensated for by reductions in existing duties had not mollified public opinion, yet despite pressure from within the party, this preferential theme was too deeply held by a devoted core of tariff reformers to be jettisoned so easily. The only alternative was to supplement preference with additional themes that might attract a greater measure of popular support.

Balfour's third point, the safeguarding of domestic industries, was an attempt to do just this and would have been familiar to his audience as a traditional justification for protection, though tariff reformers were rarely keen to use that evocative word. The domestic market could be preserved, or in some cases reconquered, by shutting out cheaper foreign products. The practice of "dumping," whereby foreign competitors deliberately sold goods in Britain at below cost to drive local firms out of business, could be halted. "Many industries now dying out would be revived" ran this argument, "and others, long since dead, would be brought to new life."[68] The result would be a significant reduction in unemployment; as the *Daily Express* rarely tired of repeating, "Tariff Reform means work for all." Here seemed a way of countering the apprehension that the imperial aspects of tariff reform would only raise the cost of living. Even those already regularly employed would benefit, tariff reformers predicted, as wages rose in a newly buoyant economy. Like the issue of food taxes, this contention was open to serious challenge, in regard to both the probable deleterious impact upon the volume of British trade and the effects upon those industries that neither relied primarily upon the domestic market nor displayed signs of imminent decline (the cotton industry being the most frequently cited example).

The fourth point in the tariff reform program reflected the changing emphases of the movement as dictated by political realities. In packaging the fiscal issue for popular consumption, the original imperial aspects that Chamberlain had stressed would be overshadowed by the paramount necessity of demonstrating that tariffs would be cheap and effective. Enacting social reforms and meeting the nation's security needs were to be financed by a fresh source of revenue, namely, that arising from protective duties on imported manufactured goods. "England expects that every foreigner should pay his duty" was one league slogan (and a suggestive one, too, evoking the patriotic sentiment of Nelson's famous signal at Trafalgar and nicely illustrating some of the interrelated concerns of the nationalist agitation), which implied that the basis of taxation could be broadened to tap the unfair competitors whose ill-gotten gains had caused honest English workmen such misery. Estimates ranged between £10 and £20 million as to the amount that might be raised by this device alone. Tariff reform attracted attention as a revenue device because it could be bent to traditional ends: utilized to deflect demands for greater direct taxation, which the Unionist party's prosperous supporters would otherwise be forced to bear. Tariffs, as presented in late 1907, broadened the basis of indirect taxation, which, to that same core of party support, appeared to be a far more palatable alternative.

There were, to be sure, problems with these formulations. The link between diagnosis and cure had yet to be established with sufficient plausibility for many skeptics. As the Unionist free trader Ernest Beckett explained:

> Now, those who argued that our industries were being ruined had to prove, first that the proportion of ruined industries as compared with the flourishing industries was something more than infinitesimal; then that the ruin of industries was foreign competition, not home competition and effete methods and business inefficiency; and finally that the disappearance of such ruined industries was not soon followed by the emergence of others better equipped, with larger profits, and affording greater employment.[69]

Although each side in the debate characteristically focused on those industries that displayed the clearest indications of growth or decay, the nation's diminished share of total world production was irrefutable. If there was a glaring weakness in the tariff reform program, it stemmed not from the persistent assertions of economic pessimism, but rather from precisely those revenue implications that the Tariff Reform League and the Unionist party had begun to articulate with such vigor in 1907. The mystery was how tariffs could raise significant revenue from duties upon imports while simultaneously protecting domestic industries by reducing the volume of imports. Asquith posed this dilemma with particular clarity, remarking acidly in the Commons that "as an instrument of revenue it [a tariff] can only succeed to the extent in which it fails as an instrument of protection."[70] Yet revenue was a critical issue, and potential solutions were not to be discarded lightly, even if they might exemplify dialectical dexterity rather than perfect logical consistency. In May 1907 Asquith had announced that the Liberal government would press for old age pensions, and it was incumbent upon the Unionist opposition to meet Liberal revenue devices with counter proposals, and, in the absence of anything better, tariffs might serve this purpose.

Indeed, tactical considerations were also critical, and, whatever the ideological ramifications of Balfour's rapprochement with the tariff reformers, his move was bound to affect the tariff reform campaign in the constituencies. That work in the country, undertaken in its more notorious instances by the Confederacy, was devoted—as it had been in Durham or Greenwich or Croydon earlier—to ensuring that Unionist free trade MPs forsook their fiscal convictions in favor of tariffs. Failing this, it aimed at denying unrepentant free traders official party support and opposing them with declared tariff reform candidates. That task, however, would become easier, as tariff reform figured more clearly in the party's program. Austen Chamberlain staunchly defended the logic behind Confederate intervention. Were a Unionist free trader reelected, "he will count as one of our supporters, but in all the divisions on the most critical point of your future constructive policy [Chamberlain reminded Balfour], he will vote against us. He is a soldier in the ranks who in critical engagements will fire on his general instead of on the enemy."[71] Moreover, he continued, "as he openly disavows and rejects your policy those who agree with that policy among his constituents have a clear right, and may even think it a duty, to run a candidate against him."

Tariff reform's electoral credentials appeared to receive confirmation with whole-hogger triumphs at Mid-Devon on 17 January 1908 and Worcester several weeks later (for which arch-Confederate Edward Goulding, "Joe's Man Friday" was returned).[72] An economic downturn lent some credence to their predictions of the imminent woes of free trade, and prospects appeared likely that the Unionist free trade ranks would be thinned if not eradicated altogether by further defections, defeats, and retirements. Renewed pressure on George Bowles at Norwood in mid-1907 had been temporarily suspended by a letter of support from Balfour, but, with this prop now gone, he was an isolated target. Bowles' appeals to the Conservative Central Office now met with stony silence or with the pointed advice to follow party policy as laid down recently by Balfour at Birmingham; failing that he could expect no support nor even neutrality should a tariff reform candidate be run against him. When Bowles discussed the matter with the president of the Norwood branch of the Tariff Reform League, a "kindly, if silly, old man" who "understands nothing of tariff reform," he was assured that another letter from Balfour might resolve the situation.[73] Yet this particular local whole-hogger, Colonel Campbell, was irrelevant to the process. Whether kindly or not, he was regarded by the Confederates as "an old fogey who must be stirred up," and neither he nor Bowles carried any weight with Balfour, who was in any event most unlikely to rupture the recently affirmed semblance of party unity stemming from his Birmingham speech. Pressure was consistently applied, and, in April 1908, the executive of the Norwood Unionist association voted against Bowles by 44–12, an action concluding a process that had been "in entire accordance with the wishes of the Central Office."[74]

Efforts of a similar nature occurred in most other constituencies with sitting Unionist free trade members. Their capacity to resist was diminished. A Central Office anxious to restore an unambiguous "fighting" policy was in no mood for concessions. Threats by free traders to retaliate by opposing tariff reform candidates in three-cornered contests or to seek some centrist coalition were similarly ineffectual. Opportunities to negotiate an alternative settlement appeared unlikely, given the inflexible public stance of the Confederates and the developing electoral muscle of the Tariff Reform League. In fact, behind the scenes, negotiation was an option explored by several Unionist free traders and pursued by the Confederates as well. At Marylebone, for example, Lord Robert Cecil exercised a degree of leverage, whether through his lineage or, when Balfour tired of his letters, through his undoubted talent, which the party could ill afford to lose, or the distaste for proscription that a number of the senior party members exhibited when applied to a Cecil. As Goulding reported to Joseph Chamberlain, "you will have seen that we are active in Marylebone and everything has been done through the local people. Most if not all the Chairmen in the wards where they love a Lord and that Lord being a Cecil has made our difficulties very great."[75] In March 1908, Cecil and his local association compromised: Cecil would stand as a Unionist but would resign his seat if unable to support a tariff reform budget once the Unionists were back in power.

Even this accommodation proved to be short-lived. In January 1909 tariff reform pressure was increased another notch. An article in the *National Review* entitled "The Confederacy" and attributed to "A Confederate" announced that a deadline for decisive action had finally arrived. "The last proselyte has been made," and the remaining heretics were to be rooted out.[76] On 18 January the *Morning Post* published a blacklist of eleven Unionist free traders who were presumed to be seeking reelection and a further five who were not. The article applauded what it perceived to be the correct steps to eliminate the threat to party unity which this obstinate handful continued to pose:

> We have reason to believe that the attitude adopted by the Principal Agent of the Conservative Party, Mr. Percival Hughes, shows that he fully realises the danger and is doing his best to meet it. . . . We are able to state that the Conservative Central Office will decline to give its official support to any candidate who does not unreservedly support the leader of the Unionist Party in the policy then laid down.

Orthodoxy on the fiscal issue was the sole determinant of continued membership in the Unionist party, as the paper reemphasized the following day. "There can be no room in the ranks for laggards and waverers in this cause, whatever their abilities or qualifications in other spheres."[77] And well might the paper be satisfied with the attitude of Hughes, for the article "was altered and approved by Hughes and his superiors (I [Goulding] presume Hood) and was kept by them for that purpose four days before even Ware (as Editor) saw it and consented to insert same."[78] The clear implication was that any deals being worked out with free traders should be abandoned in the greater interest of the party. It was a curious argument. Party discipline was being asserted, namely, the primacy of commitment to party policy, yet defined in a way that ignored every issue on which politicians had customarily divided until some 6 years before. A particular nationalist issue had been broached, criticized as a threat to party unity, yet reappeared triumphantly cloaked in appeals to Unionist harmony. It was a remarkable achievement, yet it imperfectly concealed two crucial facts. First, a fair proportion of Unionist members or candidates, the precise figure as yet undetermined, was soft on tariffs. They had only accepted tariff reform reluctantly, either in deference to external pressure or in dismay at the lack of alternative policies with which to counter the Liberal program. Second, despite whatever gloss might be placed upon it, no less than navalism, tariff reform had served to divide rather than to integrate Unionists as a political force. Tariff reform may have been adopted as the "first constructive policy of the party," but it clearly had led to bitter internecine warfare, which, in the short run, weakened rather than strengthened the party. In 1907 and 1908 there still appeared, to many in the party, good reasons to doubt the urgency of implementing the solutions demanded by the nationalist agitation. An argument could be (and was) made that an appeal to more traditional Conservative issues was sufficient, that the party's difficulties stemmed from too great a tolerance for those nationalist types who condemned any such traditionalist appeals as outmoded and ineffectual.

Proponents of a more forward, agitational direction with regard to naval policy were a distinct minority, but were forced to secede from the bulk of the navalist movement. Within the tariff reform movement, a body comparable to the dissidents of the Imperial Maritime League emerged, namely, the Confederacy, yet they largely succeeded in implementing their stance as the policy adhered to by a majority of the party. In part, this reflected the greater variety of avenues through which tariff reformers could operate, ranging from league branches to local Unionist or Liberal Unionist associations to sympathetic, prominent individuals. No doubt too the fact that the demarcation between the parties on fiscal policy was sharper than on naval policy contributed, as did the fact that expert opinion on tariff reform was more fractured. Economists could be found to justify all shades of opinion.[79] And while there was incontrovertible proof that the nation's grip on economic supremacy was rapidly slipping, the Royal Navy remained without question the strongest fleet in the world.

The commitment and resources behind the tariff reformers' political activity often infuriated but invariably impressed contemporary observers. One individual who was well placed to evaluate those efforts was J. Wallace Carter, the organizing secretary for the rival Free Trade Union who, in the midst of the troubles brewing with Marylebone, assessed the situation in a confidential memorandum for Lord Robert Cecil:

> The Tariff Reform campaign has assumed enormously greater proportions since the General Election. Previous to 1906 the Tariff Reform League would send from six to twelve workers into the by-elections. Now they may be numbered by hundreds. . . . Since the general election the Tariff Reform League has among other things:
>
> a. Conducted a large proportion of its propaganda from public houses
>
> b. Imported large numbers of alleged "unemployed" who have lost their occupations owing to Free Trade (this is in a sense true, since owing to Free Trade they have become agents of the Tariff Reform League!)
>
> c. The Tariff Reform League workers no longer carry on a separate campaign, but work from Unionist committee rooms.
>
> d. Apparently there is no limit to the number of their agents or the extent of their financial resources. The result of all this is that the Corrupt Practices Acts might as well be torn up. . . .[80]

"The tariff reformer conducts his nightly campaign on extremely skillful lines," warned another recipient of league attention. "His appeal is cunningly varied to suit the locality in which he is operating; and always some decaying local industry furnishes the text."[81] The basic message, "more work and higher wages," was repeated, whatever the circumstances. On occasion, however, the medium might change even if the message did not, as in South Hereford, for example:

A miserable specimen of humanity makes his appearance at a public house. Apparently he is a tramp, and a miserable object at that, of doleful visage and clad in a grimy, greasy, ragged attire. He addresses a pathetic plea for food or for any help the kind gentleman in the kitchen may be pleased to bestow. He tells a pitiful story of prosperous days clouded by unemployment brought about through the importation of foreign goods. To the baneful practice of dumping he attributes the wretched condition in which he is obliged to present himself. Then naturally enough, under the stimulating influence of the drink offered by sympathetic yokels, a discussion on the great remedy, Tariff Reform, is started. The stranger waxes eloquent on the need of broadening the basis of taxation, the utter harmlessness of little duties, the skill with which the charges upon taxes are to be rung, the joy of fleecing the foreigner and the like . . . [if there is a suspicious person present] he notices the visitor wears sound waterproof boots, and . . . sound, warm underclothing. In fact he is really a Protectionist emissary playing a part.[82]

Armed with official party cooperation to supplement these sharp practices, tariff reformers could present a formidable combination. Walter Long recalled that in 1906 it had been "common talk in the Head Whip's room that the organisation of the Unionist Party was being interfered with and frequently checkmated, by the action of the extreme Tariff Reform Party." By 1908, though, "apparently the latter has swallowed up the former."[83] Chief Whip Acland-Hood was "coming round" to tariff reform late in 1907, and the following year "appeared to have gone over bag and baggage to the extreme tariff reformers."[84] The party's principal agent, Percival Hughes, was, at the very least, "in close touch" with members of the league and "fully aware of their wiles."[85] Sir Joseph Lawrence, a member of the Tariff Reform League's executive committee, reported that "we save money and increase efficiency of all Unionist parties by avoiding duplication of lecturers and literature, and helpfully interchanging services and concerting our efforts."[86] When the Unionist Organization Committee conducted its inquest during 1911 into the state of party machinery, a number of witnesses praised the league's prior service to the Unionist cause. Party lecturers were compared unfavorably with those dispatched by the league, and H. Imbert-Terry claimed that the league functioned so smoothly in harness with the party organization that there was no need to locate it in the Conservative Central Office![87]

Critics deplored this increasing coziness as further evidence of the degenerative moral tone tariffs inevitably produced. Lord Robert Cecil's primary objection to tariff reform was his revulsion against its "way of looking at politics. It appears to me to be entirely sordid and materialistic, not yet corrupt, but on the high road to corruption."[88] Tariffs produced a politics of trusts and cartels whose lamentable influence was both alien to the principles of English behavior and characteristic of the vulgar tone of American ways.[89] Likewise, the Duke of Portland, spurred to action by the Confederacy's pressure upon his brother in South Nottingham, condemned the Tariff Reform League's activities as "not only most impolitic but at the same time most unpatriotic."[90]

The Language of Tariff Reform

Yet, as its adherents were at pains to point out, tariff reform was articulated as a specifically nationalist or patriotic policy. At its most basic level, it involved sharpening the distinction between "us" and "them," between Englishmen (or, as an occasional variation, Anglo-Saxons) and foreigners. Definition of an out-group as a focus for hostility and blame was essential to the perception of a nationalist community whose existing bonds needed to be strengthened to assure repelling the threat from outside. The enemy might be identified as any foreigner, or, more specifically, German, or even an Englishman whose erroneous beliefs no longer entitled him to consideration as one of the patriotic community. These sorts of people shared an adherence to English free trade, possibly from conviction, but more likely from self-interest, as they benefitted at the expense of the broader community. If there was a "sordid" or "materialistic" aspect to political life, then, it would not be introduced by the tariff reformers but vanquished by them, for it already existed under the guise of free trade. Foreign nations, profiting at England's expense from her misplaced expectation that other countries would adhere to her standards of ethical business conduct, had a vested interest in England's continued adherence to free trade. And those unscrupulous individuals often owed allegiance to no particular nation. "Cosmopolitan interests," they were labeled, as they bled England dry in the name of free trade.

"Herr Dumper" was a stock figure in tariff reform literature, and the same theme was illustrated in "dump shops," rented rooms where the Tariff Reform League displayed German or other foreign goods that undersold their English counterparts and eliminated English jobs. These shops were quite literally E. E. Williams' warnings made tangible, but in the hope that they might soon serve as trophies from a species of competition rendered extinct by the revival of native industry. For the lyrically inclined, there were songs such as the popular "Herr Schmidt's advice" with its refrain, "Ach, Cobden vos a vondrous man."[91] These anti-Germanic sentiments harmonized well with the developing concerns of the nationalist agitation and appeared to receive further confirmation from reports of widespread German espionage within the country. In retrospect, such reports appear to have been highly exaggerated, but, within the contexts of German naval and economic competition and the intended reaffirmation of English nationalist identity, they seemed to make some sense.

H. A. Gwynne, for example, editor of the *Standard*, confided to Bonar Law that "there are a good many level-headed and not a bit excitable people who are getting rather nervous about the German danger. This nervousness is, I assure you, in no degree hysterical, but is due to a well-founded dread of a possible raid in such numbers as to threaten our existence as a nation."[92] Gwynne claimed to have evidence that German staff officers were exploring Essex, that German waiters and publicans were congregating near Aldershot, and that Germanic tourists' professed enthusiasm for natural beauty seemed always to be taking them within range of military installations. Popular fiction broached the same themes. Alan Burgoyne, a Navy Leaguer and a Confederate, produced a typical example of the genre in his *The War Inevitable.* "Two years of Teutonic arrogance and deception over certain features of our foreign policy had left an ineradicable mark upon the British populace," he wrote.[93] A surprise German attack was only repelled by the inspired leadership of Sir John Angler (a none too subtle pseudonym for Fisher) and Lord Roberts, who tapped the latent strain of English courage. In the Tory utopia that followed— for the Liberals had been discredited by their inattention to the nation's needs—tariff reform was enacted and socialism "recast and reconstituted" to foster individual self-reliance.

On occasion, anti-German sentiment shaded into anti-Semitism. Tariff reformers pilloried banking and international finance as unregenerate cosmopolitan interests, and the Jewish presence in such institutions was significant. Foreigners depicted in Tariff Reform League literature or posters sometimes took on stereotypical Jewish features or accents, and journalists such as Arnold White, who wrote on behalf of the various nationalist organizations, made little effort to disguise their anti-Semitic prejudices. Moreover, the tariff reformers' pledge to preserve employment for English workers (reminiscent of the Navy League's efforts to restrict the manning of British ships to British seamen) implied limiting imports of foreign workers as well as foreign products. Safeguarding domestic industries, then, entailed restricting immigration. When Joseph Chamberlain pledged himself to do just that in London's East End, in practice this meant, and was understood by his receptive audience to mean, restrictions upon the entry of East European Jews. Ugly scenes did occur. In Scotland, in one example, "some people [canvassers insofar as the investigator could determine] . . . created a bother and set up the backs of the Jews at Tradeston by calling them bad names." These "canvassers" were "Tariff Reform League people," though Steel-Maitland, who was pursuing the matter, was advised that the person most likely to understand the situation "was a well-known Jew there who did a great deal of work for us in organising meetings, etc."[94]

The language of the tariff reform movement and the cluster of meanings and associations it sought to involve exhibited a number of interconnecting strands. The primacy of nationalist symbols was evident in the frequent display of John Bull and the Union Jack, and the contrasts between English habits and individuals and those of foreign countries were vividly demonstrated. Among these specified English virtues were not the familiar ones of law or sweet reasonableness so much as those habits that were deemed critical to the survival of England as a great nation in a hostile environment: masculine behavior, an uncompromising stand on issues, and a willingness to retaliate for unfair commercial attacks (images of the boxer in the ring or use of the "big revolver"). In so doing, tariff reformers sought to appropriate the moral high ground by investing their campaign with an aura of commitment to principle while shifting the notion of corruption and sordid self-interest to their Liberal free trade opponents.

Even hesitant Unionists could, if dilatory in expressing their enthusiasm for tariffs, expose themselves to criticism along these lines. Balfour himself was open to charges of an effete political style predicated on olympian philosophical sophistry, not the practical straightforward style associated with his successor, Bonar Law. The fact that much of Balfour's style was deliberately cultivated and concealed a ruthless streak did not detract from tariff reformers' efforts to emphasize this line of attack. Moreover, the stress upon English common sense and practical skills, reminiscent of the contested terrain within the Navy League, could sustain an aversion to the amateurish landed elites under whose limp guidance industrial supremacy had departed and in whose stifling atmosphere Balfour and the Cecilian line had been nurtured. In contrast, tariff reform would address the interests of common people, both by its supposedly sincere commitment to living standards and economic regeneration and through its professed preference for more democratic means of political organization.

Less visible perhaps, but nonetheless frequently implied in private correspondence, was a stream of religious imagery that suggests that tariff reform had assumed the status of a secular crusade. Leo Amery had described Chamberlain's Birmingham speech as a challenge "as direct and provocative as the theses which Luther nailed to the Church door at Wittenberg" with the result that even moderate men began "hating free trade with all the intensity with which any Calvinist ever hated the Church of Rome."[95] Sir Joseph Lawrence declared that the prospect of a tariff reform-based Unionist party "serving well-ordered progress at home and the unity of the Empire" was "a faith more inspiring than any form of religion."[96] The Confederacy spoke of proselytes and heretics, and one of its leaders, Henry Page Croft, compared visits to Birmingham with pilgrimages to Mecca.[97] Austen Chamberlain noted, with evident pride, that "where a man has become a convinced Tariff Reformer, nothing will shake him. It is a religion and he becomes its ardent missionary."[98] There are a number of possible factors at work here.

In an age of declining formal religious commitment, it is likely that tariff reform absorbed energies that formerly would have been channeled into organized religion. Or, given the centrality of Anglicanism to so many Conservatives, this religious-like sense of a community of believers may have proven congenial to non-Anglican Unionists (and, of course, the Chamberlains were among the most prominent examples of this latter category). But the most striking aspect is the degree to which tariff reform could be embraced as the critical core of an encompassing nationalist ideology, virtually a gospel according to Chamberlain. The nationalist agitation, if it gained a measure of coherence at all, derived it from the sense that a prevailing set of assumptions—free trade, voluntarism, Little Englandism—had dictated the tone of English life for decades and were strongly entrenched. The whole of this tenacious culture, this orthodoxy, had to be uprooted. Englishmen had to be taught to challenge their customary and cherished assumptions and made to recognize that radically different circumstances (a set of new and terrifying economic, military and political challenges) required a new faith. It was the sense of seeking to discredit outworn but prevailing norms (another Reformation) and dread of the consequences of failure (the submersion of English identity to continental authority) that led Amery, quite consciously, to stress the parallels with the sixteenth century, the era of the English Reformation and the consolidation of the Tudor state. Perhaps some tariff reformers felt guilty about seeking to displace defense of the church as a primary Unionist issue, and they thus came to see their commitment to tariff reform in moral terms as a means of compensation. And to those profoundly distressed by the erosion of formal religious observance among the working class, tariff reform might redress matters if it were invested with a strong moral component.

Reaching the working class was, as the whole-hoggers acknowledged, a tricky matter. Sir Joseph Lawrence reacted to criticism that Tariff Reform League literature was too simplistic by explaining that the league's staff, "some of whom are experienced in political propaganda work and in elections, say that owing to the dense ignorance of a large mass of electors, it is only possible to reach their intellects through simple leaflets and cartoons."[99] Material, he continued, "has to be doled out in homeopathic doses, and adapted to a particular constituency." Certainly the Trade Union Tariff Reform Association had enjoyed less than conspicuous success in its efforts to mobilize workers. "Opinions as to its efficiency and value in the Tariff movement differ very widely," reported Hewins to Balfour in 1908. "In the places I have visited they are doing very good work," he explained.

> I may for example mention Dudley, where I attended a meeting of the Branch some weeks ago and found that they have 400 bona fide Trade Union members—a body of voters of very material value in a contested election. On the other hand, I think branches might be mentioned which are of very little value, and naturally in any controversy as to the claims of the Trade Union Association, critics insist very much upon such branches.[100]

By early 1909 the association had attracted two enthusiastic sponsors in Amery and Lord Milner, who hoped to form a committee "behind the scenes" to launch it properly and to assist it both "financial[ly] and otherwise." Amery claimed that the Trade Union Tariff Reform Association contained "quite a number of really intelligent and capable working men" and suggested that "if a small and energetic committee devoted itself to working the thing up as an organisation, and also helping it by insisting on getting some of its men into the House, the thing might at the end of a few years stand entirely on its own feet and compete effectively with the existing Labour party."[101] Privately, however, Amery recognized that it would not be the solution, for "many of its views are thoroughly distasteful to a great body of working men."[102]

Once again it was the problem of "socialism." Nield had raised it during the dissension in the Navy League; Balfour mused over it while preparing his Birmingham speech; Burgoyne's wishful thinking recast and reconstituted it. The 1906 election, by bringing into the Commons a significant group of Labour MPs, and the industrial disputes fueled by the decline in real wages sparked by rising prices (though this trend had by no means reached its peak) focused attention on the social issue. Even the normally imperturbable Balfour interpreted the results of 1906 as "the faint echo of the same movement which has produced massacres in St. Petersburg, riots in Vienna, and Socialist processions in Berlin."[103] The nation was facing, if "in a milder form," the "Socialist difficulties which loom so large on the Continent," and the election therefore inaugurated "a new era." To many of those who fancied themselves patriots, no greater threat could be posed to the fabric of the nation than a doctrine that stressed the primacy of international loyalties and seemed calculated to mobilize workers as a class enjoying an overwhelming preponderance of numbers.

The Sudden Urgency of Anti-Socialism

Unionist appeals to a tradition of Tory democracy would prove of little immediate practical significance. A properly nationalist response could take a negative form by seeking to construct an anti-Socialist bulwark of the frightened classes to ward off the masses, or the opportunity might be seized to launch a positive, constructive alternative in which tariff reform would figure as the central plank, but as a means to a broader end.[104] Lord Milner was a prominent advocate of the second approach, insisting that collectivist social reforms constituted the best way to attract and preserve working-class support. Only a wider state role would finally restore the fundamentals of British military power and domestic tranquility, while the outdated policies heretofore presented by the Unionist leadership amounted to little more than an ultimately ineffectual rearguard action.[105]

Demands for a more forward, comprehensive Unionist policy that would meet the coming crisis were encapsulated in a book published in 1908 entitled *The New Order: Studies in Unionist Policy*. The ostensible editor, Lord Malmesbury, introduced the volume of essays as "an attempt to discuss a number of questions of immediate public interest in a spirit consistent with Unionist traditions, and at the same time without hostility to reasonable innovation."[106] Anticipating one line of criticism the volume could likely arouse, he emphasized that "however difficult it may be for the more rigidly Conservative cast of mind to accept it, the necessity for new institutions and new movements in harmony with the changing spirit of the times has never been more imperative than at present; and just in proportion as the Unionist party proves itself capable of this adjustment will be its power of continued usefulness to the Country."[107] The essays, the editor hastened to add, were practical rather than purely philosophical, but were intended to guide the party through the disintegration of the organizing principle of previous decades (laissez-faire), the emergence of collectivism, and a "revolution in the theory of international trade."

Both the timing and the authorship of the essays were as important as the arguments propounded within them. Chapters such as that on "Ships" by Alan Burgoyne clearly were prompted by recent events. Burgoyne described himself as "a hardened Tory and enthusiastic Navy Leaguer." While acknowledging that "the Navy League has, unfortunately, suffered in the past from an excess of zeal on the part of certain members," he stressed "the danger" that lay "not so much with the Navy as with the politician."[108] "There has arisen a class of Parliamentarian," he continued, "to whom the words Patriotism or Imperialism appear a blasphemy, and these gentlemen are making their way steadily to the front in the ranks of the Radical Party. To them as allies have come the Labour section, and lastly that incomprehensible political hermaphrodite, the Socialist Independent."[109] Malmesbury chose a biological metaphor: "organisms are subject to malignant growths, . . . and from this rule the political organism is not exempt. We have in our midst a growth which has sprung into a poisonous weed of huge proportions." Socialism's "evils are found in almost every direction," he maintained, "destroying our national defences and warping the strength of the nation by its insidious and seductive teachings."[110] Thus in its attention to the naval issue, the socialist issue, and the legacy of free trade as a doctrine whose philosophical underpinnings had collapsed, *The New Order* was highly topical and reflected the concerns in 1907–1908 of the nationalist agitation to fashion an effective political platform. Owing to the admirably patient and thorough detective work of Alan Sykes, it is now clear that *The New Order* was in fact produced by members of the Confederacy and that it represented the public, articulated justification of the necessarily more shadowy work being undertaken in the various constituencies.[111]

When, however, Socialist candidates won by-election victories at Jarrow and Colne Valley in July 1907, some of the dangers dimly apprehended in January 1906 now appeared to be all too imminent.[112] The same month the National Union appointed a subcommittee to explore the possibility of mounting a special anti-Socialist campaign. Those chosen were all ardent tariff reformers: Viscount Ridley, Edward Goulding, and Sir Harry Samuel.[113] Three weeks later the London Municipal Society took up the challenge. It had been founded in 1894 to assist Unionist candidates in municipal elections and possessed considerable experience in campaigning against "municipal socialism."[114] It had, of course, been restricted to the metropolitan London area, and other existing anti-Socialist organizations that might work throughout the remainder of the country were small, ineffectual, and poorly coordinated. Accordingly, the London Municipal Society announced that

> the strenuous work which organised Socialism is now doing all over the country demands a wider and equally vigorous educational campaign. With a view to combined action by the various forces which are opposed to Socialism, a meeting of the Executive Committee of this society will be held on Wednesday next to consider the necessity of convening a conference of representatives of the different bodies interested in the question.[115]

The resulting conference on 24 October 1907 in London was attended by representatives from over 200 organizations, largely local rate-payers' associations or property owners' groups, but also including delegates from the Primrose League and the Liberal Unionist Council.[116] Despite the obviously Unionist complexion of the audience, there were the customary appeals to consider the matter in a generous nonpartisan spirit. The sense of urgency, however, was the dominant tone. Herbert Jessel, chairman of the London Municipal Society, wasted no time coming to the point, declaring that "he had no doubt in his own mind that at the next election it would be a straight fight between those who were opposed to Socialism and those who were not."[117] In so doing, he echoed George Wyndham's claim that only "Socialists and Imperialists are living men: the others are old women and senile professors. Let them clear out of the ring for what would be a fight to the finish."[118] So pressing a problem required a response that was both prompt and effective. Here the tenor of the meeting suggested that only a policy offering a constructive alternative to Socialism would serve. W. Hayes Fisher, who had sought to carry the naval issue to the working class, explained that "I would not stand on my platform to combat Socialism if I had to rely on a policy of pure negation."[119] Archibald Salvidge, the influential chairman of the Liverpool Working Men's Conservative Association, had likewise stressed that "it is not enough to call the Socialists names. Send us arguments."[120] The conference concluded by establishing a committee to monitor Socialism's progress, provide the desired critical literature, and prevent overlap through the coordination of existing approaches.

This committee met initially in the offices of Ralph Blumenfeld, editor of the *Daily Express*, and included Jessel, Harry Cust (who had helped to launch the Navy League), Conservative MPs Wilfrid Ashley and Claude Lowther, and a prominent writer, W. H. Mallock, who served as the first secretary.[121] Their deliberations, which did not commence until February 1908, were affected by the results, remarkable to ecstatic Tories and doleful Liberals alike, of the London County Council elections in October 1907. In sharp contrast to their party's recent decimation in the general election, candidates in the Unionist interest wrested control of the London County Council. Much of the "credit" went to the London Municipal Society, which had assiduously worked to produce such results. If so dramatic a Unionist recovery could be achieved on the local level, this appeared to validate the society's methods and to hold out the prospect of major additional gains if those efforts were extended on a nationwide basis.

Progress toward this goal, however, was slow. Funding was the first major hurdle. Given the variety of existing approaches to combating socialism— indeed, it had been the fact that anti-Socialist groups were so plentiful but uncoordinated that prompted these efforts—it was not the easiest matter to convince new subscribers loyal to existing organizations that fresh contributions were necessary to fund an association that might seem to duplicate previous efforts. Not until the autumn of 1908 was sufficient backing secured to proceed with founding the Anti-Socialist Union on an official basis. This contrasted with the swift response from members of the political and business communities to donate toward the Tariff Reform League; even the Navy League, while hardly financially secure, stimulated a prompt groundswell of support, which seemed to be lacking in the case of the Anti-Socialist Union. There was a second distinction unique to the experience of the union, namely, the financial role that the Unionist party adopted from the outset. W. H.

Mallock, as secretary, negotiated with Acland-Hood, the party's chief whip, and the financial guidelines they eventually adopted were evident from Mallock's report. "I am happy to be able to tell you," Mallock explained to Hood,

> as I told Sandars the other day, that the Anti-Socialist Association has at last received promises of support from private donors to the extent of £5,000, so that, with the addition of the £5,000 promised from the party fund, the total—viz. £10,000—estimated as the amount requisite for starting the Association on a practical basis, has been secured. The money will not be requested for actual use before October, and there will be no need to ask for the party donation till then. Meanwhile I shall be collecting the funds promised by the private donors. There is much preliminary work that ought to be begun at the earliest date possible; but it is practically impossible to make an efficient start until there is an assurance that the funds required will be forthcoming at a definite date. What, therefore, I am writing to ask you is this—that you should let me have a memorandum to the effect that, upon your being satisfied that the Association has in its possession cheques to the amount of £5,000, the additional £5,000 will be forthcoming, if necessary by, but not before, October. I wish to add further that the Association will be provided with a definite legal constitution, which would be shown you for your approval.[122]

Nor was the contribution an isolated windfall. In 1912 Wilfrid Ashley was understandably anxious whether the Union would "get our £5,000," and his apprehension was justified for the new party chairman, Steel-Maitland, had already proposed that "the enormous subsidy presently paid to the Anti-Socialist Union should be discontinued, proper notice being given them."[123]

Until 1912, however, the Anti-Socialist Union could proceed on the basis of the 1908 Mallock–Hood settlement, yet there remained the question of to what ends the funds should be directed. There was, for example, the possibility that the union would function solely as a sort of "think tank" to produce anti-Socialist literature to then be distributed by other agencies. It might, therefore, aspire to a role analogous to that of the Tariff Commission, as an ostensibly nonpartisan, deliberative body of experts whose considered opinion would embody the solutions to pressing economic and political circumstances. The lessons of the 1907 London County Council elections, however, seemed to point in another direction. While confirming the benefits to be reaped from an anti-Socialist platform, the elections also indicated that beneficial results could be obtained only through the intensive and sustained electoral intervention undertaken by the London Municipal Society. The ideas themselves were not enough; they had to be hammered home, methodically and persistently. If the very success of the London Municipal Society inspired imitation, it would also presumably strengthen the hand of those who espoused the genuine article. Indeed, it was legitimately contended that the London Municipal Society should extend its activities rather than entrusting responsibility to an untried organization. Eventually a compromise was effected, and the party leadership was kept apprised. "I think the little trouble between Jessel and the Anti-

Socialist Union has been smoothed away," a member of the union's executive assured Balfour's private secretary. He continued:

> after a long powwow we arranged that Jessel and the London Municipal Society were to have the administrative county of London for their anti-Socialist activities and that we [the Anti-Socialist Union] were to exploit the rest of Great Britain. This seems to satisfy Jessel and I hope he will keep the peace. . . . It does seem so silly to quarrel instead of pulling together.[124]

By early 1909, the Anti-Socialist Union had begun to establish a bureaucratic presence and elaborate its position. Despite its pledge to the London Municipal Society, the Anti-Socialist Union's headquarters and initial branches were established within London; indeed, even by April 1909 the only branch outside London to which references were made was in Manchester. The union focused on training speakers and providing literature to isolate "plague spots of socialism," most of them again identified as within the metropolis.[125] No membership totals were cited, nor circulation figures for its monthly journal, *The Anti-Socialist*. It subsequently claimed that an original order for 20,000 copies of the inaugural issue had to be supplemented by an additional 50,000, but provided no evidence (nor any claims) that these levels were maintained.[126] In fact, most copies were not sold on a subscription basis but displayed at newsstands (such as Temple underground station, presumably for the edification of the barristers and solicitors who hurried past). Nor were any suggestions aired as to the union's financial health, and there was no mention of the subsidy from the Unionist party. Rather, the intention was to foster the impression that patriotic Englishmen spontaneously had come together to decry the dangers inherent in socialism and to implement constructive remedies for the particular social ills on which Socialists had happened to fasten.

The Anti-Socialist Union was at pains to explain that it did not "enter the field to fight for reaction and to uphold vested interests against human rights." Instead, the union contended:

> Our policy is a popular policy. We are out to defend the cause of the people against Socialism, because we believe that cause to be identified with public freedom and private property. The State has a province of its own, and in that province it can do great things for the welfare of the people . . . [but] the State cannot embark on industry without loss, on universal control without tyranny, on expropriation without robbery, and on Socialism, in short, without disaster. We shall, therefore, support the cause of Social Reform, . . . the whole system of private production, private industry, and private ownership under which the Empire has grown great.[127]

This approach defined Socialism as incompatible with the best English traditions and the nation's survival as a prosperous and stable power. But in convincing complacent Englishmen of the terrors that lurked before them, it was essential to demonstrate exactly how multifaceted and imminent the threat was. E. E. Williams, his reputation secure from his earlier identification of the German commercial threat, contended that "men who recoil in horror from the appellation of Socialist as applied to themselves . . . do far more to advance Socialism than the most raucous wearer of the red tie."[128] In a piece entitled simply "The Menace," Williams warned that "the citadel of individual freedom is being betrayed from within," and, even if unwittingly, Socialism was nonetheless "coming under the guise of ordinary legislation."[129] It was not simply property owners who had been deluded, but working men as well. A typical Anti-Socialist Union illustration portrayed an honest workman made to dream of a leisured existence with free meals and cigars and without the threat of unemployment or depressed trade (the utopia some tariff reformers were willing to promise!) While one Socialist hypnotized the honest worker, his unscrupulous comrade rifled the worker's pockets, suggesting exactly who society's real exploiters were.[130]

As articulated at the outset, though, the Anti-Socialist Union's identification of the Socialist menace posed several problems. Its very elasticity, namely, socialism conveyed as despicable intentions disguised in ordinary forms, presented a real difficulty of interpretative focus. Furthermore, the union's initial brief, of demonstrating the repellent features of even innocuous individuals, intentions, and institutions, only served to emphasize the negative aspects of the union's platform in which constructive alternatives were relegated to a distant second. Moreover, along these same lines, there was the difficulty of elucidating the distinction between socialism and social reform in a way that could be grasped by the public and be seized upon by politicians as a basis for legislative action. Herein lay a dilemma and, in part, the Anti-Socialist Union's early significance.

For the question could be raised, as indeed it had been by the London Municipal Society, of the necessity for an Anti-Socialist Union. Clearly the Unionist party already served as a bulwark for private property against the allegedly rapacious designs of those committed to radical politics. It was equally true that the party had responded slowly to a specifically Socialist challenge, but eventually the National Union and then even Balfour himself had taken up that challenge. Coordinating existing anti-Socialist overtures or organizations could, arguably, be achieved as effectively under party auspices as under a newly founded association. To argue that the Anti-Socialist Union represented a sudden eruption of spontaneous capitalist anti-Socialist sentiment in defiance of an obstinate party seems unwarranted, given both the delay in securing donors and the degree to which the Unionist party itself participated in the union's foundation. Rather, the Anti-Socialist Union was another response to the dilemmas of the nationalist agitation. Opposition to socialism appeared to offer the prospect of extending and consolidating the political weight of property owners. If pursued in the correct manner, it might draw timid, prosperous members of the Liberal party whose habits of political participation prevented them from immediately rallying around the Unionist standard, yet who might be willing to take this hesitant, but ultimately significant, first step toward the right. In short, socialism might achieve what home rule had done some two decades earlier. Alternatively, if anti-socialism were purged of its partisan connotations, it might sustain construction of a durable centrist coalition to deal with the Socialist threat on a broader and more effective basis. These were similar to the alternatives posed by the efforts to secure national regeneration through fiscal reform or naval expansion, yet the room for maneuver had constricted.

The mere fact that the Unionist party controlled the Anti-Socialist Union's pursestrings suggests that any members who sought to deflect the issue from partisan gain were likely to wield little influence on the union's executive. It is more likely that the union was intended in part as a screen behind which to criticize the Liberal party as well, as an anti-Liberal union too. After all, the union consistently emphasized that the threat to individual liberty and private property derived not just from those who clutched copies of Karl Marx, and it implied that those who looked to T. H. Green or to L. T. Hobhouse were suspect also. At least this was the logical conclusion of the union's elastic definition of socialism and the mechanisms by which it sapped the finest English traditions. In fact, the union's opening salvo might even have reverberated within the citadels of tariff reform, for the state intervention in economic matters that tariffs entailed certainly seemed to qualify as an example of the misguided collectivist legislation that anti-Socialists were pledged to oppose. On the other hand, "constructive policies" represented, within Unionist circles at least by late 1908, a code word for tariff reform. And, of course, tariff reform was being touted as precisely the most effective basis for anti-socialism.

Evidently the relationship here was fraught with ambiguity. It would be going too far to regard the Anti-Socialist Union as an effort by Unionist free traders to restore their waning position. It was true enough that the Ninth Duke of Devonshire was prominently displayed as president of the union from 1909 onward, and certainly his father's free trade convictions had been inflexible. There had also been considerable sentiment at the London Municipal Society conference (from which the union ultimately emerged) in favor of avoiding that "King Charles' Head" of tariff reform.[131] And a handful of Liberals, such as Harold Cox, joined the union and remained firmly committed to laissez-faire. But Acland-Hood, whose role was critical in launching the union, had come round and then "gone over" to tariff reform. Likewise, the National Union's committee, which helped to lay the groundwork, was populated by firm whole-hoggers. Blumenfeld, under whose auspices, and in whose offices, the details were settled, continually preached the therapeutic value of tariffs for the nation's economic ills. The Anti-Socialist Union, then, was intended not to subjugate or negate tariff reform—the union scrupulously avoided directly contradicting protectionist arguments—but rather to supplement or complement the work of the Tariff Reform League.

It may have begun, however, as an effort to advertise those aspects of a Conservative program that did not involve either the singular focus of tariff reformers, namely, their emphasis on doctrinal purity with proscription of unrepentant free traders if necessary, or even any admission of party affiliation at all. In mid-1907, given that the Unionists were languishing in the doldrums, a position testified to by the discontended noises emanating from the Confederacy, there was something to be said for an initiative to foster party unity and recruit new support. By late 1908, when the Anti-Socialist Union officially emerged, tariff reformers had laid strong claims of their own to being able to accomplish both tasks. Tariff reform was acknowledged as the first constructive work of the party, opposed by only a handful of MPs, and touted, or at least accepted, as a means of bettering trade and thereby attracting working-class votes. The emergence of the Anti-Socialist Union, therefore, reflected the party's desperation at being confronted from an unfamiliar but evidently dangerous angle (Socialists who won by-elections as well as Liberals who abetted them) and also the continuing dilemmas of the nationalist agitation: loyalty to policy over party, to proscription and prescription rather than accommodation. In any event, the union had barely entered the fray when the situation was to be transformed, with profound implications for efforts to isolate Socialist issues, to identify Socialist support, and to clarify the respective roles of the Unionist and Liberal parties in any anti-Socialist campaign. The reason was the explosive interconnection of the naval and social questions on the agenda of the recently installed Asquith ministry.

4

Revolt From the Right

Despite the divisions that still persisted within the Unionist party late in 1908, the Liberals seemingly had failed to turn these to maximum political account. Balfour's selective use of the Unionist majority in the House of Lords to emasculate Liberal legislation may have verged on the indiscriminate, but it was effective. Liberal leaders could not always utilize their large majority in the Commons, and they could not hope to retain the full measure of their support there if they could not deliver on the statute book. But the impudent impediment of their Lordships was not the only issue facing the Liberal party. Maintaining the nation's defenses at frequently escalating levels posed a particular challenge to a party influenced by the "new Liberalism." Armaments had been controversial, as both a moral and a financial problem. But, given the Liberal party's stated commitment to implement and fund social reforms, critics were quick to argue that the Liberals would either deprive the military of its deserved share of the budget or else strain the nation's finances beyond a tolerable limit.

Accordingly, from late 1908 onward the nationalist agitation grew even more vituperative in its criticism of Liberalism's alleged inadequacies, more vociferous in its advocacy of battleships and tariffs, and more direct in its commitment to partisan action on behalf of the Unionist party. The debate only intensified as a result of the Committee of Imperial Defence's investigation of the possibility of invasion. Its lengthy examination had offered publicists and experts, self-appointed and otherwise, ample opportunities to peddle their particular views. In the bewildering atmosphere of charge and counter-charge between advocates of the rival "blue water" and "bolt from the blue" schools, the dangers seemed all too tangible, the solutions all too evanescent. The duplicity of a kaiser who corresponded with Britain's First Lord of the Admiralty to deny aggressive designs, belied by tensions in the Balkans widely attributed to Germany, only stoked the controversy to a fever pitch. When Lord Roberts contended that nearly 80,000 potential German troops already were stationed in England, there were few efforts to correct the old general's obviously faulty figures. There was still less than universal agreement, however, about his particular solution, namely, the introduction of national service to provide an adequate citizen defense force (in Roberts' view, at least 1 million trained men).[1] Did military priorities dictate that internal threats—from German spies and saboteurs—and the likelihood of German infantry wading ashore at Dover and in East Anglia were to be countered by producing trained soldiers at home? Or were these threats irrelevant as long as Britain preserved its mastery over the waters of the Channel and North Sea?

Yet the identification of defense priorities could not be confined to the services themselves. When Campbell-Bannerman's health failed in 1908, the Liberal government was reconstructed. Asquith's assumption of the post of prime minister might be interpreted to mean a more sympathetic ear toward imperial or defense issues, but the ineffectual Tweedmouth was replaced at the Admiralty by Reginald McKenna, whose reputation as a "Treasury man" implied that he would push with greater zeal and talent to contain naval spending. Moreover, the Asquith government's introduction of Old Age Pensions in 1908 signalled that social services would absorb an important share of the budget, leaving the military services to justify their respective claims upon the diminished remainder.

This situation posed awkward problems for any efforts to mobilize a nationalist agitation. However desirable it might appear to combine national service and massive naval building (especially now that the *Dreadnought* had persuaded many observers that the nation's existing naval lead had been rendered ineffectual), it did not appear practical. To find money for defense at the expense of Old Age Pensions would not be a sound move electorally, and indeed it would be perverse for many nationalists to deny such pensions in view of their earlier stress upon the deterioration of Britain's population. In late 1908 and early 1909, the best alternative was to demonstrate the moral bankruptcy of Little Englandism by reiterating the threat posed by the ever increasing likelihood of German aggression. In October 1908 the Kaiser, an asset of incalculable value to the nationalist agitation, again intervened to tactless effect. The *Daily Telegraph* carried an interview with Wilhelm II that, although supposedly proofread by the German Foreign Office prior to publication, contained a provocative mixture of bland assurances of personal goodwill coupled with assertions regarding the depth of anti-English feeling among Wilhelm's German countrymen. It did nothing to dispel the impact of the Reichstag's ratification several months earlier (June 1908) of a new naval building program with provisions for an increased building tempo and a reduced interval before older ships were replaced.[2] If anything, the Kaiser raised suspicions that Germany's real aims were being concealed. And it was this atmosphere that lent credence to the repeated warnings of one H. H. Mulliner.

Repercussions of the 1909 Naval Scare

Mulliner, managing director of Coventry Ordnance Works, had spun a tale of secret acceleration in the German building program. He claimed to have evidence that the Krupp works were turning out far more armor plate, guns, and mountings than would be required by the ships officially laid down. The obvious deduction to be drawn from this, Mulliner explained, was that Germany was stockpiling these items (the acknowledged bottlenecks in any naval building program) so as to complete additional battleships with far greater rapidity than normal.[3] Because most naval experts and politicians talked solely in terms of recently introduced Dreadnoughts, an unexpected increase of even a handful of such ships on one side could drastically affect calculations of relative strength. There was, though, a seamier side to Mulliner's accusations, for, while his claims were ostensibly based on visits to Germany, it was undeniable that the Coventry Ordnance Works was seeking new orders to utilize idle capacity. Nonetheless, Mulliner's charges were seized upon as final and conclusive evidence by interested parties, especially by Admiral Fisher, always anxious to preserve or increase his naval estimates, and by anybody looking for an opportunity to criticize the Liberal government.

The Liberal cabinet, as it contemplated the scattered bits of evidence and innuendo, sought a solution that would be compatible with financial realities, Liberal traditions, and German designs. The resulting compromise was to proceed with four scheduled Dreadnoughts and to declare construction of four more contingent upon their demonstrated necessity. Despite this decision, which in effect constituted a defeat for the "little navy" faction within the cabinet, the introduction of the revised naval estimates in Parliament in March 1909 offered the prospect for further navalist agitation, or what was quickly to be termed the "naval scare" of 1909. Critics of the Asquith government could insist that this compromise did not go far enough in that the situation demanded the immediate construction of the four contingent Dreadnoughts as well, or, as this was simplified for public consumption, "we want eight and we won't wait."[4] The Liberals' naval estimates, published on 12 March 1909, called for an increase in the estimates of £3,000,000 to £35,000,000, but again stipulated the construction of four Dreadnoughts, not eight.

In contrast to the many previous occasions when the passage of the naval estimates occasioned little more than barely stifled yawns and empty benches in Parliament or modest notices in the press and public indifference, the naval program of March 1909 aroused a storm of comment. One focus of this renewed attention was the borough of Croydon, just across the Surrey border to the south of London. When its sitting member, the Liberal Unionist H. O. Arnold-Forster, died in early March, the resulting by-election was regarded as an opportunity to gauge the public mood and to elicit a national verdict on Liberal naval policy. And, when the votes were counted in Croydon on 27 March 1909, the Liberal candidate was soundly defeated, while his Unionist opponent polled nearly 4,000 votes more than during the previous election (1906) and increased the Unionist majority from 3 to 19 percent. At first glance these results lent themselves to a navalist interpretation, namely, that the stronger Unionist showing could be attributed directly to the Croydon electorate's dissatisfaction with Liberal naval policy and to support for the Unionist opposition's advocacy of a bigger fleet.[5] Upon closer inspection, however, Croydon's verdict was a good deal more complex.

The Unionist candidate, Sir Robert Hermon-Hodge, had been vacationing in Madeira when the vacancy occurred, and his hastily organized campaign upon his return began by emphasizing tariff reform and home rule as the primary questions, to which the naval issue was often appended as a postscript. The protectionist *Morning Post* was confident that "everything" pointed to tariffs as "the principal issue," and the borough was, as a result, soon submerged in a sea of conflicting interests and organizations without Dreadnoughts rising to undisputed prominence.[6] "Croydon has suddenly become a dumping ground for cranks and faddists of all descriptions . . . [as well as a] resort for the more serious politicians who come to push their views," complained the local Liberal paper as it surveyed the invasion of speakers from the Tariff Reform League, Free Trade Union, Anti-Socialist Union, pro- and antisuffrage groups, and temperance societies.[7] Voters who went to the polls in Croydon took with them not only the varied prescriptions of conflicting interest groups, but also the traditions of the borough as well. Croydon, since its creation as a parliamentary constituency in the redistribution of 1885, had elected only Unionist MPs, so the return of Hermon-Hodge in 1909 was in itself neither particularly surprising nor significant. It was the ways in which the course of the campaign and the relative vote totals were construed that lent to the by-election the character of a navalist referendum.

In both cases, however, the grounds to support such an interpretation were shaky. While the naval issue eventually figured prominently in the campaign, it was not the sole issue, or even necessarily the most important one. Moreover, the by-election was by no means an "ordinary" two party fight that could be compared straightforwardly with a similar contest in 1906. Croydon had withstood the Liberal landslide in January 1906 only because the presence of a Labour candidate split the progressive vote and enabled the Unionist to win, despite Unionist abstentions and a mere 41 percent of the vote. Municipal elections had grown increasingly bitter as Liberals responded by seeking revenge through the defeat of local Labour councillors. During the by-election of 1909, therefore, the Unionist vote was bound to increase as 1906 abstainers returned to the fold (without necessarily being attracted by the naval issue), while the Liberal turnout was likely to be depressed by the acrimonious Liberal–Labour rivalry on the municipal level and the reemergence of a Labour candidate in the field. Both features artificially inflated the extent of the Unionist majority, which, by comparison with an inappropriate base year (1906), appeared more impressive than it really was. Indeed, the Unionist share of the poll in 1909 was lower than in 1895 or even 1892, when the Unionists had held the seat during a Liberal general election victory.[8]

Most observers, however, were unfamiliar with Croydon's municipal affairs and, noting the coincidence of the naval scare and the increased local Unionist majority, presumed that the two were causally related. Nor was Sir John Fisher particularly anxious to dispel the validity of any such connection, for he perceived that the navalist hysteria offered a golden opportunity to press for larger than anticipated increases in the naval budget.[9] Professional recommendations from the Admiralty and partisan clamor from the Unionist benches thus reinforced one another and consequently circumscribed the ability of reductionist Radicals to contain the naval estimates. Indeed, in July 1909 the Liberal cabinet authorized the laying down of the four additional battleships it had already sanctioned on a contingent basis. This decision would appear to constitute a notable navalist success and clear evidence of the effective resonance and integrative capacity of the naval issue in English society. And indeed it was, but only to an extent whose limits one should take care to note.

The Navy League's executive committee, for example, concluded that the naval issue had not penetrated deeply enough and that, more specifically, this disappointing situation was reflected in the Navy League's own inability to mobilize a satisfactory level of public support. While the Asquith government approved increased naval construction in July 1909, the Navy League's membership simultaneously met to debate a scheme of reorganization intended to broaden and sharpen the league's appeal. The league's leadership did not attempt to conceal its displeasure, admitting that "the league has failed so far to establish a firm hold upon the interests of those in whose hands lies in the last resort the responsibility for the maintenance of our supremacy of the sea— the lower middle and the wage-earning classes."[10] And while stressing the league's "inestimable service" and "acknowledged success" (its advocacy of an educational policy, its insistence upon the withdrawal of muzzle-loading weapons from ships, its commitment to improved gunnery and support for the two power standard), the committee insisted that the league had been "too aristocratic, too far above the level of the crowd."[11] The familiar refrain of ignorance and educational necessity required a new populist inflection. The Navy League argued that future sacrifices on behalf of the navy were inevitable, and it surmised that those who refused would do so from ignorance rather than a lack of patriotism. But a basically decent population could be misled by "the class of pernicious demagogue which democracy never fails to produce." The best method, then, of insulating the people from such misleading appeals was to acquaint them with and involve them in the league's affairs. "The league itself must be democratised. Its ranks must be freely thrown open to wage earners . . . and from the wage earners who join it earnest and patriotic men must be chosen to preach the gospel of Sea Power to their fellow workers."[12]

This vision was embodied in a report presented to the leadership by a special reorganization committee whose composition belied the democratic rhetoric. Three peers—Lords Ridley, Elcho, and Wilton—were hardly calculated to provide a perspective from below, though Ridley was lauded for his effective contribution to the working of the Tariff Reform League.[13] The report their lordships had prepared recommended three particular reforms: the reduction of the regular subscription to one shilling, the establishment of new provincial councils and a grand council, and the incorporation within the league of any activities previously conducted independently by the auxiliary Women's Navy League. These recommendations prompted a lively debate when they were presented to the membership for a vote in a manner that precluded prior discussion or consideration. But it was more than mere annoyance that set tongues wagging. For the proposed reforms bore directly on the

most critical concerns of the nationalist agitation as it had developed since the
1890s, namely, the reciprocal relationship between popular mobilization and
popular participation and the complementary relationship between patriotic
agitation and partisan gain.

When he introduced the reorganization committee's report, the league's
president discounted the need to provide a detailed explanation of its proposals. The committee, and indeed the larger executive committee that endorsed
the proposals, were, in Yerburgh's view, animated by the principles of "demo-
cratisation, representation, and decentralisation." Setting the basic fee for
membership at one shilling would sweep away "the invidious monetary distinction between members and associates" and ensure that all subscribers who met
this minimum fee would be entitled to exactly the same privileges. Along the
same lines, the Navy League endeavored to correct the problem that most
members could not participate directly or vote at league meetings (because
either the site, London, or the time was inconvenient) by substituting "a system
of representation of every individual member" by means of a grand council of
delegates selected by provincial councils whose members would be elected by
particular branches. Yerburgh also applauded any provision for tapping female
energies in the league's service, arguing that "men and women give their best
work when they are working together," but he could not resist drawing attention to an aspect "which appears to be essentially the province of women, and
that is the invaluable work connected with the juvenile branch." He was
confident that these brief remarks would suffice and that the proposed reforms
would be duly adopted.[14]

Yet, before a vote would be taken, the executive had to endure a barrage of
queries and publicly stated reservations. One member raised the issue of the
effect on league finances if subscription rates were lowered, for the reduction
might well make the league more dependent on generous individual donors and
thus negate one of the ostensible aims of the reforms. Another speaker reminded the audience that while membership privileges were now uniform,
distinctions nonetheless persisted, given that the league had introduced the
designation of "fellow" for contributions of one guinea, "the smallest mess of
pottage for which a man was ever asked to sell his birthright."[15] In this sense,
the reforms reformed nothing. Furthermore, their overall thrust was to reduce
representation; voting was now indirect, and popular input filtered through a
membrane of various restrictions. Controversial proposals from below would
be laundered by this process because the local delegates to the provincial
councils who in turn selected grand council representatives would, in all
probability, be chosen by a minority within local branches. Dissident members
would be denied their opportunity for direct representation at league general
meetings.[16] Moreover, the league proposed to invest the provincial councils
with the responsibility to oversee the distribution and disbursement of funds,
effectively constraining the initiative of local branch treasurers. And, as if this
were not enough, the executive committee had also suggested that all MPs be
appointed *ex officio* members of the grand council. Because the number of
MPs was roughly equivalent to the size of the prospective grand council

(around 200), this was tantamount to turning over responsibility for shaping Navy League policy to the House of Commons. Moreover, given the preponderance of Unionists among such Navy League MPs, this proposition in turn raised the familiar issue of the league's independence (or lack thereof) from partisan politics.

Together these points constituted a powerful indictment of the proposed reforms. Nonetheless, there were, apart from the committee itself, members willing to refute these charges. One participant, himself an MP, advised his fellow Navy Leaguers to "have all the Members of Parliament you can." With them, he explained, the league could carry matters through, but, he warned, "if you do not welcome them, and try to keep them out, your measures can never attain success."[17] On this reading, popular mobilization was ultimately irrelevant (and probably undesirable anyway) as long as a majority could be sustained within the Commons. Walter Long, who continued the debate, admitted that it was widely, if in his view mistakenly, accepted "that agitation for a strong navy has a very large party bias attached to it." In an uncharacteristic show of generosity he conceded that "many" Liberals were in fact supportive of a proper fleet, but he seemed to think that this admission mitigated any appearance of impropriety that might result from incorporating all current league members from the Commons on the grand council. Like the previous speaker, Long could not conceive of any effective strategy that did not revolve around parliamentary majorities. "You may have all the leagues in the world," he lectured his fellow navalists, or "you may get as many members of your league as you please, but unless you can get the right feeling predominating in Parliament you will do no practical good whatever."[18] He thus ignored objections from the floor to the substitution of control by MPs for the degree of local autonomy that had characterized the league, and he failed to provide satisfactory assurances on the issue of the impartiality of the proposed grand council. As matters stood, the MPs currently enrolled as members of the Navy League were overwhelmingly Unionist, and thus to transfer so sizeable a bloc to the grand council was to deliver the latter into the hands of one party. This preponderance of Unionist MPs was not new, but to invest them as a body with the decisive influence in league affairs would constitute a significant departure from prior league practice and would surely hinder efforts to portray league policy as being derived from impartial judgement.

The secretary of the local branch in Ealing (itself a strongly Unionist constituency) protested along these very lines and cited examples of potential members who had been dissuaded from joining because of the strong presence of Unionist MPs. "You are part and parcel of one section of the House," was the way one possible recruit had put it.[19] Accordingly, the secretary urged that the Reorganisation Committee's report be reviewed and that any decision be postponed. Yet these reservations were brushed aside, and the members present voted to implement the proposed reforms. The critical factor in their willingness to do so was not the conviction that Walter Long's parliamentary strategy was valid or that the reduction in subscriptions would democratize the league, but rather the sense of urgency that something had to be done. Eton's branch

secretary reminded the audience that "while we are talking the Germans are
acting. (Cheers.)"[20] "There is a hurry," argued another member, who pointed
out that few voting members would be available during the upcoming late
summer months to revise the report. It was virtually now or never:

> Those of us who are interested in the work of the Navy League know that by
> almost every post we get letters from people in different parts of the country
> asking to form a branch. . . . There is not so much enthusiasm and readiness
> to work in this country that we can afford to damp people down and say to
> them, "wait four or five months until the Committee has evolved a scheme,
> and the executive committee has approved of it, and a general meeting have
> passed it, and then you may begin to start your branch." That is why I do
> earnestly ask you to insist upon this scheme being put into operation imme-
> diately, to begin tomorrow.[21]

Perhaps the tide of navalist mania had indeed crested and was now beginning to ebb. Certainly the broader context within which the nationalist agitators were accustomed to operating had just been transformed by Lloyd
George's introduction of his celebrated "People's Budget" in April 1909. It was
a tactical masterstroke that regrouped a squabbling party and redefined the
terms of political argument. Navalists had sought to expose the moral bankruptcy of Little Englandism and to demonstrate its continuing hold on the
policies of the Liberal government. Lloyd George's budget, however, indicated
that recent Liberal assurances about the maintenance of naval supremacy were
indeed to be fulfilled. Tariff reformers, many of whom were also navalists, had
devoted much of the previous campaign to the demonstration that free trade as
practiced by the Liberal government was not simply outdated but also unable
to generate the revenue required by twentieth-century conditions. In short, the
Liberals would be bankrupted by the escalating demands of both defense and
social reform. Free Traders would have to state their priorities, to identify
either Germany or poverty as the principal enemy, for they could not, tariff
reformers alleged, afford to conquer both and remain true to free trade. Yet
Lloyd George's budget, if its provisions were validated, seemed able to achieve
both; it was therefore especially incumbent upon tariff reformers to secure its
rejection if their own case was not to be irrevocably discredited.[22]

Less directly, but no less unavoidably, the People's Budget challenged the
proponents of national service. The Liberal government stated its commitment
to naval strength in terms that implied the Blue Water credo. Each Dreadnought laid down, according to that line of argument, made a successful
invasion less plausible and an extensively trained citizens' defense force less
essential. Furthermore, the budget's reaffirmation of the principles of free
trade finance directly affected the many conscriptionists who were also tariff
reformers. The connection was not fanciful, at least not to Sir Edward Grey's
private secretary, who presumed that tariff reform would provoke a commercial war with Germany that, in all probability, would escalate into a military
conflict. That in turn would necessitate a conscript army, and he therefore did
not see how Britain "can go in for protection without some form of compul-

sory service."[23] With the Liberals apparently regaining the initiative in the spring of 1909, it was essential that advocates of national service make their voices heard before their cries were drowned out by a sea of Dreadnoughts or direct taxes.

The Constriction of Conscription

The National Service League, for its part, had not been doing that poorly. In 1908, its organizational reach had broadened and its membership had increased dramatically. The league counted some 21,500 members by December 1908 and claimed another 30,000 "adherents." Circulation of the *Nation in Arms* reached 17,500, while the number of branches doubled from the mere eighteen of 1906.[24] Nonetheless, the outlook was not entirely rosy. The National Service League was strongest in rural areas; it was the county branches with their retired military officers as secretaries that formed the backbone of the organization. Urban areas, with a few exceptions, had not responded to the league's appeal. "Little progress" was reported in Sheffield, for example, while that in Manchester was admitted to be "slow."[25] By comparison, county associations such as that for Essex witnessed rapid and dramatic growth: founded in 1907, it numbered 560 members and associates in 1908 and over 1,000 by 1909.[26] Yet it was the urban working class, that sector of society whose bodies and sense of patriotism appeared to be underdeveloped, whose sympathies had to be engaged. Or, at the very least, it was their compliance in a system of national service by parliamentary statute that had to be secured.

The logical consequence of this intention to reach the working class and mobilize parliamentary support was a familiar one and had been faced by the other patriotic societies as well, namely, the definition of an agitational role with regard to partisan politics. By 1908, the National Service League's professions of nonpartisanship were wearing thin. It found the attitude of Labour MPs on defense issues "so extraordinary" that it felt "obliged to comment." "It appears," the league contended, "that the Labour party are determined, on the one hand, to protest against compulsory military training and, on the other, to object to any advantages being given to those who would voluntarily undertake to protect the country, thus doing their best to destroy the voluntary system."[27]

However vocal the opposition from Labour, though, and however offensive or distasteful the league might find Labour representatives to be, they did not constitute the greatest impediment to the realization of the National Service League's aims. For, despite increasing sympathy on the Unionist benches, neither party was willing to include compulsory service as part of its formal platform. It is as a reaction to this dilemma that the bizarre Stratford by-election can best be understood. Although it degenerated into a farce, it revealed with brutal clarity the necessity for the nationalist agitation to come to terms with the relative inflexibility of the country's partisan boundaries. Initially the Stratford affair seemed an ideal test case. Stratford's sitting member, Captain Malcolm Kincaid-Smith, was both an executive member of the National Service League and a Liberal. To everyone's complete surprise, Kincaid-Smith announced in April 1909 that he was resigning his seat and would then contest the subsequent by-election solely on the basis of his support for national service.[28] He was, to be sure, a most unusual Liberal who had alienated his local association and frequently flouted his party's policy, but his decision to stand in 1909 on national service presented difficulties for both the Unionist party and the nationalist agitation. Should the party oppose him, on the grounds that a "fully Unionist" MP was preferable to Kincaid-Smith with, in theory at least, his occasional Liberal predilections and connections? Or was Stratford the opportunity to lay partisan divisions aside in favor of the greater national interest?

Lord Milner was appalled at the very prospect that so delighted the Liberal *Daily News*, namely, that of Unionist navalists and Unionist conscriptionists squabbling among themselves and with the party leadership. In this instance, Milner urged Balfour to persuade the party and the party machine not to oppose Kincaid-Smith.[29] While he recognized that the Unionist chief would not commit himself unreservedly to national service, Milner readily appreciated the damage a Unionist candidate opposing Kincaid-Smith would do. Lord Roberts, the *Morning Post*, and several Tory back-benchers all argued along the same lines.[30] As one correspondent to the *Times* put it, "Defence of country is Captain Kincaid-Smith's battle cry. The Unionist party claims it also as theirs." The party had finally begun, he believed, to rebut the charge of "making party capital out of the naval necessities of the country," only to find "to our amazement that one of the two Radicals who voted for the Unionist view of the situation is to be opposed by a Unionist."[31] This course of action would do little to demonstrate the sincerity of the Unionist party's recently and effusively stated convictions about the country's defenses.

Yet the situation was not perceived in Westminster as quite so clear cut. Even if Kincaid-Smith stood as an independent candidate without official Liberal support and even if his views on this particular aspect of defense were sound, the definitions of what constituted an acceptable candidate (to either the Unionist party or the nationalist agitation) were more stringent.[32] Navalists would want to verify his views on the fleet, anti-Socialists would seek to identify his stance on welfare measures and the Labour party, and tariff reformers would be determined to clarify his attitude on fiscal matters. Moreover, technically Kincaid-Smith's particular issue was not even part of the party's official program, and he was, therefore, as J. S. Sandars reminded Balfour, "a man who is against us on all the main principles of our case."[33]

Sandars' advice on this occasion was that Balfour rely on the same excuse that had been employed so often in the past when that fastidious politician had been confronted by sharply contrasting viewpoints, each articulated by factions too influential to ignore. Responsibility for any official Unionist reaction to Kincaid-Smith's candidacy could naturally and legitimately be devolved upon the local Southwest Warwickshire Unionist association. Balfour thus washed his hands of the affair, and the local association readopted its former member, P. S. Foster, who opposed compulsory service but supported tariff reform. Balfour then did his duty, duly endorsing Foster in lukewarm terms without reference to the issue of conscription. The voters of Stratford then did theirs, returning Foster and inflicting a humiliating defeat on Kincaid-Smith (who won only 479 of the 8,600 votes cast).[34]

The results suggested echoes of the Hampstead by-election of 1902, in which commitment to the issue of national defense had failed to dislodge the primacy of partisan loyalties. In some ways, Stratford seemed a replay with a similar finale. But there were critical differences. Hampstead's results had been dictated by the character of local relations between Conservatives and Liberal Unionists, whereas in the Stratford case Kincaid-Smith's defeat was sealed by his advocacy of an issue that was both more problematic and less popular than navalism. Furthermore, at Stratford compulsory service fell victim to the officially sanctioned Unionist candidate, but one whose party label was predicated on acceptance of the terms imposed by another grouping of the nationalist agitation, namely, the tariff reformers. While members of the nationalist opposition hoped that ideally their movement could advance on broad lines and secure naval supremacy, conscription, and tariffs simultaneously, it was evident from Kincaid-Smith's defeat that the various components could well splinter with a set of conflicting priorities emerging. In April 1909, it was not that party loyalty as such was so strong as to defeat Kincaid-Smith, but that party loyalty as shaped by the tariff reform movement was of particular significance. His effort to dismiss fiscal or other aspects of nationalist concern as subsidiary or irrelevant lost him the support he might otherwise have received.

People's Budget Versus Tariff

Unfortunately for Kincaid-Smith, his quixotic aspirations were compounded by his poor timing. His by-election campaign was conducted at precisely the point when the Unionist party was seeking to close ranks on the fiscal issue in response to Lloyd George's provocative budget. There is a view, subscribed to by Lloyd George only in retrospect, that he had framed the 1909 budget so as deliberately to provoke the House of Lords into rejecting it and thus initiating a constitutional crisis in which the Liberal party could campaign as representatives of the people seeking in the national interest to free the country from the retrograde grip of the peerage. It has been more convincingly argued, however, that, as the chancellor of the exchequer, Lloyd George found himself confronted by heavier than anticipated expenses and that he sought not so much a confrontation with the lords as the passage of the budget itself and thus a solution to the government's financial predicament.[35] He did, however, intend the budget to bring tactical benefits to the Liberal party, for it promised to provide the necessary revenue without resorting to the tariffs that the Unionist opposition touted as the sole means of funding the nation's escalating military and social programs. And thus when the budget's provisions introduced higher taxes on the wealthy and the prospect of land valuation as well, both of which produced animated opposition from within Unionist landed circles, the threat was felt most keenly by tariff reformers. As Lloyd George wrote to the Liberal journalist J. A. Spender several weeks after introducing his budget, "the Tariff Reformers are especially depressed as they are convinced that if the Budget goes through, their cause is lost."[36] On behalf of the whole-hoggers, Austen Chamberlain acknowledged the connection even while rejecting the idea that the bill "is the final triumph of Free Trade and the death blow to the policy of Fiscal Reform." He proclaimed himself, and his fellow tariff reformers, confident and "ready to go to the country at any moment upon it."[37]

There was little doubt that tariff reform sentiment was more extensive in the country and its prospects for success were far better than at any point since 1903. A number of signs pointed toward tariff reform's greater strength. The most obvious was Balfour himself, whose public conversion brought with him the machinery of Conservative Central Office and thus facilitated the exclusion and proscription of remaining Unionist free traders. There was also a string of impressive by-election victories by whole-hogger candidates, culminating in the defeat at Manchester NW in April 1908 of that prominent defector from Unionist ranks over the fiscal question, Winston Churchill.[38] The distribution of league propaganda increased dramatically: over 6,000,000 leaflets in 1908 compared with one-fourth that number in 1906; the circulation of *Monthly Notes on Tariff Reform* doubled to 120,500, and 38,500 copies of the league's updated notes for speakers were distributed.[39] New branches were founded to augment the 309 which the Tariff Reform League had mustered in December 1906, and existing ones flexed new muscles. The league's association in Kensington claimed to add 383 members in 1907 alone, that in Deptford quadrupled its membership to 200 within 18 months, and various local branches and regional federations weighed in with similarly optimistic reports.[40]

More tangible evidence that the Tariff Reform League was mobilizing considerable resources could be derived from its own financial situation. The league had never endured the financial stringencies that plagued the Navy League. Instead, its income, while never matching the inflated figures circulating in the popular press, was quite substantial. Between 1905 and 1908 annual revenue fluctuated between £14,000 and £20,000, with a significant gain perceptible in 1908.[41] In 1909, however, the league enjoyed unparalleled success by raising in excess of £42,000.[42] The upsurge reflected both an expansion of tariff reform sentiment and a conviction that such support was critical with a general election imminent. In other words, there were new donors who were willing to give the issue a chance at the next election. It was incumbent upon the league to make something of that opportunity, for more skittish subscribers or fickle donors might not be so patient or so generous a second time around.

With the introduction of the budget, therefore, tariff reformers strove to portray it as the last, futile expedient of an expiring fiscal strategy. Free trade was, on this reading, incapable of providing the necessary revenue except by the resort to flagrant increases in direct taxation that unfairly penalized the wealthy classes. Lloyd George's budget was condemned as little more than a thinly disguised effort to legitimate outright robbery. On this score, the tariff reformers could quote the chancellor himself, who earlier in the year had suggested, perhaps with a Welsh twinkle in his eye, that he would have to find new "hen's roosts to rob."[43] Tariff reformers promised a less painful remedy— taxing the foreigner instead, who through import duties would contribute the necessary additional revenue.[44] Tariff reform would not increase indirect taxes on popular consumables such as tobacco and alcohol as the Liberal budget had done, so it was therefore fallacious to insist that only tariff reform would raise the cost of living for the working class. Even if protection would escalate prices on consumables (the "food taxes"), tariff reformers countered that such modest increases would be overshadowed by the greater prosperity of the economy as a whole under protectionism. Higher wages and more regular employment were touted as the real product of colonial preference, not shrunken loaves of black bread as Liberal free traders alleged.

To counterpose the People's Budget and tariff reform as the two critical elements of the political debate, the tariff reformers had, inevitably, to secure the rejection of the budget itself, even if to do so would raise questions of constitutional propriety and legitimacy. After the budget's provisions were made clear, there remained significant sections of the Unionist and Liberal Unionist parties that harbored grave doubts about the wisdom of rejecting it. While there were no statutes expressly forbidding the House of Lords from rejecting money bills, a tradition of noninterference in such matters had evolved since the 1860s. For the lords to throw out the budget, then, might enable the Liberals to present rejection as the petulance of an overprivileged few and as an unwarranted interference with the nation's finances. By late August 1909, however, Balfour had decided in favor of rejection as the only means to consolidate his authority against tariff reform pressure and to maintain a measure of party unity and morale.[45] The difficulty, though, would be how to ensure that the by now inevitable campaign was fought on the fiscal issue rather than the constitutional issue produced by the lords' unprecedented rejection of the budget on 30 November 1909. A general election was now set for January 1910.

The strict constitutionality of the lords' action could not be entirely evaded as an issue. Unionists tried to cloud the matter by contending that the House of Lords and the occasional exercise of their veto power were essential to the preservation of democratic politics. The budget, they argued, was the real violation of traditional practice and was to be pushed through without reference to an electorate whose mandate had been granted too long ago (nearly 4 years) and on different terms. Their lordships were merely affirming the people's right to be consulted on a political innovation of supreme importance. Naturally, this self-serving rhetoric did little to deceive either its intended audience or its opponents. The lords had vetoed or mutilated a string of Liberal legislation in which partisan hostility rather than democratic altruism figured as the clear motivation. Indeed the House of Lords was being employed by the Unionist leadership to negate the initiatives of a popularly elected House of Commons so much that it no longer functioned as the watchdog of the constitution but as "Mr. Balfour's Poodle." Yet despite the obvious discontent generated by the lords' obstruction, there was sufficient ambiguity regarding the defined limits of their role in regard to the budget that it was not easy to translate the constitutional question as such into all the necessary Liberal votes.[46] Accordingly, there was an incentive for Liberals to stress the primacy of the free trade budget versus tariff reform issue with the same fervor as the Unionists, although from opposite ends, of course.

By late 1908, the Unionist Free Traders had virtually been reduced to a negligible force, certainly in view of their dwindling numbers if not the brilliance of their articulate spokesmen. But their relegation to the margins of the party, and the Central Office's insistence upon adherence to fiscal reform, did not necessarily mean that tariffs would remain the single issue of the Unionist campaign. Tariff reform was a multifaceted issue, and therein lay much of its attraction to nationalist agitators who could envision and portray tariffs as a means to the restoration of British economic supremacy, the reduction of unemployment, the dispersal of socialist sentiment among working men, the consolidation of imperial bonds, the reconstruction of systems of imperial defense, and the provision of revenue essential to meet the costs of both social reform and naval defense. Hammering away at the themes of the People's Budget as extortion and tariff reform as the equitable alternative of indirect taxation seemed, however, to relegate many of these alternative benefits to temporary oblivion. Lord Milner, for example, whose contribution to tariff reform was not in doubt, complained that "in the hubbub one gets little attention for anything except tariff. The Liberals shout 'Budget' and we shout 'Tariff' and the question is who shouts the loudest. It is horrid."[47] On the other hand, some tariff reformers felt they had been maneuvered into a position in which they appeared to be refusing to pay for the Dreadnoughts they had clamored for in the previous spring. There were thus conflicting currents of often discordant views, which made general acceptance of the persistent primacy of the tariff issue unlikely.

National service, in the wake of the Stratford fiasco, clearly did not yet qualify as practical politics, was recognized as such by most Unionists, and was therefore excluded from any significant role in the election campaign. One might have thought that the naval issue would be similarly muted. After all, the scare of 1909 had subsided, the public appetite for Dreadnought stories was presumably jaded, and the Liberals had eventually acceded to navalist demands and laid down eight new battleships. Furthermore, Anglo-German relations had eased slightly in the wake of von Bülow's resignation as Germany's chancellor in July 1909 and his replacement by the ostensibly "pro-English" Bethmann Hollweg. And yet, despite all this, early in December 1909 the naval issue again vaulted to prominence. In part, this reflected the fortuitous conjuncture of unrelated events. H. H. Mulliner returned to the public eye with the publication in the *Times* of selections from his correspondence, while simultaneously Lord Beresford was adopted as a Unionist candidate for Portsmouth (an ideal constituency from which to harp on the sorry state of the fleet under the misguided leadership of his great rival, Admiral Sir John Fisher). Assistance also arrived from an unexpected source, the eccentric

Socialist, Robert Blatchford, whose *Clarion* had commanded a wide reader-ship. Blatchford inaugurated a series of articles on the German peril in the *Daily Mail* in mid-December 1909 that rivalled anything yet written by Maxse and other ardent Germanophobes (indeed, Maxse, impressed, "freely plun-dered" Blatchford's work). It was an odd trio, as Fisher aptly noted, "to engineer a scare. A discredited Socialist, a shady company promoter, and a blatant Admiral."[48]

The critical role in resurrecting the naval issue, however, was not that played by any one of that peculiar trinity, but the prompt and sympathetic response of both the navalists and Arthur Balfour. Independently they exercised only a sporadic and isolated influence in this matter, but operating in conjunction they temporarily eclipsed tariffs with navalism as the primary question before the electorate. Balfour's personal interest in defense matters, his discomfort with whole-hogger pressure and policies, and the urgings of journalists all inclined him toward reviving the naval issue. Immediately after the Croydon by-election, H. A. Gwynne of the *Standard* had advised Balfour that a prompt and sustained utilization of navalism would "secure for many years the su-premacy of the party."[49] This advice was echoed later in the fall by J. L. Garvin, who, claiming by virtue of his editorial position an ability to divine the popular mood, condemned much of current party literature as ineffective. Tariffs coupled with a supreme fleet were the essentials to attract voters. In an appropriate choice of imagery, Garvin argued that the "two-keels-to-one stan-dard" could serve as an "election cannonball," the kind of issue comprehensible to the "dullest elector" and that would "inspire enthusiasm in the party and would take the country."[50] Garvin's powerful advocacy of this strategy reson-ated in the columns of the *Observer*, but no less so on Unionist platforms in the country.

There was no clearer indication of the final convergence of the nationalist agitation and partisan calculation than the ways in which the naval issue was reintroduced in December 1909 and January 1910. This was certainly the lesson of the Navy League's efforts during the election campaign. In contrast to its indecisive stance on the occasion of previous elections, the league's journal unequivocally advised its readership that "a definite opportunity to the Navy League and its members to bring their influence to bear upon the Government will be afforded by the forthcoming General Election."[51] Implicitly, it was the Liberal record to be influenced. The league circulated three test questions requiring candidates to recognize that command of the sea alone ensured the essential imports of food and should therefore be considered a question above party politics, that maintaining command of the sea inevitably rested on the two power standard, and that additional measures were necessary to ensure the provision of British seamen for British ships. The Navy League then published a list of eighty-three candidates who had given affirmative replies and who were therefore entitled to official support. Of the eighty-three, all but six were Unionists; no sharper demonstration of the reality now underlying professions of nonpartisanship was necessary.[52] Extracts from various answers were juxta-posed in such a way as to prompt a particular inference: the Unionists' firm commitment to naval supremacy contrasted with their opponents' disrespectful, almost contemptuous, dismissal of the Navy League's concerns. Indeed, the final quotation was from a Labour candidate for Crewe whose succinct answers to the first two questions admitted of no ambiguity. Where Unionists answered in the affirmative, he replied "rubbish" to the first and "certainly not" to the second.[53]

This sharpening partisan inclination had been implicit in the debate over the league's reorganization the previous July, but during the election campaign itself it became all too explicit. Previously the Navy League had simply wrung its hands over the reluctance of most Liberals to meet its definition of the big navy advocacy incumbent upon all true Englishmen, but had not ventured much beyond that. In January 1910 a note of hysteria intruded. "Unless the electorate fulfills its duty at the polls in January 1910," the Navy League insisted, "it is very unlikely that England as a free country will see another parliamentary election."[54] Duty in this case was not left to the dictates of individual conscience; it quite unambiguously meant voting only for those candidates who had pledged to support a two-keels-to-one policy. According to this interpretation, and to the Navy League's own list, only a Unionist victory could ensure the survival of a free people. As if anyone might fail to grasp the necessary distinctions, the Navy League posed the stark alternatives in posters and its own journal—"Patriot or Traitor."[55] There was no longer any latitude for dissent over the notion of an independent patriot who eschewed party labels in the purity of his nationalist commitment. The navalists' arguments had taken on an abrasive and hectoring tone far removed from the olympian reasonableness that the Navy League originally had sought to substitute for the ceaseless struggle for party advantage.

Originally, too, the Navy League had refused requests for speakers from the Primrose League on the grounds that they wished to avoid public identification with that body.[56] Such scruples by 1910 had been long abandoned.[57] Meetings at Conservative clubs were increasingly common, and eventually the league agreed to print in its journal material favorable to tariff reform. It had become ever more difficult for Liberals to participate comfortably within the Navy League's confines. For example, Lord Nunburnholme, a former Liberal MP for Hull, wrote to Reginald McKenna, the First Lord of the Admiralty, seeking his advice on whether to accept the presidency of the Navy League's Yorkshire East Riding branch. Nunburnholme had been "assured that it is to be run entirely as a non-political league for increasing the general knowledge of naval matters," but he feared that "it will be only used for political purposes by the other side."[58] In response, McKenna conceded that the league had made some efforts to remain neutral, but in the changing climate he felt that it was "unavoidable that unfair criticism would be made of the Liberal government," and he therefore advised Nunburnholme to decline the offer.[59] While Unionists contended that they had been forced (with the greatest regret) to consider the naval issue as a party question "by the failure and neglect of the Radical government," their efforts to claim the virtue of necessity were transparent.[60]

The campaign also reflected a xenophobic strain introduced by the nationalist agitation. The contrasts between parties were defined more tightly and sharply than ever before. The Unionists, so they assured themselves, represented only English virtues and national interests, while the Liberals inevitably were guided by the predominance of their support from the non-English Celtic fringe and cosmopolitan free trade interests. The ubiquitous Garvin urged the Tories to identify the "freely importing foreigner" as the bogey, and a like-minded Maxse fulminated against a Liberal Britain "governed by Scotsmen, kicked by Irishmen, and plundered by Welshmen."[61] Edward Goulding believed that no Parliament had contained so many "new made Englishmen speaking in broken accents" as that elected in the Liberal landslide of 1906, so this ardent tariff reformer was not surprised by Liberal opposition to the resolute anti-German measures advocated by the nationalist agitation.[62] Unionists congratulated themselves on their decisive and vigorous attributes, such as Henry Page Croft, a brewer's son of boundless energy on the platform or behind the oars who persisted in expanding the East Herts Tariff Reform Federation despite "fierce antagonism" (in this case, from the ossified local Conservative association).[63] Or there was Sir William Bull, aptly described by the *Daily Citizen*, which remarked that "the heavy lowering head, the massive shoulders and bulky lumbering frame are all characteristically bovine, like the dull but truculent eye."[64] The sturdy Bull, "the embodiment of anti-socialist feeling" and "a magazine of Tariff Reform ammunition," did not dispute the bovine and truculent attributions, for his "recreations are those of the Englishmen who made the Empire. He shoots, sails, and swims."[65] To this list might have been added boxing, a talent that the right honorable member for Hammersmith was only too eager to demonstrate. Called a "lying lawyer" by a local hairdresser during the January 1910 campaign, Bull promptly claimed to be "an Englishman before a gentleman" and landed several punches on the unfortunate heckler "whose silk headgear [was] sent flying."[66] The associations on this particular occasion were not particularly arcane: Bull as the redoubtable exponent of masculinity and Englishness, his opponent as one who lacked conviction (heckling rather than debating) and manifested particularly effete characteristics in his choice of occupation and headgear.

Tariff reform encompassed much of this cluster of attitudes and inferences, but complementary emphases wriggled free from the tariff reformers' efforts to concentrate upon the fiscal issue. "Herr Dumper" seemed to be a good start toward mobilizing anti-German prejudices, but the logical conclusion of this approach was the prospect of invasion. So too the stress upon quintessentially English virtues raised the issue of popular patriotism's nemesis, namely, socialism. Even efforts to portray Lloyd George's budget as a form of robbery, an unjustified expropriation of legitimate income, and an unwarranted extension of direct taxation all conjured the specter of socialism. Because socialism preached class confrontation and international proletarian brotherhood, it was deemed especially poisonous. Yet, because of its breadth, in both theory and practice, nationalist agitators rarely agreed on what they meant by the term *socialism*.

On the whole, the Unionist party was responding with only moderate speed to what it came to regard as the "Socialist menace," and the delay provided more scope for the efforts of the Anti-Socialist Union. Physical violence was a facet of some Union Meetings, no less than of the Hammersmith campaign, especially as the Anti-Socialist Union's objective was to penetrate hostile communities with trained speakers.[67] Some 175 speakers were enrolled in the first speaker' classes and an additional 596 by the end of 1909. Graduation was by no means assured, however, for of 200 students examined in October 1910, only 32 survived to the final round.[68] New recruits were intended to sustain an agitational campaign far larger than the Union's modest efforts to date (177 meetings and 172,000 leaflets distributed between October 1908 and March 1909).[69] In the spring of 1910, the Union anticipated the enrollment of 2,000 speakers for 6 week courses who would then be dispatched in a special northern campaign.[70]

Exactly how anti-socialism was to be explained without appearing to be entirely negative was, of course, a good deal more problematic than giving volunteers a rudimentary acquaintance with public speaking and elementary economics. Pamphlets and lecture topics reflected an odd mixture of scandal, sensation, and social thought. "What Price Your Baby?" (pamphlet No. 98) implied that the state would supersede the family in matters of infant care; "Was Jesus a Socialist?" was typical of efforts to discredit any links between the communal experience of religious groups and the aims of Socialism (as in pamphlet No. 94 on "Christianity and Socialism Contrasted"); "Englishmen, Which Will You Choose?" (No. 40) posed the choice between the Union Jack and the Red Flag; "Socialism and Sea Power" attempted to explain that any ship functioned effectively only with a hierarchy of command and that any effort to institute abnormal equality on board would have the most disastrous consequences. A series entitled "What Socialists Have Said" cultivated a string of quotations from avowed Socalists, often wrenched out of context, but always casting the worst aspersions on the monarchy, the church, the family, or private enterprise. The Union continued to avoid the fiscal issue, claiming that "we have no more to do with tariff reform than we have with vivisection or votes for women."[71]

Other contemporary issues could not be so easily avoided, even if the Union's response was often gratuitous. "The Patriot's Creed" attributed 90 percent of existing poverty to "laziness, dishonesty, and incompetence," and the remaining 10 percent to "bad harvests and national misfortune." The Liberals' new budgetary policies were decried as having been necessitated by extravagance and the cost of increased state expenditure.[72] Such attitudes only fostered a misconceived predilection to look to the state for the means of individual advancement when, in fact, the Union contended, the real means for improvement lay much closer to hand. To emphasize the point, the Union published a number of potted biographies reminiscent of Samuel Smiles' *Self-Help* entitled "Success Without Socialism, Short Stories of Men Who Have Risen." A typical example of these was the account of the career of Sir Alfred Jones, the Liverpool shipping magnate (active in both the Navy

League and Tariff Reform League), which the Anti-Socialist Union found most instructive:

> The life story of Sir Alfred Jones is a striking example of how hard work and enterprise will enable the humblest British citizen to climb the ladder of commercial success to its topmost rung. Sir Alfred was born in 1845 of poor parents. Had he been possessed of the same flabby constitution as the present day Socialists, he would no doubt have lived an idle life, and spent his days denouncing the purely imaginary gulf that is fixed between the rich man and the man whose means are small.[73]

Here again was the vigorous, no-nonsense, self-reliance that wove its way as a continuous strand throughout the varied prescriptions of the nationalist organizations. Socialism was tantamount to pacifism, and the Anti-Socialist Union—taking its cue from the naval scares in March and December 1909— predicted that "if Socialism were given a free hand ashore and afloat, in twelve months every ship of the fleet would be rusting in desolate dockyards, and every soldier would have been exchanged into the army of the unemployed."[74] This last phrase would have pricked the ears of whole-hoggers, who were eager to intone the prescription emblazoned on the front pages of the *Daily Express*, "Tariff reform means work for all." Unionist energies, then, were fragmented in that different sections of the party (or sympathetic but extraparty groupings) identified different agitational foci, and the overall blend varied at different points in the campaign. The same could be said for the Liberals, too, but both parties were fairly clear about where their allies and enemies stood. Certainly the Unionist party was, temporarily, more united than at any point since the Boer War, and it was apparent that groups that defined a nationalistic agenda sought shelter under the Unionist umbrella.

The campaign itself, therefore, was hotly contested. It is generally agreed that the Liberals dominated the early stages, but there was an unusually long interval between dissolution in early December 1909 and actual polling because the Liberals elected to wait until January 1910, when a fresh electoral register would be available.[75] Perhaps inevitably, Liberal momentum sagged, and the Unionists recovered ground with their appeal to the naval issue in mid-December. When polling finally concluded, though, the Unionists found the results ultimately disappointing. The party recovered many of the seats it had lost in southern England in 1906, but it made little headway in the north or in the Celtic fringe.[76] Thus, while the Liberals and Unionists were almost evenly matched, Asquith and Lloyd George's party retained office by virtue of their support from Labour and the Irish Nationalists. The Unionists failed to achieve a decisive breakthrough despite unprecedented assistance from a range of nationalist organizations and sympathizers. The Navy League had made it quite clear which party it believed deserved the support of citizens anxious for the security of their country. Likewise, the Tariff Reform League had mobilized the full weight of its considerable resources by providing speakers for more than 15,000 meetings in 1909–1910 and disseminating more than 80,000,000 leaflets and pamphlets during the same period.[77]

Even the Anti-Socialist Union had generated a remarkable upsurge in electoral work. It had intervened in 120 constituencies, dispatching speakers, canvassers, and quantities of literature. Metropolitan London was the most heavily worked (44 constituencies).[78] Beyond the confines of the capital, the union's efforts were rather more selective. Ireland and Scotland were ignored, and Wales received only perfunctory attention. Most of its efforts were devoted to the north of England, including 13 constituencies each in Lancashire and Yorkshire, and a further five in Durham and Staffordshire. Generally, although not exclusively, these were constituencies with a Labour candidate. Union canvassers and lecturers toiled ardently on behalf of whole-hoggers such as E. Ashton Bagley at Leicester or Henry Page Croft at Christchurch. Indeed, Croft specifically assured the union that its assistance "largely contributed to our astonishing victory" and that he had "long watched" its work and "realized how much service it is doing for the Imperial Party in this country." Similar endorsements, always from professedly grateful Unionists, were carefully culled and reported. Navalists like Admiral Beresford insisted that the union had "helped very materially" at Portsmouth, while Hermon-Hodge at Croydon concurred that the Anti-Socialist Union was "of great value and materially contributed" to his reelection.[79]

The Dilemmas of Defeat

And yet the Liberals retained office. Publicly, the Unionist party and the assorted nationalist groups sought to cast the results in the most favorable light. This usually involved touching briefly on the larger number of seats won than in 1906 and then dwelling upon the great work that remained. Certainly the Tariff Reform League strained to detect a silver lining in the cloud of January 1910's defeat:

> Tariff reformers have no reason to be dissatisfied with the results of the general election. In parliamentary numbers they are now equal to the Radical party proper, and they are far more united in their principles and their aims. While we regret that these principles have not triumphed to a still greater extent, a survey of the progress made since 1906 inspires us with the confident assurance that ultimate success cannot be long delayed. To overthrow the fetish of Free Trade and to uproot doctrines which for many years have been coexistent with the prosperity of this country, and to which its industrial and commercial success has been falsely attributed, is a work which cannot be carried through without difficulty and delays. But a great deal has been accomplished, and no one doubts that, if there is no slackening of effort on our part, Tariff Reform will sweep the country at the next election.[80]

Stung by an increase in the Labour party, the Anti-Socialist Union responded by announcing that the "stiffest fight will be in the industrial centres of the north, and in this field the Union is immediately entering upon an important campaign. Lancashire and Yorkshire, in particular, will be thoroughly worked."[81] It appealed for some £3,000 to fund the 2,000 speakers it intended to train and dispatch without delay. The Navy League attributed the reduction of the "Radical majority" to Liberal failures on the naval issue and urged continued vigilance.

Some Unionist party strategists responded by reiterating the notion of two elections. First formulated in the wake of the intial reactions to Lloyd George's budget, this strategy presumed that the Unionists could not hope to win the first postbudget election, but that they could reduce the Liberals to dependence on their Irish and Labour allies and also popularize tariff reform to an extent that a second election could be won once the initial popularity of the budget had worn off. The operating assumption was that another election was imminent, because the monarch would insist on a second verdict before acquiescing in any reduction of the powers of the lords or any expansion of their numbers. Therefore, failure to oust the Liberals in January 1910 was in one sense of secondary importance, so long as more favorable ground had been prepared on which to wage the following campaign.[82]

Of course, January's campaign would amount only to procrastination if measures were not taken to adapt and implement the apparent lessons of consecutive defeats in 1906 and 1910. How this was to be achieved was less clear. Certain aspects of a properly nationalist focus would retain their relevance, including the threats to English liberties and authority posed by Labour and the Irish. Indeed, the resonance of the latter issue might be enhanced, given that another home rule bill was the logical concomitant to any elimination of the lords' absolute veto. The difficulty with this issue, congenial as it might be to the party's squires, was that its very familiarity would obscure the imperative to reshape the nation's economic and military structures in order to meet the mounting threat from Germany. Furthermore, after nearly a year of recurrent Dreadnought mania, coupled with the eventual passage in April of the Liberals' expanded provisions for the fleet, who could be certain that public interest in the naval issue had not been exhausted? Army reform, or at least the case for national service, was hardly calculated to draw the masses. Even if the target was the wavering minority in the borderline constituencies who might ultimately decide an election, national service appeared to alienate as many voters as it attracted. Therefore, regardless of the "two election strategy," it could not confidently be predicted early in 1910 that conditions were necessarily more favorable in the event of a second contest, and this apprehension was shared by modernizing peers, backwoodsmen, and party mandarins.

The traditional "Hatfield" view of the party's dilemma was eloquently put by Salisbury, who anticipated the second election as an attempt to "risk everything upon the next throw." The prospect of failure was almost too terrible to contemplate:

> If we fail this time the power of the House of Lords must go, and with it the Union, the Church, the whole realm of religious interests to which we are attached, and the barrier against Socialism; and at the same time if it be true

that the present government cannot be trusted in Imperial defence, perhaps
the very existence of our Empire. Is it reasonable, is it possible, to ask us to
enter into this struggle except upon the best ground we can find? If we can
win without food taxation, but may very possibly be shattered with it, can we
hesitate which choice to make?[83]

To the ardent tariff reformers, however, it was not the fiscal issue but the
traditionalist baggage that hampered the party. In their view, tariffs had nearly
overcome the handicaps that an unresponsive party persisted in retaining.
Austen Chamberlain, perhaps predictably, passed over the disappointing re-
turns from Scotland, London, and Lancashire to emphasize that "tariff reform
was our trump card. Where we won, we won on and by tariff reform. Even
where we lost, it was the only subject in our repertoire about which people
really cared."[84] Bonar Law responded to Salisbury's argument by reminding
him that "a large section of the party . . . regards Preference not as a political
opinion but as something almost sacred," and he emphasized that any concessions on the matter would probably produce "a wholesale revolt among the
rank and file which would cause a division in our Party more complete and
more hopeless than has existed at any time since the fiscal controversy was
raised."[85]

These confessions of faith did not answer the question of what was to be
done. Finding better electoral ground in Scotland, for example, was unlikely.
Austen Chamberlain termed the Scottish results "very bad," while Salisbury
felt that tariff reform there "seems to have made little way."[86] Guy Speir, the
conservative agent for Scotland, advised prospective candidates to put home
rule and constitutional questions at the forefront, "while not necessarily omit-
ting tariff reform."[87] The Scottish Tariff Reform League was unable to control
its branches, experienced "difficulty in maintaining the interest of men who
have hitherto been active," and proved incapable of overcoming "old party
influences and prejudices . . . too strong to give the new opinion the full force it
would otherwise have cut at a general election."[88] Nonetheless, the loss of
much of Scotland could be contemplated with a degree of equanimity that was
not the case for London and, above all, Lancashire. Industrialists in the middle
of the nineteenth century had been fond of claiming that when Manchester
sneezed, the remainder of the country caught cold. To the Unionist party, in
particular, its performance in Lancashire usually served as a reliable guide to
its capacity for office.[89] Reasonable showings in the north, coupled with the
party's traditional strength in the south, would give the Unionists a majority.
Without a firm turnout in the north, however, the party's southern support
would amount only to a substantial minority.

Lancashire had reliably contributed toward recent Unionist majorities until
1906, at which time, and again in January 1910, it had not done so. Chronolog-
ical convergence and political rhetoric indicated that the Unionist party's
impaired performance there was attributable to tariff reform. More specifically, the disappointing results reflected the hostility to protection by Lancashire's cotton bosses and to food taxes by the working class. Salisbury, in the

process of clarifying his earlier remarks, argued that "of course far and away the most notable adverse results have been in the industrial districts of the North, where Tariff Reform may have reduced majorities in some cases—though not in all—but where it has signally failed of success."[90]

To improve the party's electoral prospects in Lancashire, then, some way had to be found to minimize the unappetizing aspects of tariff reform, namely, colonial preference (food taxes). Fabian Ware, the *Morning Post*'s editor, was quick to spot the "rot" emerging in the later stages of the January election. In some ways, he believed, the situation was comparable with that in 1906. "But now," he explained, "the enemy, instead of endeavouring to throw over the whole question of Tariff Reform, desires merely to jettison the imperial side." In Ware's estimation, the "enemy" was the "Central Conservative Office clique" whose principles crumbled before their estimates of temporary electoral advantage.[91] Bonar Law spoke for many whole-hoggers when he tried to meet such arguments on their own terms. Dropping food taxes from the Unionist program would divide the party and antagonize agricultural voters who had responded favorably to the issue. The party would risk "losing the advantage we have gained in the Counties, without any guarantee of securing an equivalent advantage in the towns."[92]

Lurking behind this discussion was, as Bonar Law suggested, a potentially broader disagreement over the nature of partisan commitment, the role of patriotic doctrine, and the resonance of public reaction. These were familiar issues that the Unionist party's temporary unity over tariff reform had as temporarily concealed. Implicit in the debate were the questions of whether the Unionist party was necessarily the best or even the sole guarantor of national interests; of whether properly "national" interests were familiar constitutional ones that threatened to reassert their hold now that the House of Lords was to be the focus of political conflict; and whether the national interest was best served by resolute commitment to a full program even if certain aspects were deemed unpopular or if judicious pruning and juggling to catch votes was ultimately more productive. Initially it had been tariff reformers who had preached the virtue of independence from precise party doctrine in the fulfillment of a higher national purpose. However, as their arguments converged with those of the party leadership, they began to encourage a more precise identification of party and patriotic interest, with the consequence that Unionists who failed to satisfy their primary test of loyalty on the fiscal issue were effectively repudiating their rights and responsibilities as party members. It was this inflexibility, this perverse fixation on a single issue that fueled the resentment of free fooders such as Lord Robert Cecil. He found himself impaled on the "old controversy whether an MP is a delegate or a representative." Recognizing that any individual would "differ on some points from those with whom he is generally in political agreement," Cecil predicted that artificial unanimity (the insistence "that each member of a party in every important question . . . defer to the opinion of the majority") would produce the gravest results. "Honest and intelligent men would be conspicuous by their absence," a situation Cecil deemed already characteristic of the Irish and Labour parties.[93]

   The thrust of the nationalist agitation had been that conventional party politics permitted MPs, however honest or intelligent or well-intentioned, to disregard issues so critical to the national interest that agitation and mobilization of the electorate was justifiable to ensure that appropriate remedial measures were discussed, defined, and implemented. If dictation to a party hastened the achievement of national security and if such "artificial unanimity" relegated other important issues of long standing to a subsidiary role, this was a small price to pay, given what was at stake. Taken to their logical conclusion, such views seemed catastrophic to those who regarded parties as the essential instrument of political action and conceived of their debilitation as tantamount to national collapse. In early 1910, after the Unionist party had lost two successive elections, these latter considerations regained their urgency. Salisbury's priorities—the lords, the church, the union with Ireland whose defense gave the party its name—were superficial, not directly responsible for the maintenance of British power, which depended on economic and social reorganization. At least this is the way in which ardent tariff reformers perceived the situation. And yet the failure to achieve an electoral breakthrough on the basis of the Unionist party's commitment to tariff reform could not be gainsaid.

   There were at least two possible ways to sidestep this wrangle. One might involve a breathtaking effort to slice the Gordian knot of partisan intrigue at a single blow. The possibility of achieving bipartisan consensus on major issues was explored during the summer of 1910. Prompted by the death of Edward VII in early May, the subsequent "constitutional conference" embodied private meetings between major figures from the Liberal and Unionist parties.[94] They sought to resolve the House of Lords question without necessitating a Liberal resort to the new king, George V, to demand the creation of enough new Liberal peers to secure passage of legislation restricting the powers of the upper chamber. The fundamental hurdle was neither the status nor the sinews of aristocratic power, but rather the lords' position as a barrier to Irish home rule. To circumvent that impasse, Lloyd George in August 1910 produced a startling memorandum that reflected his own impatience with the fixation of lesser minds on lesser problems and that appeared to meet many of the most prominent objections of the nationalist agitation. Lloyd George proposed a coalition to implement compulsory military training, secure naval defense, and introduce colonial preference. These propositions were all attractive to the Unionists, but they were to be coupled with the unimpeded progress of national insurance, land reform, and other social legislation, as well as devolution ("home rule all around"). To some historians, Lloyd George's initiative has seemed to indicate the potential for a drastic restructuring of the British state along "social imperialist" lines, but several points must be borne in mind that restricted this possibility.[95] Lloyd George did not have the authority to grant such concessions, and his memorandum was perhaps more a way of thinking aloud than a specific basis for detailed reconstruction. Furthermore, most Unionists would not have so readily conceded home rule, and, in any event, the party itself was not consulted. F. E. Smith's enthusiastic reaction, for example, was in no way representative of the attitude of the Unionist rank and file or even of that of Balfour himself.[96]

The second possibility appeared more practical and derived a measure of plausibility from the Unionist party's new tactical situation. In attempting to justify the lords' rejection of the budget, the Unionists had retreated from stressing the responsibility for the upper chamber to stand firm of its own accord and instead had played up the decision for rejection as a sorely needed plebiscitary initiative that protected the people's right to be consulted directly on critical issues. In 1909, the argument was that the electorate had no inkling of a potential constitutional crisis when it had gone to the polls in 1906. In 1910, this sort of argument was harder to sustain, for the electorate was informed during the January campaign about the major issues, especially about "the core of the argument," namely, the choice between direct, redistributive taxation or tariffs (an indirect means) as the means of financing social reform.[97] Nonetheless, the notion of placing a single issue directly before the public as a referendum eventually gained currency within the party as a way of excising the demonstrably unpopular element of the Unionist program, namely, food taxes, without appearing to compromise principles. Tariff reformers could have their big loaf and eat it too. Or so they were told. Prominent whole-hoggers continued to hold firm on preference and resist the idea of a referendum. As Austen Chamberlain reminded Balfour, "Tariff Reform and Imperial Preference, Imperial Preference and Tariff Reform must be the burden of our song. . . . When all is said and done," he added optimistically, "they make a very popular refrain."[98] It was, in a way, an indirect tribute to this opposition that the referendum idea received official party sanction in so odd and hasty a manner.

The decisive signal came in late November 1910 from Lancashire. To breach the citadel of free trade, Bonar Law had agreed to leave his safe seat at Dulwich to contest Manchester NW. In an interview with a local journalist, Bonar Law expressed sympathy for submitting tariff reform to a referendum (pledging not to implement food taxes unless first approved by the electorate), and this commitment was relayed to Garvin, who had already privately been advocating such a course. Garvin promptly endorsed the referendum scheme in the front pages of the *Observer*, and the remainder of the Unionist press followed with varying degrees of enthusiasm. But Balfour, whose decision of course would be critical, was used to this sort of clamor in the press. What carried particular weight with him was the apparent support for the referendum by Bonar Law, an authentic whole-hogger spokesman and presumably someone also consonant with the immediate situation in Lancashire.[99] On 29 November, therefore, before a packed Albert Hall, Balfour announced that he had "not the least objection to submit the principles of Tariff Reform to Referendum."[100]

One member of the audience promptly shouted, "That's won the election," and the vast majority of his fellow listeners appeared to have agreed.[101] Would the ploy work, and would it be sufficient? Certainly other approaches had been in the works. October 1910 witnessed the emergence of the "reveille" movement, which, as its name implied, was intended to regroup and revitalize the party on a vigorous program of tariff reform and national security. While embodying nothing new, apart from offering Leo Maxse yet another opportunity for his bitter invective and incandescent prose, the reveille signified the unease with which some Unionists continued to regard the possible vacillation of the party's leadership.[102] It also reflected their conviction that a strategy of principles rigidly adhered to would pay greater dividends than the adoption of tactics of expediency or opportunism. The Anti-Socialist Union intensified its own efforts in the north. One of the union's executive committee members, Wilfrid Ashley, assured Balfour's secretary that "our anti-Socialist campaign in Yorkshire makes progress. It costs the devil of a lot of money but as nearly half the Socialist votes last election came from these two counties, one must not grudge it."[103] By August 1910, Ashley detected further progress and claimed that the union "on the whole is markedly stronger than it was a year ago, both financially and numerically." Its seaside campaigns (in Blackpool and elsewhere) "attracted large crowds," and, though Ashley conceded that these efforts did not match those of the opposition, he nevertheless contended that the union was "preventing large numbers of people from *becoming* Socialists."[104]

Navalists too were seeking to keep their issue before the public, even if it meant widening the rifts that already fragmented the movement.[105] The Imperial Maritime League, eager to regain the offensive, began a vigorous criticism of the Declaration of London (1909), which had defined foodstuffs as contraband and thus liable to seizure during wartime. To the Imperial Maritime League, this decision merely legitimated the likely efforts of enemies to threaten Britain's jugular, while the Navy League's acceptance of the declaration offered another opportunity to portray that rival as supine and ineffective. The "navier league" repeated its desire to "attempt to lift National Defence above the clang of controversy into the serene atmosphere of patriotism and expert knowledge," but its efforts belied its assurances.[106] The Imperial Maritime League had labored to collect signatures for a petition urging the Lords to "throw out the budget" by which the Liberal government was alleged to be undermining the nation's security.[107] Regarding the budget as a violation of fiscal integrity, the league advocated a £100 million loan specifically for naval defense as a more practical way of meeting the country's immediate military requirements. In this way, issues of constitutional legality or fiscal purity could be avoided by a sharper concentration on the most pressing question at hand.

Yet "serene patriotism" was inevitably constrained by the existing contours of partisan debate. The Imperial Maritime League could not remain aloof. Its annual report, published in October 1910, was explicit in its prediction that "Unionist candidates and Unionist agents may rest assured that in the loss of our naval supremacy through the neglect of the Liberal government—if and when that neglect is brought home with knowledge and persistency—lies a weapon which can vie with tariff reform itself as a means of winning the suffrages of electors."[108] Recognizing that this stark declaration might offend more tender nonpartisan sensibilities, the report clarified the league's position:

If criticism be levelled at this direct reference to the Unionist party, your
Committee reply again that the object of the Imperial Maritime League is to
save the Sea Power of Britain and restore the Two Power Standard, and that
previous experience has amply shown that no argument under the sun has
any weight with the present Ministry save the fear of losing votes.[109]

A poster introduced at the Croydon by-election had put the matter more
concisely. "Our naval strength has been fooled away by the Radicals and
Socialists," it read. "What guards your food? Our Navy. Then kick out the
Radicals, or when war comes you will starve."[110] A statement justifying the
possible candidacy of Harold Wyatt as a Unionist summarized the Imperial
Maritime League's stance in the wake of the disappointing results of January
1910. It warned that candidates should not run as independents or "counter to
the usual party arrangement." Instead, "it is essential that these candidates
should belong to the Unionist party for the sole but in itself sufficient reason
that the present Liberal government are for all practical purposes in the hands
of their Socialist, Irish Nationalist, and 'Little England' supporters."[111]

It therefore would be the party, its leader and organization, that dictated
the agenda of the second campaign. Unlike the January election, in December
1910 the various nationalist agitators could not succeed in dislodging the
constitutional question as the dominant one before the electorate. Tariff reform was no longer quite considered by many as "practical politics," given
Balfour's referendum pledge and the economy's continued improvement.
Under a free trade government, tariff reformers required evidence of considerable economic distress if they were to persuade voters of the necessity for
fiscal change. When presented with exactly that opportunity in 1908 they
had made progress, though not enough, and now, 2 years later, those gains
appeared to be eroding. The Tariff Reform League found itself again confronted with the claim that tariff reform activities were unpopular and undertaken only through the sponsorship of a relative handful of corrupt-minded
donors. In late November 1910, just days before Balfour's appearance at the
Albert Hall, Lord Weardale on behalf of Free Traders challenged the Tariff
Reform League to make public the identity of its subscribers. He hoped in
the process to reveal the league's dependence on large subscriptions and to
discredit its claim to speak for thousands of committed individuals from
among the common people. The challenge provoked much discussion among
league leaders over the least damaging way of countering Weardale, who had
offered to contribute £1,000 toward the Tariff Reform League's expenses if it
would publish its accounts. T. W. A. Bagley, the league's dutiful and harried
secretary, calculated that the London central office had received nearly
£160,000 since its inception, some £45,000 of which had been spent on meetings. He strongly advised against disclosing such information, for, as he
explained to league chairman Viscount Ridley, "our opponents would only
talk of the total, and would want to know what the huge balance was spent on;
while our supporters would at once attribute waste to the office and our
movement."[112]

Instead, Bagley proposed to deflect the challenge by attaching additional conditions that, for example, free trade associations reciprocate or that newspapers devote the space to list every subscriber. Moreover, the league should insinuate that its reliance solely upon subscriptions from British subjects was not matched by its greedy opponents, who accepted money from "foreign gentlemen."[113] By December the issue had faded; Weardale ruefully noted that "the tariff reform millions will remain a mystery," but, he concluded, "the plain man knows that where things are concealed there is usually a good reason for concealment."[114]

In December 1910, then, the plain man's attention was focused on the Liberals' right to deal punitively with the House of Lords and on the Irish Nationalists' determination to exploit their own indispensability to ensure home rule once the lords' absolute veto had been abolished. Priorities were neatly encapsulated in a Tariff Reform League leaflet entitled, "What's the Game?" A crude effort to stir prejudices, it exhorted electors to "vote for tariff reform, a big navy, and no Home Rule," but despite the order in which the issues were placed (and despite the organization that issued the leaflet), the third topic dominated the text:

> It's sumnat you ought to hear,
> About this 'ere darned election
> What's going to upset all the trade
> Just to please the Irish section;
> It ain't even British-made!
> D'you think it's the Lords or Veto,
> That's making 'em play the fool;
> It's Mister Dictator Redmond
> Who's out to obtain Home Rule
> Let's start playing "Rule Britannia"
> Then act up to what it means
> And show all these Empire breakers
> We're just going to give 'em beans.

This defiant declaration was then topped off with a dose of pure Tory nostalgia. Vituperative remarks about a "gang of shifty lawyers" (a reference to the prevalence of such professionals on the Liberal benches, though they were by no means absent from the Opposition benches as well!) were used to sustain the remarkable observation that "we were better off in the old days when governed by country squires, than now with a gang of lawyers whom for truthwork nobody hires."

December 1910 did not produce the much anticipated Unionist victory. Liberal majorities were reduced in a number of Lancashire seats, but London held firm, and, when the results were tallied, they only served to confirm those of the previous January. The referendum was influential only in Lancashire. Everywhere confident Liberals pointed to it with satisfaction as another example of the Unionists' rush to avoid remaining true to principles. Ardent wholehoggers, frustrated by both the electorate's response and Balfour's move to regain tactical supremacy, wasted little time in voicing that discontent. Ridley complained that "there is understandably a great spirit of discomfort in our ranks on the Referendum, and although I personally supported it as I felt that the only thing to do in a crisis was to back our leader, I cannot help feeling that we should have done just as well or better at the elections without it."[115] Shortly thereafter he warned that some tariff reformers were "getting wobbly" and that the "referendum trick *lost* us votes everywhere and especially in Lancashire."[116] On the eve of the new year, prospects for the whole-hoggers were none too comforting. "The situation seems to me full of difficulties for the Tariff Reform League," predicted Ridley gloomily to Bonar Law, "and the adoption of this Referendum proposal will lose us a great deal of support and subscriptions."[117] Leo Maxse, as usual, could be counted upon for more vigorous statements, and he did not hesitate to assign blame. "We should have won this General Election if it had not been for Arthur Balfour side-tracking Tariff Reform."[118] Balfour had "done more harm to Tariff Reform during the past two months than he did in the previous five years." His Albert Hall speech cost, by Maxse's calculations, "40 or 50 seats. It is unpardonable. Balfour must go, or Tariff Reform will go—that is the alternative."[119]

Although eventually both would go, and although his estimates of lost seats attributable to the referendum were wildly exaggerated, the vitriolic editor of the *National Review* was quite correct to stress the growing precariousness of Balfour's position. The Unionist leader had exposed himself to the charge of renouncing convictions to catch votes. He was now vulnerable to the taunts that he had never had convictions and that he had failed to deliver the votes. Ironically, however, in early 1911, in the wake of three successive defeats for which he inevitably bore much of the responsibility, the constitutional crisis ensured that tariff reformers and other disgruntled nationalists had to defer to Balfour's leadership of the party and to accept the relegation of their particular issues to secondary status. It was a temporary reprieve, however, for if Balfour mishandled the crisis, the gravity of the situation would encourage the dissident bodies to seek their own orbit.

Asquith, as expected, did indeed introduce a bill to curtail the powers of the lords, yet—to the dismay of many Unionists—he had chosen his ground carefully by first securing from the young George V a pledge to create if necessary the additional peers to secure the bill's passage through the upper chamber. In response, Unionists had to evaluate two questions: whether for the second time in 2 years the Lords should risk rejection of a bill they considered odious and whether Balfour's leadership so lacked astuteness that the party should risk his removal. The two questions were related, of course, in that Balfour's handling of the lords crisis would probably persuade cautious or uncommitted members either to remain loyal or to disregard his authority. Balfour himself eventually found the case for submission more persuasive than that for rejection, but his preference only increased his isolation.

One cannot comprehend why he was eased out of the party leadership in November 1911, however, unless one grasps the link between Balfour's attitude to the lords and his earlier referendum pledge. The common denominator was political principle, and Balfour's Unionist detractors (figuring largely within the nationalist agitation) argued that his preference for submitting meekly rather than standing boldly for the rights of a hallowed institution was of a piece with his career. Olympian calculation, philosophic doubt, an addiction to golf, and frequent influenza had not endeared Balfour to his party. Plagued by doubt and frustrated by a political deadlock in which the Liberals contrived to remain in power, many Unionists began to find a tougher approach emphasizing cherished principles attractive. Such an attitude precluded any effort to seek innovative emphases for tariff reform and minimized the need to devise fresh appeals for an electorate that had resisted Tory charms in 1906 and 1910. Balfour did not fit the newer image. His rarified and rational approach had produced no appreciable party advantage; his linguistic dexterity and subtlety had failed. Unionist dissidents offered a straightforward, direct approach, encapsulated first by Maxse's battle cry, "B. M. G." ("Balfour must go"), and then by the "Diehards."

The reputation of the Diehards has been rehabilitated to some extent from the sneers of George Dangerfield.[120] The peers who opposed the Parliament bill in 1911 did not solely consist of "backwoodsmen," atavistic landowners who crawled from beneath the rocks of their landed estates to emerge blinking in the unfamiliar light of the upper chamber. On the contrary, despite the presence of unrepresentative Diehards such as the aged, backward-looking Lord Halsbury, they counted among themselves many of the most active peers, and they also elicited the support of prominent Unionist party members from the House of Commons (such as Austen Chamberlain and F. E. Smith). The progressive rise in the political temperature that hot August 1911 has been described many times, and there is no need to narrate it again here. The Diehards' decision to defy not just the Liberal government, but their party's leaders and political logic as well, marked the climax of a revolt from the right that had been brewing in earnest since 1908–1909, but whose diverse strands had begun to emerge in the 1880s and 1890s. It is unfair to characterize this revolt as purely reactionary, for many of the Diehards, as well as members of the various nationalist associations, were willing to contemplate measures that appeared to diverge from Conservative political practice as it had been conventionally understood. Exactly what had been at stake and what had been achieved would not be clarified, though, until the dust had settled, so to speak, in the aftermath of August 1911.

5

Disintegration

In August 1911 the Diehards were defeated. The Liberals secured passage of the Parliament Act without recourse to the king's pledge, thus preserving the upper chamber's social exclusivity while emasculating its legislative power. For the Diehards themselves, the results were especially bitter, and there were recriminations against the Unionist peers who had voted in favor of the bill (the "rats" or "hedgers") and Balfour and Lansdowne who had urged such a course. Briefly there was sentiment for retaining the Diehards as a distinct grouping separate from the Unionist party, which manifested such insipid behavior.[1] But it was not enough to fulminate against supine leaders and acquiescent followers, and even Balfour's resignation as party chief in November 1911 would not clarify the nationalist dilemma.

For one thing, there was the problem of unity. The various Diehards shared only an announced commitment to defiance; they could not agree on the substance of a subsequent program. In other words, their significance was primarily tactical and their convergence was a matter of convenience. As Alan Sykes has argued, they were all extreme, but they were not all radical.[2] Furthermore, this lack of consensus, and the absence of a coordinated strategy which that entailed, complicated the Diehards' relationship with the party. Defiance, of simultaneously the Liberals and the Unionist leadership, reinforced the lesson that, as a minority, the Unionists desperately required cohesion. In this regard, 1911 was important in that it demonstrated the political impotence of a squabbling party. Yet a familiar dilemma remained.

Irish home rule was obviously once again to be at the center of political debate. To conduct a campaign against it would certainly draw the party closer together. But for more than a decade the nationalist agitation had been seeking to identify other issues that were, perhaps, of greater long-term significance: industrial competitiveness, military security, the weight of organized labor in mass politics. The lessons of 1911 seemed to be that the agitation "for country," as it were, had weakened the party and that immediate tactical realities dictated that dissent be subordinated to harmonized partisan action, even if this entailed focusing upon home rule. Would such a strategy, however, alle-

viate a gnawing doubt, namely, that to opt "for party" could delay the implementation of those measures the country so urgently required? A defensive,
negative posture, one of a unified but cautious opposition, would serve the
Unionist party's immediate interest. But would it serve the country's? Would
not a regenerated agitation, dissonant if necessary, remain the best alternative?
If desirable, was such an agitation still practical? From 1911 until 1914 each of
the nationalist pressure groups struggled with these questions.

The Popular Dimensions of Navalism

Judged solely on the basis of its published figures, the impressive growth of the
Navy League should have suggested that, far from vanishing after January
1910, the naval issue continued to hold out the prospect for sustained agitation.
From some 20,000 members in 1908 the league ballooned to 100,000 in 1912
and nearly 125,000 by 1913.[3] Likewise, by 1912 the league counted 127
branches, a figure that would exceed 150 on the eve of the war.[4] The Birmingham branch expanded from 352 in December 1912 to 718 a year later, the
Nottingham branch grew from 40 in May 1911 to 671 by July 1913, while the
Glasgow branch quadrupled its membership within the same period to 1,600.[5]
The accelerating totals appeared to bear eloquent testimony to the success of
the league's efforts to democratize its structure.

Appearances could be deceiving, of course, and there is evidence to indicate
that spiralling membership figures provided only a partial impression, and in
many ways a misleading one, of the Navy League's affairs. Despite the secession in 1907 of the dissidents who subsequently constituted the Imperial
Maritime League, dissatisfaction with the league's leadership persisted. "The
truth is that the Head Office has long been synonymous with incapacity,
muddle, petty jealousies, intrigues, inefficiency, amateurishness, and do-noth-
ing[ness]."[6] This litany of abuses was embodied in a memorandum to be
circulated among fellow league members by a critic who proceeded to amplify
his charges. He condemned the "vacillating incapacity of those who draw
salaries in the Head Offices" and believed it to be "treason of the worst to allow
the public to imagine that in the Navy League is a vigilant and adequate
organisation." Some responsibility lay with the president, Robert Yerburgh,
whom he characterized as "a pleasant gentleman, but he is not the man for the
Navy League, and not the man for a president."[7] Other critics were even more
specific. Carlyon Bellairs, a former Liberal who had crossed the floor to the
Unionist benches, left the league because it "would not put in a big, influential
go-ahead man but elected Yerburgh as President, Chairman, and Trustee! A
most hopeless ass as a sort of Pooh Bah who goes in for being a sort of guinea
pig President of small leagues and so gives the world the idea that he occasionally works!"[8] Yerburgh, his income secure from a marriage to a brewer's
daughter, favored "hunting and country pursuits generally" and never exhibited any particular imagination or vigor. One of his kinder Unionist colleagues
described him as "an able man, who had by many years of party service earned

that intangible thing called the 'gratitude of the party,' but who for all that remained on the back benches."[9] Lord Hugh Cecil less charitably labeled him "Mr. Pliable" when Yerburgh justified his own support of tariff reform on the grounds that it was a policy of free trade.[10] Likewise, in Lancashire tariff reform meetings, Yerburgh was the only dissentient from "a bold advocacy" of whole-hogger policies, despite Yerburgh's own admission that, as a representative of the Tariff Reform League, he could not very well be suspected of being "lukewarm."[11]

In the league's defense, it could be argued that Yerburgh had not been the first choice as president, that other candidates had refused the executive committee's offer, and that he was irrelevant to league policy. When Yerburgh died in 1916, Arnold White presumed that "the days of shop window dressing presidents are over."[12] Clearly, it was the secretary who played a more important role, given the division of administrative duties, which was reinforced by Yerburgh's preference to act in a reticent and advisory capacity. The Navy League's longtime secretary, William Caius Crutchley, was a retired naval officer, as was his successor, Brian Hewitt. Neither made a particularly strong mark, and Hewitt was portrayed as a creature of the Admiralty, an "absurd situation," and "a poor compliment to the intelligence of the members."[13] It had been Spenser Wilkinson, Herbert Wrigley Wilson, and Arnold White who—in various ways—had done more to shape the league's public image, while daily maintenance often devolved upon energetic local branch secretaries. Little wonder that a "reformer" called for "a clean sweep of the Head Office to put in command men pledged to act, and to be straightforward as well as patriotic."[14] But, in July 1911, came a decisive break with mediocrity.

The Navy League's new secretary was unlike his predecessors. Patrick Hannon had not entered upon a naval career, and he was a Catholic and an avowed Unionist and tariff reformer. In December 1910, he had stood as a Unionist candidate for Bristol East (considered an unwinnable seat) and managed a respectable showing in defeat. Indeed, he was praised for giving "a new impetus to the activities of the local Unionist and Tariff Reform Association," and it was the same energy and enthusiasm he was to bring to the Navy League.[15] In 1912, he personally addressed 121 meetings and impressed Yerburgh with his "perfect genius for organisation, ceaseless energy," and "abundance of tact."[16] Even Sir John Fisher, someone a good deal less easily persuaded, concurred, noting that Hannon was "just doing wonders" for the Navy League.[17]

No doubt Hannon's vigorous example benefitted Navy League organizers in the country, but here too the situation was not entirely satisfactory. The league's annual report for 1911 admitted that "much trouble has been experienced in finding honorary secretaries with the necessary public spirit and the time at their disposal to infuse real vitality into local branches," though the committee contended that, with public attention focused on the constitutional conflict and the National Insurance scheme, 1911 could not be considered "a normal year."[18] The situation in Scotland confirmed such admissions of stagnation, at least according to Lord Ampthill, who toured the Scottish branches in 1911. "Scotland knows very little and cares very little about the Navy," he reported to the league's secretary:

> My tour was a great disappointment to me from the point of view of my concern for the Navy League. As I had been invited with some circumstance and formality, and at no less than four months notice, to speak at the great centers of Edinburgh, Glasgow, and Dundee, I had naturally hoped that the meetings would be well organized and would have a considerable effect. But in this hope I was entirely disappointed although the time chosen for the meetings could not have been more favourable, seeing that the Navy Estimates had just been under discussion in the House of Commons.
>
> The meeting at Glasgow was not so bad. There were about 600 people present but the hall would have held four times that number. The meeting at Dundee, however, was contemptible in size and that at Edinburgh was beneath contempt. In all three places the members of the local branches made the great mistake of thinking you can hold a big public meeting without previous organisation. I told them all that organisation, that is to say, systematic canvassing of individuals must come first and that the big meeting then serves as the reward and encouragement of the workers and a public demonstration of the work which has been done.
>
> The local secretaries had no idea of such organisation; they all thought that when they had secured a speaker, published advertisements and invited 'a platform' they had done all that was possible or necessary to ensure a big meeting. These remarks do not apply so much to the Glasgow secretary, Mr. James Walton, who as I have already said was not altogether unsuccessful, and who is a really good man. The secretary at Dundee, Mr. J. O. Duncan, is as keen as possible, but he is young and entirely inexperienced. He has, however, learnt a lesson from which I am sure he will profit.
>
> The secretary of the Edinburgh branch, Mr. C. W. A. Tait, is 'no more use than a sick headache.' He is incompetent, idle, and timid, and until he is superceded that Branch will do no good. The meeting which he provided was simply an insult—twenty men and about twice that number of a hopeless class of females.[19]

Once again one might be tempted to dismiss this sort of account as accurate but insignificant, for the naval issue had never figured as prominently in the Celtic fringe. Yet Glasgow was not so easily overlooked. With its massive shipbuilding works on the Clyde and substantial mercantile community, it would have seemed to be more receptive to the league's message. Moreover, the Navy League pointedly emphasized the Glasgow branch's rapid growth and active schedule. Ampthill conceded that its meeting was "not so bad" and that its secretary was "a really good man," but the branch did have a curious history. It had originally been founded in 1898, but evidently foundered, for it was refounded in 1910. As a means of trying to recruit additional members after that refoundation, the secretary distributed an appeal undersigned by the first 116 members, which thus affords a glimpse into the branch's composition. The league itself described the branch as being composed largely of businessmen ("of the highest grade"), and the list generally bears this out.[20] The largest group (twenty-two) might be classified as merchants, with those in the wine and spirits trade particularly well-represented. The branch also numbered a variety of professionals and manufacturers and a strong contingent of stock-brokers/chartered accountants. Surprisingly, there was only one representative of marine insurance, a figure curiously low in light of the Navy League's arguments about the likely collapse of marine insurance if British naval supremacy was threatened. British commerce would be uninsurable or hard-pressed to afford the sky-rocketing premiums. The presence of a Liberal Unionist agent and the absence of any Liberal officials reflected the general political tone characteristic of other league branches. In all, these social groups were not unrepresentative of those that supported the Unionist party in the 1910 general elections.

Increases in the numbers of meetings, branches, or members were all heartening when compared with the Navy League's dismal performance in these areas in its early years, but the league increasingly had begun to insist upon the supreme importance of attracting working-class support (as in its plan of reorganization). Up to 1909, by its own admission, the league had failed to do so in significant numbers. The Glasgow branch's list from 1910 strongly suggests that workers did not figure prominently among its early members, though the sources upon which one must rely to reconstruct that membership are heavily weighted toward the more prominent, affluent, and stable strata in society. In its three annual reports immediately preceding the outbreak of the war, however, the Navy League expressed great satisfaction at the rapid rise in its membership and claimed that the vast majority of these new adherents were working-class.[21] It could not be argued, though, that the Navy League's program had changed dramatically enough to account for the undeni-ably substantial upsurge, nor could tense foreign relations and clearer appreci-ation of the German menace account for the whole of the increase. While tension and anti-German sentiment were conducive to recruitment in 1911–14, were not the navy scares of March and December 1909 equally conducive? A critical factor was the reduction in subscription fees that permitted local secretaries formally to enroll in the league members who could not have afforded the more restrictive, higher fees it had previously maintained.

Of course, much of the working-class participation could have been purely nominal. Certainly the Navy League continued to act as though its hold on workers was tenuous. One of its indefatigable lecturers, a former railway trade unionist named Marshall Pike (a fact advertised so strenuously as to suggest that his example was unusual), worked persistently to secure a broader follow-ing for the league. In itself that was not entirely unexceptional, but his lectures often fostered the impression that the Navy League was still recruiting poorly in 1912 and 1913 among the broader groups it hoped to reach. Pike's appeals to trade unionists implied that in their devotion to higher pay and sporting statistics they overlooked the state of the fleet. This unfortunate situation he found difficult to reconcile with union members' positions as "the best and most intelligent of the workers."[22] Apart from flattery, Pike played upon the trade unionists' recognition of the benefits of collective action, and he urged them to employ the same principle in joining the league. He conceded that workers might be more interested in domestic reform, but reminded working-class audiences that "reforms themselves depend upon national security. And with England national security depends upon sea power. If that is lost all is lost."[23] To be on the safe side, the league supplemented Pike's efforts with a program (undertaken in consultation with the Admirality and the Anti-Socialist Union) to arrest the spread of socialism within the fleet. Action was concentrated in Portsmouth, Plymouth, and Torquay.[24]

Even among the petite bourgeoisie, usually considered easy prey for nationalist demagogy, the Navy League fell short of its standards. Styled by Marshall Pike as the "four pounds a week class," this social grouping was hailed for its embodiment of essential national characteristics, yet assailed for its lack of navalist enthusiasm. Pike, as well as other league members, found the situation both curious and distressing. "Self-respecting, industrious, frugal, sober, and strictly honest" and "no less patriotic than any other class of the English . . . they have managed to persuade themselves that such questions as that of naval policy and strength are nothing whatever to do with them."[25] The league presumed that the majority worked in clerical positions in "the great mercantile houses" and therefore appealed to them "on the lines of business and not of sentiment." It discounted the influence of sentiment because this "four pounds a week class" had little direct contact with a fleet manned "almost entirely by the working classes" and "officered by the wealthy classes. . . . So, represented neither on the quarterdeck nor upon the lower deck, as a class they lack that tie of interest that personal service establishes between whole families and the Fleet."[26]

It was essential, therefore, that the petty bourgeoisie recognize that their position, their careers, their very lack of contact with the fleet were all secured by the Senior Service (which as the "Silent Service" they were all too likely to take for granted). This last point was a familiar one, of course, but lecturers like Pike embellished upon it more uncompromisingly than the league had been wont to do in the past. "All questions if you get to the bottom of them become economic questions . . . and naval rivalry is only another form of economic rivalry." Stressing the inevitability of economic competition, Navy League speakers drew parallels between the struggle for naval supremacy and efforts to achieve economic advantage through tariff wars. Without specifically favoring or denigrating protectionism, Pike contended that Britain's commercial success (and thus the salaries of the nation's clerks) could not be maintained without assuring continued British naval superiority. Again, elements here were familiar, but, given this particular twist, the argument could appeal to either of the warring fiscal factions within the Unionist party and to those disgusted with fiscalitis altogether.

Ironically, despite its undoubted growth, regardless of the extent to which the lower middle class was involved, the Navy League's financial situation actually deteriorated. The secession of members in 1907 and early 1908 had dealt a financial blow from which the league had only just recovered by 1910 (when it reported an annual income of £8,640). Yet for 1911 the total slipped to £5,750. A reluctance to match the special generosity of an election year no doubt contributed to the decline, but the primary reason was, as the league's treasurer explained, the revision of its fee structure. Subscription rates fell faster than membership totals rose. Even in 1913 the Navy League's annual income totalled only £7,814.[27]

The Navy League's position after 1911, then, was in some respects a curious one. It succeeded in attracting many new members, but only at the cost of foregoing the higher subscriptions it required to finance expanded agitation. More critically, as the naval issue faded as a means of strictly partisan mobilization, as it became clear that the Liberal government would retain British naval supremacy, and as it seemed that Conservative victory was thus not the only reliable assurance of a Grand Fleet, a Navy League itself might appear less relevant. Not surprisingly, therefore, some navalists who sought to preserve the "cutting edge" of the issue found themselves being forced to consider a more radical posture. This was the case within the Imperial Maritime League, which had to deal with the migration of former colleagues back to the Navy League. In 1913 there were suggestions from both leagues that reconciliation or even amalgamation was now possible, especially since both Wyatt and Horton-Smith had resigned as secretaries of the Imperial Maritime League. Even F. T. Jane resurfaced with his familiar offer of mediation, but the prospect was impractical.[28] For instance, the chairman of the Navy League's active Bristol branch responded with a warning that "the Imperial Maritime League is inspired by lawyers who treat the defences of the country in the legal fashion such as 'when you have no case abuse your opponent's counsel.'"[29] Support for amalgamation within the Imperial Maritime League largely reflected its desperate straits. The *War Office Times and Naval Review*, noting the recent pronouncement by the *Pall Mall Gazette* that "the egregious organisation, the Imperial Maritime League, was moribund if not actually defunct," reminded readers of its similar recent assessment:

> Three months ago we published an indictment of the Imperial Maritime League under the heading of "Imperial Impudence.' We referred to the desperate efforts being made by the league, or the league's organisers, to rake in cash by the bait of offering persons who sent along cheques or postal orders the empty distinctions of Supporter, Associate, Member, or even Vice-President of the League. . . . The Navy League, like its offshoot, can only exist by constant agitation. Its demands are accordingly based not upon policy but on the need of whipping up subscriptions if the league is not to become moribund or defunct. . . . The only advice we can give in regard to them is that their appeals should be relegated to the waste paper basket . . . instead of financing these ludicrous leagues and providing salaries for their officials.[30]

Indeed, the Imperial Maritime League approached Walter Morrison (often a generous donor to Unionist organizations) in the hope that he might contribute the funds "immediately essential" to its continued work.[31] The league also prepared a circular for Indian princes that hinted toward, even if it did not directly solicit, minimum contributions of £1,000.[32] Total annual expenditure hovered slightly under £4,000 but, more ominously, income from subscriptions was declining and membership figures gave little indication of rising.[33] When Captain Mathias, Wyatt and Horton-Smith's successor as secretary, privately calculated the number of copies he required of a league publication due to each member, he arrived at the figure of 1,460 distributed in twelve branches.[34]

Frustration at the league's inability to secure funds or members, or to exercise much influence, manifested itself in several ways: in tart letters to editors denying that the league was defunct, in announcements that league officials had attended meetings organized by other associations, and in radicalized rhetoric. The Imperial Maritime League persuaded Lord Willoughby de Broke to serve as president, and thus linked its image to a Diehard who defied party calculations. This idea was to become the league's new theme. As a 1913 circular announced, "this league is everyday becoming more impressed with the fact that neither political party will take a strong line on the question of national defence. . . . Therefore the IML [Imperial Maritime League] are anxious to build up a great body of public opinion, free from all political bias."[35] Just 3 years earlier the league had urged close cooperation with the Unionist party, but this previous strategy was now rejected. Perhaps the Imperial Maritime League's executive believed the Unionists were powerless after three consecutive defeats and that tenacious independence was the best course. But the lack of support that greeted its extremist stance was all the more obvious when compared with the Navy League's absolute growth and relative success.

Tariff Reform's Change of Course

For whole-hoggers, the situation after the constitutional crisis was likewise uncertain. Balfour's resignation and the accession of Bonar Law augured well, for the latter had been strongly committed to tariff reform, to the efforts of the Tariff Reform League, and even linked to the Confederacy.[36] On the other hand, Bonar Law's protectionist inclinations were inevitably circumscribed by his inheritance, namely, a party whose focus had recently been directed elsewhere, and, more obviously, by Balfour's referendum pledge. Would Bonar Law be bound to honor his predecessor's pledge, especially in view of the critical weight of his own opinion in persuading Balfour to consider the idea in the first place? And would the Tariff Reform League be able to sustain its level of electoral work after so many elections, so many defeats, and such ambiguity in the fiscal issue's priority?

Money was again the best indication. In 1909 and 1910 the Tariff Reform League had flexed its financial muscles to impressive effect, raising more than £40,000 in the first year, over £30,000 in the second.[37] But Ridley's prediction that the postreferendum situation would be "full of difficulties for the Tariff Reform League" was amply borne out.[38] Donations withered to barely one-fifth of their former peak, and total income plunged in half. "This is a horrid situation that we are in," lamented Austen Chamberlain in October 1911. "The

TR League have recently issued a fresh appeal for money (they are very short) in my name. Of those who reply, one half refuse alleging that we are anti-Balfourian, and the other half out of disgust at Balfour's surrender last August. Result £700 of outstanding contributions paid up, but only £17 of fresh money."[39] The Tariff Commission faced a similar situation.[40] Up to this point both organizations had jealously guarded the nature and extent of their revenue; even when Lord Weardale had dangled his bait of a £1,000 challenge in November 1910, the league refused to lift the veil of secrecy from its accounts.

One year later, however, the Tariff Reform League abruptly reversed its policy by publicizing its own income and comparing the figures to those published by its rival, the Free Trade Union. The league's secretary, T. W. A. Bagley, contended that the Free Trade Union's "Fighting Fund" alone exceeded the league's total revenue for the first 9 months of 1911, £10,043 to £9,703. He presumed that the disparity between the total income of the two organizations was greater still. Moreover, the Free Trade Union's revenue was drawn from 966 contributors, in contrast to the Tariff Reform League's 1,323 donors.[41] The resurrection of the issue of the league's income was, at first glance, puzzling, in light of both the league's previously studied secrecy and the minimal differences between the published accounts of the two rivals. *Monthly Notes on Tariff Reform* provided part of the explanation:

> Opponents of Tariff Reform have constantly asserted that the Tariff Reform League possess an enormous revenue and spends millions which are contributed by wealthy supporters whose interest it is to obtain 'Protection.' The objects of such assertions are obvious. They are intended to discredit the league with the working classes and to check the progress which Tariff Reform is making among them. They are also meant to suggest to would-be supporters that, as the league has such abundant funds, their subscriptions are not needed.[42]

In 1911, with the position of tariffs as a Unionist desideratum ambiguous, the Tariff Reform League clearly had to attract fresh revenue. Yet efforts to glean new donations or to secure new subscribers were hindered by one of two common perceptions: either that tariffs were, in the wake of three defeats, no longer a real issue or that the Tariff Reform League was propelled by the perseverent generosity of a few wealthy men in whose interests and by whose munificence alone the league functioned. Either way there was little incentive for the average individual to contribute. To do so would be either ineffectual or irrelevant. Therefore, it was essential to the league's financial health that it dispel its image of nearly limitless wealth, but without portraying itself as a lost cause or a broken reed. Revealing the number and amounts of its own contributions was the price to be paid in order to transfer to its free trade opponents its own image of an organization whose major donors offset limited popular support. Little wonder that the Tariff Reform League's exposé was entitled "The Tables Turned."[43]

Of course this new public posture did not prevent the league from seeking to prolong its survival by appealing to wealthy dignitaries. A meeting hosted by the Duke of Westminster in July 1912 at Grosvenor House raised an "Imperial Fund" of £21,250 from just seventeen prominent Unionists.[44] Yet half this sum was already depleted the following year to cover an operating deficit. It was a revealing commentary on the league's difficulties that its treasurer, Sir Alexander Henderson, was excluded from any role in securing the Imperial Fund.[45] A fellow whole-hogger, Sir Joseph Lawrence, was convinced that Henderson was partly to blame for the league's financial difficulties, as he explained in response to one of Leo Maxse's queries about the political influence of the "Plutocrats":

> Now to answer your question about the TR League and the millionaires. It is hopeless to expect Bagley or the staff to supply the information. They are recruited from a class who know nothing of wealth or social status outside their own circle. The only man who could help with information is Sir A. Henderson, but he won't give it or does not care to put us on to wealthy people, any more than he would tap them for subs as to TR. He will beg for the party from the Rothschilds etc. but *not* for TR, although he is our Treasurer! That dirty work falls to Paddy Goulding, myself, Ridley, or Duncannon.[46]

This sort of explanation was too easy. While personal contacts might lubricate the flow of funds from wealthy individuals, and while the league's image as a brash newcomer rocking the foundations of traditional gentility might dissuade apprehensive subscribers, the crux of the matter was popular perception of the prospects for tariff reform. If tariffs appeared impractical or unlikely, why contribute? By 1912 the league's predictions of imminent victory had begun to wear thin. This was not from lack of repetition. Its annual report for 1912, for example, referred to "the ominous signs of an entire breakdown of the Free Trade financial position, so plainly to be read in the more recent acts of the Liberal party in connection with both Finance and Defence."[47] The conspiracy of optimism extended to the local federations as well. The executive committee of the Kent County Tariff Reform Federation assured readers that "there has been no diminution in the ever-increasing labours for 'The Winning Cause' in Kent" and that "'The Forward Movement' has made great headway in the county during 1912."[48] Corroborating testimony was not hard to find. The Northern Tariff Reform Federation claimed that "at no time during the last eight years has there been greater enthusiasm or more fidelity for the cause of Tariff Reform amongst the workers in the North Country than at present."[49] And both Yorkshire and critical Lancashire were, if the local leadership was to be believed, swinging toward protectionism as well. "The year under review has been one of great progress for the movement," contended the regional federation, which now numbered 209 branches and 62,500 members and associates.[50]

There were, however, contradictory and more credible indications that by 1911 tariff reform was not progressing. Certainly the Trade Union Tariff Reform Association barely flickered on. Without the persistent assistance of Leo Amery it would have collapsed, as indeed he explained to Ridley. Together with J. W. Hills (the candidate who had ousted Arthur Elliot at Durham in

1906), he had "saved it from utter wreck," but now found that he had "reached the limits of our useful working effectiveness unless we can get hold of some fresh source of income."[51] Amery's grandiose vision of an organization that "might at the end of a few years stand entirely on its own feet and compete effectively with the existing Labour party" was negated by his periodic admissions that it lingered only with the aid of the Tariff Reform League itself and that its pretensions to independence were meaningless.[52]

Unionists in the constituencies, outside the league's inner sanctum, also repudiated the glowing predictions of the league. Walter Long reported in 1912 from Manchester that "there is practically a unanimity of opinion that Tariff Reform has not made any headway since the last Election, and nearly everybody I spoke to on the subject was convinced that there is a great hostility to the Food Taxes."[53] Another MP put the matter bluntly, that "to advocate food taxes [in the North] is to court disaster."[54] A local clergyman foresaw no hope for tariff reform in Lancashire because the area was "gorged with prosperity," advice duplicated by Lord Galway, who explained to Austen Chamberlain that with trade "booming . . . the electorate do not care a straw about Tariff Reform and you cannot win a general election on that cry."[55] These warnings carried greater urgency, though, because they were coupled with disturbing revelations about the league's clumsy or inefficient operations. In Yorkshire, for example, the local West Riding Tariff Reform Federation resisted dictation from London, prompting subterfuge and producing dissension.[56] Walter Long, touring the constituencies in connection with efforts to investigate the condition of local Unionist party organization, reported to Bonar Law that "a considerable amount of friction at present exists," and he detailed examples of the two organizations working at cross purposes.[57]

This dissension was publicized in September 1912 when F. C. Thomas, the secretary of the West Riding federation, wrote to the *Yorkshire Post* to condemn the league's interference within what he considered the federation's proper jurisdiction. Local resentment against the London head office was widespread, he indicated. A recent Tariff Reform League meeting in Leeds, for example, was a fraud, for it "consisted of a mere handful of people, a number of loafers having been given 6d. each to stand around and form a crowd, . . . [and] the attendance of the so-called delegates was obtained by issuing free tea tickets."[58] Moreover, "as to the league's numerous branches," Thomas contended that "no one in the West Riding can discover them, as they exist only on paper."[59] A Lancashire organizer for the Tariff Reform League (a Tom Smith who "did an immense amount of work" in that capacity) was cited by Long for his admission that "the Tariff Reform League organisation in Lancashire was mainly a paper one and that the supposed great improvement which had taken place in the prospects of the Tariff Reform League was entirely mythical."[60] Naturally, the Tariff Reform League repudiated these charges and blamed the West Riding federation for maliciously disrupting the league's own meetings.[61]

An undue concentration on this pattern of charge and countercharge can obscure the ebb and flow of the public mood. Gerald Arbuthnot, an MP for

Burnley in 1910 and the chairman of the Lancashire Federation of Junior
Unionist Associations, symbolized the shift in attitudes to tariff reform. Prior
to the January 1910 election, Arbuthnot had written that the primary issue
"must be tariff reform and bad trade."[62] In 1912, though, his tune changed, as
he explained to his party's leader:

> many of our party in other parts of the country are being badly deceived over
> Lancashire by the tactics of the Tariff Reform League and the T. R. Press.
> . . . What has happened is—1) many more branches of the league have been
> established. That means nothing: the members are our own men. 2) our
> opponents are apathetic on the subject, for the moment, as they are wild over
> the Insurance Act and want to show their annoyance. Anyhow the Tariff
> Reform battle is not won in Lancashire and the policy of the league to claim
> great victories for themselves must not be taken to mean that such victories
> are evidence of any widespread change of feeling.[63]

Bonar Law had begun to perceive much the same situation. He confessed to
the "aboriginal protectionist," Henry Chaplin, that "the change which has
taken place is really remarkable—even for politicians. The strongest Tariff
Reformers are all coming to me saying that it is impossible to fight with food
taxes." The party leader insisted to his fellow whole-hogger that "so far as the
present is concerned, I am not going to depart in the least from the policy we
have laid down."[64] By this he meant the private assurances he had given in
February 1912 that Balfour's referendum pledge was no longer operative.
Nonetheless, having already qualified his stance ("at the present"), Bonar Law
admitted to Chaplin that "(between ourselves), I am convinced that it must in
the end be modified."[65] The Unionist leader found himself under great pressure, not just from much of the rank and file, but from the major figure in
Lancashire Unionist politics, Lord Derby, to do something to excise food taxes
as an issue at the next election.

It would not be a very easy step to take. Bonar Law doubted in December
1912 "whether this modification will be possible under my leadership," but, he
added significantly, "that is a bridge which I need not cross till we come to
it."[66] After all, he had been involved in the original elucidation of the referendum idea in November 1910, and he was sensitive to the intimations of
unprincipled behavior that had been leveled at Balfour. Moreover, he sincerely
embraced the principles of tariff reform, including its imperial aspects. Tariff
reformers had regarded him as an acceptable alternative to Austen Chamberlain for that very reason, and any signs of wobbling might disrupt the party's
recent but still tenuous unity. In essence, Bonar Law fought a rearguard action,
but by January 1913 he too had come to the realization that dropping food
taxes was essential, even if this meant reinstating the referendum. A clever way
to withdraw without losing face was now the priority, and it materialized in the
form of a petition to him signed by virtually the entire parliamentary party. It
reaffirmed that party's commitment to tariff reform and imperial preference,
but urged that any imposition of food duties be postponed until after a second

election. Bonar Law's subsequent speech at Edinburgh in mid-January ratified the proposals, and, after a decade, it seemed that perhaps the dear loaf bogey had been laid to rest.[67]

Adjusting to Ambiguity

Whether reluctant or not, Bonar Law's action was taken as both party leader and prominent tariff reformer. It suggested that henceforth tariff reform, while not omitted, would no longer be the principal plank of party policy. Tariff reformers would have to adjust their expectations accordingly. Throughout 1913, the Northern Tariff Reform Federation, Ridley's regional grouping, confined its efforts to constituencies with narrow majorities.[68] The Hertfordshire Federation experienced "unavoidable difficulties" and admitted that "to regain a sound financial position our resources therefore during the past year had to be carefully husbanded."[69] The vast majority of reports of local activities in 1913 were remarkably uninformative, even for an organization that sought to conceal its total membership and revenue. There were, to be sure, occasional by-elections in 1912 and 1913 at which the league's claims to have exercised a decisive influence were not too far-fetched.[70] But the overall impression was a dismal one. Sir Joseph Lawrence, himself a tariff stalwart, "pitied" the Lancashire federation's secretary, who was "in a desperate plight with people ringing him up on the phone to know what it all means." In Lawrence's view, the postponement of food taxes meant "chaos."[71]

The perspective from inside the organization pointed to the same conclusion. On the eve of the new year, the Tariff Reform League's chairman had confided to Austen Chamberlain that "things look very bleak to me."[72] Throughout January 1913 his assessment grew increasingly pessimistic. Early in the month Ridley mused that he "had not got the health to put up a proper fight for the Tariff Reform League," and, revealingly, he argued that too many Unionist MPs had simply been "organized" into support for tariffs rather than systematically convinced.[73] It was fitting testimony to the league he chaired, even if it reflected less favorably on its methods. By late January, after Bonar Law's Edinburgh address, Ridley had been advised by the league's treasurer to curtail operations as much as possible. He himself recognized, as did Austen Chamberlain, to whom he was communicating, that the Tariff Reform League could no longer "proceed on 'Confederate' lines." The remaining alternatives were all unpalatable:

1. The party that can be stampeded away from part of the policy can be stampeded away from the rest; and I have no doubt that attempt will be made; especially as the present position will prove untenable.
2. If we stick to our present full policy, someone will start a League with only the party policy on its programme.
3. If we take up the party policy, someone will start a League for the whole policy.

4. If we do neither we shan't know what to say.

5. If we dissolve the League we shall do serious harm to the Unionist Party. And yet many men feel, like me, that the present programme isn't worth fighting for.[74]

It was not long before the hard choices that Ridley posed in private were put to the test in public. The occasion was a by-election in Westmorland South in March 1913, the vacancy having occurred with the death of the sitting Unionist MP, J. F. Bagot. The constituency was a marginal one, although traditionally the firmly Unionist rural areas of the division were just sufficient to outweigh the large Liberal turnout in Kendal, the major town.[75] In 1913, Westmorland was scrutinized for what it might reveal about Unionist prospects in the northwest of England, but it took on particular significance in light of the independence of the local South Westmorland Conservative Association. To replace Bagot the association adopted Colonel John Weston, commander of the local Territorial battalion, chairman of the Westmorland County Council, and "a large employer of labour" in the manufacture of gunpowder.[76] Weston was both influential and popular, styling himself as "a traditional Tory" and a staunch opponent of home rule. The rub, however, was Weston's resolute espousal of free trade, even though he denied that this should pose any problems for his Unionist supporters on the grounds that tariff reform was not a practical issue within the span of the current Parliament. Nonetheless, this view differed considerably from the policy laid down by Bonar Law at Edinburgh, which had only postponed food taxes, not jettisoned the remainder of the tariff program. But Weston was saying what many Unionists were thinking. When tariff reformers sought to force Weston to withdraw, they failed. Indeed, the chairman of the local association, Lord Henry Cavendish Bentinck, had himself previously resisted intimidation by the Confederacy, and saw no reason to change his mind now.[77]

The Tariff Reform League appeared to win a modest victory when, under pressure, the party machinery in London agreed to withdraw official support for Weston.[78] Speakers and literature were packed up and shipped back to the capital because he refused to accept party policy on the fiscal issue. Yet the ground had changed since 1909 when, if this had occurred, Weston's campaign would have been crippled. Both the candidate and his association remained unrepentant, while the Unionist agent for the division continued to work on Weston's behalf. Departed speakers and canvassers were quickly replaced by their counterparts imported from neighboring constituencies. The campaign itself was brisk, for Weston's opponent was also a local employer. Weston further outraged Westminster by committing himself to compulsory training, to which the Liberal candidate, W. H. Somervell, responded by attempting to persuade the agricultural community that conscription would wreak havoc with the labor supply at harvest time. Observers on both sides agreed that normal party lines were somewhat blurred by cross-voting, but the eventual verdict from Westmorland was clear enough. Weston was returned with a majority of 581, a margin slightly greater than that in either contest in 1910.[79] He had won in defiance of Tariff Reform League criticism and of the party's tariff policy, and there had been no decrease in his poll or the enthusiasm of local Unionists. Indeed, all agreed that, whatever his fiscal views, Weston was admirably suited to represent Unionist interests in the division. And here was the real rub: fiscal views, as suggested by Westmorland, clearly were subordinate, perhaps even irrelevant, to the definition of correct party loyalty. Ridley's predictions were coming to pass.

The league's chairman had warned that once anything less than "the whole hog" policy was conceded by Bonar Law, a "stampede" would ensue. Anything like the *Morning Post*'s blacklist of Unionist Free Traders in January 1909 was now impractical, as much because of the reluctance of local constituency organizations as of the party leadership. An eloquent plea for toleration appeared in the *Times* simultaneously with the announcement of Weston's victory. Advocating a degree of flexibility that would have been unthinkable just 3 years earlier, it read:

> I am a tariff reformer and, I hope, a supporter of party discipline. I am an active member of the executive in my own constituency. Our local chairman, I am sorry to say, does not yet feel able to go the whole way with us in support of Mr. Chamberlain's policy. But he is, and has been from the first, a tower of strength in the upholding of the Unionist cause over five counties. And are we now to be visited with pains and penalties because, as Unionists, we place the Union first in our programme and are prepared to wait a little for the steady growth of the spirit in favour of an Imperial Tariff? Are witch doctors from Westminster to be sent down to 'smell out' heresy in Lancashire, in the North Country, in the West of Scotland, and in Ulster, and to describe as 'flagrant and defiant mutineers' men who have grown grey in their work for the Unionist cause? We have one common task before us: to get rid of the present government, to safeguard the unity of the Empire, and to restore the Constitution . . . but if our central organisation can find nothing better to do than to drive wedges and to issue bulls of excommunication, then they shall be beaten.[80]

The Westmorland (or Kendal) incident was the major topic of discussion at the Tariff Reform League's annual meeting, which was held in the midst of the by-election campaign. At issue was how the league should react to Bonar Law's tactical retreat from a full tariff program 2 months earlier and to the current campaign in which Weston's defense of free trade might be thought a harbinger of widespread future defections. "We are seeing in Kendal today a great public national disaster ('loud cheers') because should such action be followed in other constituencies it would evidently lead to a split in the Constitutional [Unionist] party."[81] The speaker, however, did not dwell upon the forms or consequences of intraparty strife, preferring instead to paint in familiar terms the imperatives for prompt restoration of the full program, including imperial preference. "Little men, and little nations, unless they make combinations and allies," he warned, "are going to the wall." The solution, to which tariffs were essential, was to "combine and rivet the ties that bind the Motherland and the Sister States . . . [through] genuine partnership in trade and defence."[82] H. J. Mackinder, the geopolitical theorist, also emphasized the urgency of the situation and the necessary "relation between defence and trade" as inseparable elements in any satisfactory domestic or foreign policy. He stressed that too many politicians (including some Unionists) erroneously presumed that "the building of battleships and cruisers for the defence of various portions of the Empire is the alternative way of uniting the Empire in case Tariff Reform should not prove available."[83]

These arguments failed to grasp the new realities confronting tariff reformers. Reaffirming the benefits of tariffs was well and good, but simple reiteration could not disguise the fact that the relationship between the Unionist party and the Tariff Reform League, which seemingly had stabilized between 1908 and 1910, suddenly had changed. Bonar Law had reordered the priorities of the party, and in so doing he forced tariff reformers to reevaluate their own. Should the league insist upon the full program (including food taxes) and only support candidates adhering to that line, ignoring or even opposing those individuals who declined to go the whole hog? Or should it accept Bonar Law's modification and regard a reduced program free of food taxes to be its official program, on the grounds that half a loaf was better than none at all? Or could it seek some sort of compromise, permitting local flexibility?

The first of these propositions was put forcefully by one of the league's council members, Alfred Hicks of Tunbridge Wells. He was convinced that there was "no unanimity in the country" regarding the Edinburgh policy, and he therefore urged that any MP who had signed the petition to Bonar Law be ineligible for reelection to the executive committee. Quickly and efficiently, this would purge the league of false brethren. Hicks was thwarted by procedural technicalities, but, undeterred, he provoked an uproar among the audience by announcing that "the recent declaration of the Unionist party represents a betrayal of our league, and a betrayal of agriculture, and a betrayal of colonial preference."[84] Once the chairman's gavel had restored order, Hicks proceeded to argue that home rule left audiences "cold," that the Unionist party had "lost the confidence of the working classes," and that it could regain popular support only by advocating, "without shilly-shallying, the whole policy and the forward policy" of tariff reform. More controversially, Hicks continued by insisting that the Tariff Reform League must emancipate itself from party dictation:

> I am sorry to say that we have been used during the last ten years by the Unionist party—used to the full—used to the utmost. When it has suited them we have been flattered to the hilt; we have been told that we represented the first constructive policy of the Unionist party, and on more than one occasion we have been thrown over ruthlessly and hopelessly. We were thrown over at the time of the Referendum, and the recent declaration is the most complete throwing over of ourselves that has ever happened to us during the ten years.[85]

Leo Maxse found this line of attack particularly congenial. He suspected that if the Unionist party was victorious at the next election, its narrow-minded organizers and electoral strategists would quickly break any promises to submit food taxes to a popular verdict at the second election. Appreciation of the real national interest would, as it had in the past, be subordinated to calculation of narrow and transitory party interest.[86] Only patriots who cast aside their inbred deference to party prescriptions, men who thought clearly and acted decisively, could save England now; only a Tariff Reform League that pursued an independent course would serve such patriotic ends. Of course, Maxse could always be counted upon to be provocative and vitriolic, and other tariff reformers had raised similar points in the past. But the combination of Bonar Law's Edinburgh policy and the Weston candidacy in Westmorland produced a heightened sense of expectation that a critical juncture had been reached. The nationalist agitation, especially as it revolved around tariffs, would either submit or reject party policy altogether. The dilemmas of competitive cooperation now demanded resolution.

Other league members, however, felt uncomfortable with assertions that they should support Liberal protectionists against Unionist Free Traders or that they should repudiate men like Weston, whose Unionist credentials were otherwise impeccable. Andrew Maconachie, a Tariff Commission member, sprang to Bonar Law's defense by pointing to the other variables to be considered:

> Tariff Reform is not the only thing in political life, and it is not even the first thing at the present moment in the minds of many honest and sincere Tariff Reformers ('No'). Wait a moment. I know perfectly well that the view is not likely to commend itself to the hot-heads of the party, but I desire to say that it is quite possible to hold, as I do, that important as Tariff Reform is, the first requisite before the people of this country is the repeal of the Parliament Act ('Hear, hear') and the restoration to the people of England of the power to govern themselves. And, therefore, as a Tariff Reformer, I am entitled, and bound, to take that into consideration in viewing the action of the Unionist leaders in the recent crisis . . . for myself I could in no sense be a party to anything in the nature of a vote of censure for what has been done.[87]

Furthermore, Maconachie argued, as "practical people," the league's delegates had to recognize the breadth of sentiment on the issue within the Unionist party, which, after all, was "the only one from whom you can have any real expectations in the immediate future." And what about Kendal, demanded one of the MPs present? Weston was "the only Unionist candidate that the local constituency will accept."[88] His defeat, while it might delight whole-hoggers, would only prolong the tenure of the current Liberal administration, and thus further delay the eventual accession of a Unionist government and the introduction of a tariff reform budget. If he won, and if, simultaneously, the league emphasized its opposition to all candidates of dubious virtue on tariffs, it would embarrass the league. Either way, if the Tariff Reform League did not moderate its position, it would appear ineffectual.

As Maconachie well knew, the Unionist party was now the piper and the league would dance to its tune. Earlier the league had effectively managed a dissonant counterpoint. The subsequent period of harmony was brief, but the ideal persisted. To tariff reformers, harmonious cooperation was easy so long as the party maintained tariff reform to be the "first constructive policy" of Unionism. What mattered was that the party's definition of fiscal reform matched that of the league and that it was accorded priority as the criterion by which party loyalty was judged. Literature distributed by the party was often produced by the league, while on the local level Unionist associations might even merge with Tariff Reform League branches.[89] Yet, in a way, the convergence of party and league circumscribed the potential independence of the latter; the more the league stressed mobilizing Unionist sentiment in 1910, the more difficult it became to advocate repudiating party ties in 1913. The Tariff Reform League's dilemma derived from the fact that the Unionist leadership, in response to pressure from below, had redefined the "practical" (or achievable) aspects of tariff reform and had also downgraded tariffs from their once elevated position. For its part, the Tariff Reform League eventually opted to straddle the issue. While applauding and assisting those candidates bold enough to stand on the whole-hog platform, it would also support Unionists who confined themselves to the less stringent policy enunciated by Bonar Law.

Home rule was the issue that clearly was replacing tariff reform at the cutting edge of political debate. Bonar Law, an icy Presbyterian, warmed to the task of opposing Irish self-government. The Unionist party had reaped substantial benefits from playing the "orange card" in 1886, and perhaps it was natural to return to a strategy that had worked so well in the past. But that very sense of retrenchment, of assuming a purely defensive or negative posture, troubled those who feared that without a positive initiative the Unionists would inevitably be doomed to a permanent minority by the sheer weight of numbers against them. Leo Amery believed that the "meaning" of his political life lay in his effort to prevent the Unionist party from "drifting into becoming the party of a mere negative laissez faire anti-Socialism." If the party failed to avoid that trap, "it could never exercise a dominating and creative influence on the life of the country or of the Empire."[90] Nor could it prevent "political cleavage based on class, on the desire for the material gain of one class of the community at the expense of others, and of the banding together of those others in defence of their possessions."[91] Henry Page Croft, one of the Confederates, suggested much the same thing to Bonar Law:

> It seems to me we are making the same grave mistake that we made prior to the 1906 election, we are out of touch with the working classes who are absolutely indifferent to either Home Rule or the Welsh Bill; they are concerned with one and one question only which is the wage question, and unless we grapple with it fearlessly and unless our leaders can inspire all candidates to place the Tariff in the forefront, I have good reason for believing that an enormous number of our working class supporters will go over to the Labour Party.[92]

Are We All Anti-Socialists Now?

There were certainly grounds for Croft's concern. One could not dispute the fact that the Labour party's gains in 1910 were modest and that it was clearly still the junior partner in the Progressive alliance. It exhibited no obvious signs of being able to compete successfully as the primary party of the political left.[93] But its growing assertiveness, manifested in its willingness to contest three-cornered elections (even if Unionists were often the immediate beneficiary), nonetheless pointed toward the increasing hold of class as the critical factor in political life. So long as the Liberal party retained a measure of middle-class support and as the number of enfranchised voters continued to expand, Unionists need not have shared Lord Salisbury's pessimistic temperament to find this situation a disturbing one. "As you know it's not TR a bit that has lost us Lancashire," suggested a dissatisfied young Tory to the party's future chairman, "it's class feeling." He argued that workers now thought for themselves, mistrusted the party's paternalistic bent, and sought representation by members of their own class. "The organization must be made more democratic," he urged, "and we really ought to have at least a dozen working men candidates fighting proper seats, not forlorn hopes."[94]

To develop constructive policies to mitigate the political impact of class cleavage and to blunt the attractions of socialism was the intention of activists within both the Tariff Reform League and the Anti-Socialist Union. In both cases, identification of the problem proved easier than the elucidation of a solution. The Anti-Socialist Union retreated to a largely negative position. It continued to train and dispatch speakers and to produce literature. Nearly 250 speakers participated in the campaigns of 1910, while canvassers and organizers distributed a not unimpressive 3 million pamphlets.[95] Efforts continued in 1911 with a special northern campaign in which sixty union agents organized 1,500 meetings in the first 5 months of the year. Activities reached a peak in August, with some 600 meetings per week, but this pace was reduced by half by December 1911. Dwindling funds probably contributed as much to the decline as the ostensible explanation, deteriorating weather.[96]

In contrast to the often secretive financial practices of the Tariff Reform League, the Anti-Socialist Union made no secret of its financial ambitions and requirements. A public appeal for 1 million shillings in October 1909 had been the first such maneuver. "A million shillings," the union exhorted, "will enable us to cover the country with speakers and help us to free trade unionists from their fetters and give them real representation in Parliament."[97] That confidence was not altogether misplaced, but the eventual result fell well short of expectations—182,500 shillings (some £9,000) by March 1910.[98] But, at that point, the union had abandoned its insistence on cash and was willing to accept other gifts, such as old jewelry. A second fund, intended to finance campaigns in Yorkshire and Lancashire, was established in April 1910 with a target of £3,500, but it secured little more than a £1,000 contribution from Sir William Bull.[99] In March 1911, a third effort, described as a "premium" to insure

against revolution, set the lofty figure of £100,000, accompanied by the warning that "when, through the Cabinet, Socialist schemers are foisting on the
nation a Single Chamber of Government, the Anti-Socialist Union appeals to
the loyalty and patriotism of the British people."[100] This incipient populism
was immediately tempered, though, by the union's belief that socialism's "main
attack" was directed against the upper class and that it was incumbent upon
that class "to save themselves from destruction."[101]

This last observation reflected the union's failure to develop a broadly
based subscribership. The Midland Counties Division in Birmingham had
solicited pledges for £1,000 annually for 3 years, but local branches were
scattered, modest in scope, and unable to help defray costs incurred in London.[102] The addition to the union's executive of respectable persons such as
Walter Long or the Duke of Devonshire was thus all the more essential, even if
some members only tolerated their presence for the potential financial benefits.
In a caustic letter to his journalistic friend Blumenfeld, the union's chairman,
Claude Lowther, gave vent to the frustration he felt about the kinds of people
the union had attracted and upon whose largess it depended:

> I think the doctors must have removed Walter Long's brain instead of his
> appendix, they were both small and very swollen, so the mistake is quite
> permissible—we must, however, humour him, for the retirement of this
> master mediocrity from the Executive at this juncture would be detrimental
> to the Union. Although in my opinion and in yours he is a singularly foolish
> person, he is undoubtedly a clever man for stupid people, and we must not
> forget that the overwhelming majority of our countrymen are stupid. . . . If
> Long leaves us now he might carry away with him the somnolent Duke—this
> would be disastrous to the Union for it would immediately alienate every
> snob and every mediocrity and who I ask except you and I and Grisewood
> [the secretary] do not come under that category, why even our Mr. Bull
> would go. Write Long a charming letter, tell him that without his guiding
> hand and predominant genius we are lost. . . . Don't let the fool go.[103]

Because the Anti-Socialist Union lacked the extensive network of local
branches that characterized both the Navy and Tariff Reform Leagues, it is
rather more difficult to identify its social composition. The success of the
Hammersmith branch probably owed more to the belligerency of its energetic
president, Sir William Bull, than to a perfect fit between the union's message
and the borough's social structure. Bull provided a good show. At his meetings
hecklers were forcibly ejected, and members of the audience were required to
sign affidavits of their avowed opposition to socialism. The Birmingham
branch attracted a "large number of notable people connected with the social
and commercial life of the Midlands."[104] These included a mixture of peers,
businessmen, Anglican and Nonconformist ministers, and journalists (G. W.
Hubbard of the *Birmingham Daily Post* and J. V. Morton of the *Birmingham
Gazette and Express*). The union's council and executive committee reflected a
similar pattern. There were the typical ornamental peers (including familiar
names such as Malmesbury and Leconfield) and prominent Tory journalists as
well (Garvin, Pearson, Maxse, and Gwynne). Businessmen tended to be famil-

iar whole-hoggers, such as Thomas Wrightson (a Stockton-on-Tees steel magnate), Stanley Baldwin (the young Stourport ironmaster), Colonel Sir John
Bingham (a Sheffield cutlerer), and J. F. Mason (whose interests embraced
imperial mining ventures and Alfred Hickman's steel concern).[105] Despite the
presence of the Duke of Devonshire, there was little evidence that the Anti-
Socialist Union successfully embraced a range of economic or political interests that had repudiated tariff reform. The large bloc of MPs was overwhelmingly Unionist, the exception being the eccentric Liberal Harold Cox.

The presence of MPs or the thinly disguised links to the Unionist party (as
in the subsidy or provision of literature) never provoked as sharp a controversy
over the relationship between partisan loyalty and patriotic independence as
those that erupted in the Navy League (1907, 1909–1910), the National Service
League (1909), and the Tariff Reform League (virtually throughout its existence, but especially in 1913). Several factors accounted for the greater docility
of the Anti-Socialist Union. Financially it never gained independence, always
remaining tied to the umbilical cord of the annual party subsidy. It is hardly
coincidental that shortly after Steel-Maitland decided to discontinue the subsidy in 1912, the union's visibility rapidly shrank and publication of its journal,
Liberty, was suspended.[106] Moreover, the union had only aspired to a supple-
mental role rather than insisting that its definition of anti-socialism be elevated
as the sole basis of significant political choice. Although that definition was
always elastic and often vague, it had been formulated specifically to exclude
tariff reform and thus avoid internal party strife. Furthermore, the Anti-
Socialist Union's period of real activity coincided with the party's desperate
search for arguments against the incipient socialism of the People's Budget,
and few Unionists would be willing to repudiate its assistance or declare
themselves opposed to anti-socialism. By the time home rule reemerged after
1911, the union's resources and influence were waning.

Of course, tariff reform had been touted for its anti-Socialist capacities by
binding to the Unionist party ailing economic interests in search of protection,
by luring the prosperous classes with the prospect of indirect rather than direct
taxation, and by attracting workers with a program of renewed business
prosperity, expanded imperial trade, and reduced unemployment.[107] In the
short run, the Unionist party discovered that working-class voters remained
suspicious of tariff reform, whether because of the probable rise in the cost of
living or the apparent incongruity of a conservative party proposing radical
initiatives in economic policy. The Unionist party's campaign guide for 1914
consigned tariff reform to its penultimate chapter, just before "miscellaneous
questions," though this amounted more to a suspension than to a rejection of
the issue. Interestingly, despite the flurries surrounding Bonar Law's Blenheim
pronouncement about the forces greater than parliamentary majorities and the
undefined but unlimited extent to which he would support Ulster's defiant
Unionists, the largest entry in the 1914 guide was that on socialism. It had been
prepared with the assistance of the Anti-Socialist Union and pointed toward
the terrain that the party expected to contest at the next election.[108] The change
reflected one of means rather than ends, but it was an adjustment that might

facilitate the coordination of the energies, sentiments, and activities of the Unionist party and the nationalist agitation.

The Challenge of the Great War

The outbreak of war in August 1914 confirmed, insofar as the nationalist agitation was concerned, the validity of its prewar warnings. Leo Maxse, for example, published in 1915 a collection of his earlier articles under the title *Germany on the Brain* as a none too subtle reminder to his many critics that he had not been a hysteric obsessed with a nonexistent foreign threat, but rather a perceptive sage whose insights were ignored or misconstrued. The great conflict both catalyzed the various associations into ever greater demonstrations of their patriotic commitment (something facilitated by the temporary suspension of normal partisan politics) and disrupted the familiar patterns of branch activity. The rush to the colors in the autumn of 1914 robbed the leagues of many of their most active members, even though initially the primary task of each organization was to sustain the steady flow of volunteers to replace the rapidly mounting casualties at the front. War made strange bedfellows, as even bitter rivals like the Navy League and the Imperial Maritime League cooperated in the greater national interest. It was not too long before the leagues also began to solicit funds for the relief of widows and orphans and to encourage members to assist the morale of fighting men. This might mean writing letters or donating chocolates, tinned meats, and clothing.[109]

As the scope and likely duration of the war became apparent, the various nationalist organizations worried about morale on the home front. Themes familiar from before 1914 now took on added urgency. Arnold White was convinced that a number of non-native Britons "were Prussian in heart, and were in the Prussian pay."[110] Navy League officials were slightly more cautious, but suspicious too, noting with satisfaction that "members of the League throughout Great Britain watched carefully the movement of enemy aliens and doubtful cases were at once reported to the proper authority."[111] The organizations were especially apprehensive, though, that working men (British-born, of course) might exploit their now indispensable positions in war production to hamper the military effort and foment Socialist revolution. Frequently, though not exclusively, this threat was perceived as the inevitable consequence of any effort by the Independent Labour party. The Navy League solicited special "anti-pacifist" donations to fund meetings and the distribution of patriotic literature in South Wales, upon whose deposits of smokeless coal the Admiralty relied.[112] The league even sought a secret state subsidy to expand its work, while the Tariff Reform League worked Colne Valley, Stockport, and Rochdale to minimize Socialist sympathies.[113] Protectionists also urged that anti-German sentiment and a military mentality outlast the conflict. Commerce was the extension of war by other means, and tariffs would be as essential to protect British interests after the guns had ceased firing as shells were at the present time.[114]

Despite these new avenues for action, all of the nationalist associations experienced declining membership and revenue. In part this was the inevitable consequence of mobilization and mobility. It manifested itself in various ways: more women became branch secretaries, much to the displeasure of one traditionalist executive member who spluttered, "For goodness sake, don't let us have any more women. . . . They will all talk gossip, and I had made up my mind never to serve on a committee with ladies again."[115] The Navy League admitted that the funds available for propaganda or educational work were "comparatively small," while the Tariff Reform League experienced a "marked falling off in subscriptions and donations."[116] The Anti-Socialist Union had subsided into virtual silence. Branch activities declined in both frequency and complexity; by 1919, for example, the Navy League found many of its local chapters "in a state of suspended animation," and a similar verdict was in order for the Tariff Reform League.[117]

Dwindling influence, or at least declining resources, could not be condoned by nationalists as the inevitable result of greater national cohesion in wartime. To a number of the activists who remained or who served and returned, the war seemed to aggravate domestic divisions, not minimize them. Industrial conflict, production delays, and the specter of bolshevism, its dangers already manifest in Russia, all conspired to threaten the fragile foundations of British civilization. As final victory, or even a likely end to the war, continued to elude the nation's military and political leaders, dissonance within nationalist ranks began to spill over into yet another series of organizations such as the Unionist Business Committee, the British Commonwealth Union and the National Party.[118] On occasion the Unionist leadership found these groups a useful avenue for criticism that it could not itself articulate without compromising its position as a partner in the coalition government. More frequently, however, such organizations embodied back-bench sentiment that suspected the leadership of collusion, unresponsiveness, and incompetence. Such internal dissent, of course, was neither new nor necessarily surprising, given the extent to which the new organizations drew upon the programs and composition of their predecessors, especially the Tariff Reform League. They were transitory and, in the case of the National party, a spectacular failure if judged in terms of its avowed intention of forming a seriously competitive political party. But from their point of view, they kept flickering the embers of nationalist sentiment, which too many diffident Conservatives ignored and which the left only scorned or sought to douse altogether. Thus, when Stanley Baldwin stoked the fires of patriotism to forge a long-sought Conservative majority in 1924, he could draw upon techniques and a political language formulated over the preceding decades.

Conclusion

The searing experiences of the emasculation of the lords, the escalation of labor unrest, the eruption of Ulster defiance, and the unprecedented costs of the Great War, both human and financial, all contributed to the appearance of an unusual array of publications that sought to take stock of the Conservative party's past heritage, current position, and future prospects.[1] These various books and tracts differed in their analyses and prescriptions. But they all reflected an effort that had been underway for the past two decades to grapple with fundamental changes in the party's and the country's position. The party, seeking to conserve the older order, had to evaluate the probable consequences and relative merits of reactionary inflexibility or progressive adaptability. In practice, of course, the distinctions were never that clear and depended on the resonance of particular issues rather than rarified philosophical disputation. As this applied to the Unionist party before 1914, two central themes were the overall blend of familiar and fresh issues in the party program and the incorporation of new members without disrupting that programmatic blend or alienating established bases of support.

In the past, the inertia of much of its traditional constituency had appeared perhaps as a virtue, as an assurance of Tory party stability. By the 1890s, and especially after 1900, there were compelling reasons to reject so complacent an attitude. Parliamentary redistribution, extension of the franchise, and the prospect of further independent working-class electoral organization reshaped political life, and the Unionists could no longer confidently count on the inevitable swing of the electoral pendulum to restore them to power.[2] Furthermore, there was the matter of all of the frightful things that might occur in the intervals during which the Unionists were out of power: threats of squandered naval leads or of a new susceptibility to invasion, markets lost to economic competitors, or the empire or the traditional social order dismantled by wild Irishmen and Socialists.

The nationalist agitation was fueled by the conviction that the parties, especially the Unionist party from which better might have been expected, had failed to respond effectively to a new configuration of external and internal

160

threats to the maintenance of national power and stability. W. H. Mallock recalled that when he presented statistical evidence on England's social problems to "a leading Conservative statesman," he made no headway. The politician admitted to being uncomfortable with such an approach and dismissed Mallock with the observation that "columns of figures are merely so many clouds."[3] Others encountered a similar lack of sympathy or comprehension. Hewins complained of Unionist leaders satisfied if they remembered his advice for one speech, Willoughby de Broke regretted the undue influence of "static Conservatives," while Maxse railed against "docile" Conservatives who held fast to the erroneous belief that Parliament was "the hub of the universe."[4] These more traditionalist Conservatives, "mainly concerned with the maintenance of the Constitution in Church and State, and the general preservation of the status quo," could not be counted upon to implement the necessary "forward" or "constructive" policies.[5] The nationalist agitation was determined to do just this, so as to reach the broader mass of working people. No longer could the nation be presumed to be safe in the hands of country gentlemen. It was essential, therefore, to persuade workers of the direct effects on their own livelihood of naval challenges, potential invaders, foreign protectionist competitors, and the illusory remedy of socialism.

To an extent, the agitation reflected a generational conflict. The "keener elements," as Maxse put it, were those for whom the political equipoise of the mid-Victorian era had no meaning or attraction.[6] Balfour recognized that the impetus for reorganization and constructive action "has come largely from the younger members of the party."[7] The young men of Joseph Chamberlain's "kindergarten" and the activists of the Anti-Socialist Union fit this pattern, which, if not evident at first in the Navy League, was apparent there too by 1911 in the prominence of men like Hannon and Burgoyne. They sought to alter both the style and substance of Unionist politics. Favoring a more direct agitational approach, they bitterly condemned the party's backward organization and inefficient methods, its "Kentish Gang" of squires who continued to administer the party machine.[8] Substantively, the influx of young men also affected the policies pursued, as a prominent tariff reformer explained to Balfour:

> I have noticed of recent years a class has grown up, and it finds its reflex very largely in our organisations, of men who are lukewarm or indifferent on questions that, twenty years ago, used to hold the first place in our affections. I mean such matters as Religious Education, the House of Lords, and so on. Even in such matters as the unity of the Empire, the more material or commercial aspects of the question appeal to them more strongly than the aspects which called forth the outburst of opposition to Home Rule in Ireland. . . . They have a large following, and whilst they were easily swayed by Mr. Joseph Chamberlain, they are not so easily swayed by men of later date. Whatever influence I have with them is based upon their regard for me because of the interest I take in trade questions.[9]

Given their backgrounds and interests, they were convinced that paternalistic appeals to the electorate to validate the superior credentials of the traditional governing classes would carry little weight. Issues that had brought the party votes in the past were no guarantees of majorities in the present. "The genuine political questions of the old sort—Home Rule, Disestablishment, Adult Suffrage—no longer kindle the electorate," advised the hero of Keith Feilings's didactic *Toryism: A Political Dialogue*.[10] "Do you seriously propose to appeal to an industrial electorate," he continued, "who do not own the property they make, on a cry like that? Will you make the cotton spinners weep for the Peerage or the railwaymen sigh for Ulster?"[11] Sir Joseph Lawrence's experiences in Lancashire persuaded him that it was "no use to feed the empty stomachs of men with appeals about Patriotism and the rights of property," let alone the defense of ancient institutions. "Years ago," he recalled, "Cecil Rhodes told me that the future of England rested in 'bread and butter policts.'"[12]

Disraeli, of course, was often credited with having attempted to fashion a more popular, humane, caring image for the Conservative party, but his efforts amounted to rather less in practical results.[13] The diverse groups and personalities of the nationalist agitation were confident that their particular issues and remedies were not just desirable, but essential to British power and prosperity. The various leagues were, by the end of the First World War, in varying degrees of collapse or stagnation. In that sense, they were products of a particular period, the Edwardian era.[14] But they contributed to the long-term evolution of the Right. Even if the two power standard or conscription were inappropriate to the realities of the interwar decades, the notion of critical links between patriotism, defense issues, and the Conservative party had been established in political discourse and would pay electoral dividends in the future. With the McKenna duties in 1915, the defense of free trade suffered another blow, and in 1932 at Ottawa it seemed virtually vanquished. In any event, the Tariff Reform League's ability to focus debate on the uncompetitiveness of British industry and to insist that politicians address that economic issue helped to ensure that the Conservative party would not be forced to rely solely on recycled paeans to rustic simplicity. And while the Anti-Socialist Union was perennially weak, this feebleness testified to the fact that other groupings within the nationalist agitation, and especially the party itself, had begun to focus on the issue and could do more with it. Anti-socialism would eventually enable the Conservatives to reestablish, preserve, and profit from the congenial form of a two party system. Indeed, as John Strachey grimly declared when pondering the primary achievement of the Labour party, it had been "the transformation of the British Conservative Party."[15]

The outbreak of war with Germany, the consequent reliance on the fleet to protect the nation's imports and beaches, the eventual imposition of conscription and protectionist duties, and the emergence of Labour as an independent force all bore some resemblance to the nationalists' earlier dire warnings. It is undeniable, of course, that some members of the various leagues belonged to a lunatic fringe. Their blood-curdling claims and persistent paranoia suggested psychological disturbance. But the nationalist agitation encompassed a range of sentiments, and many of its adherents could not be dismissed so easily.

Much of the tension that surrounded the agitation stemmed from the fact that it posed, occasionally with brutal clarity, two critically important dilemmas.

The first could be summarized as the issue of "for party or country?" Superficially, Unionist politicians (and their Liberal counterparts, too) deprecated any such dichotomy, insisting that the choice of their party was automatically in the best interests of the country as well. This was not the case for all individuals and on all issues. One strand of thinking within the Navy League had emphasized a less stringent, more inclusive definition of nationalist allegiance, but by 1910 this tolerant attitude had been replaced by a more abrasive and uncompromising insistence on the absolute identity of nationalist and partisan interests. But it was the Tariff Reform League that pushed single issue politics to its logical conclusion, provoking complaints of "dictation" from the party's victims of this intolerance. Lord Robert Cecil, for example, believed that his role as a parliamentary representative entitled him to some leeway for the free play of his cultivated mind in the best interests of the nation. He could not accept serving simply as a delegate, espousing without variation a policy he detested, and subordinating other issues.[16] Keith Feiling also urged that there be "no formulas, no expulsion of Tories who disbelieve in a question of method."[17] Tariff reformers were repudiating the ancient ideal of the independent country gentlemen whose unfettered patriotic consciences were the guarantee of the best traditions of British public life. Indeed, the Unionist chief whip interpreted Bonar Law's defeat of Walter Long for the party leadership in 1911 as marking "the swan song of the country gentlemen."[18]

Increasingly, therefore, skeptical Unionists warned that tariff reformers, in their obsession for the country, would concede everything that the party traditionally had valued if doing so would help to achieve fiscal change.[19] The fiscal issue provoked some defections to the Liberal benches, but in general party lines were hardening, and party discipline was becoming tighter.[20] To have it tighter still, and based upon a single issue, was a situation some MPs found intolerable. But the relationship between the various leagues and the party was never simply one of dictation; rather, it involved negotiation, periodic confrontation, and eventual accommodation. The Unionist party chairman, Steel-Maitland, was especially concerned about the role of "outside organizations" when he assumed his position in 1911. As he explained to the leadership, "they represented a time when either their objects were not the same as those of the official organization, or the C. C. O. [Conservative Central Office] was not enterprising enough to suit them."[21] He advocated bringing them under central control, but, he emphasized, the party had benefitted from them: "It might be wise, while retaining or regaining control, to trade under separate names. In some cases additional subscriptions may be obtained, in others full responsibility may be avoided."[22]

"Party or country" was a dilemma energizing the "radical right," many of whom were intimately involved in the various nationalist leagues and whose collective discontent signalled a "crisis of Conservatism."[23] The controversial actions of the Diehards in 1911 were rooted in a set of deeper developments since the 1890s. But there was no single radical right with a single uncomplicated appeal to patriotism. Patriotism was a pluralistic phenomenon, for a nationalist agenda inevitably raised questions of whose nation and what national purpose?[24] The eruption of Unionist back-bench dissonance during the First World War indicated that the crisis of Conservatism had not been entirely resolved, but it had been contained: the leagues were, on the whole, willing to accept the party's lead, although there remained a residue of their previous agitation.

This residue affected the second dilemma of "property or democracy"? Nationalist appeals stressing a community of believers seemed bent on overriding the political consequences of class division. And certainly the nationalist agitation invoked the language of mass mobilization and democratic participation in preference to the sectional appeal to the defense of property. In fact, all of the leagues, whatever their rhetoric—the Navy League in its distinctions and systems of indirect representation, the Tariff Reform League in its advocacy of the prophylactic effects of tariffs against redistributive taxation, the Anti-Socialist Union in its appeal to the upper classes to save themselves from the great Red menace—accommodated themselves to the central fact of class. In the long run, the Conservative party's stability and persistence could be traced to its own accommodation to class politics, to its construction of a durable coalition of property owners. But survival was one thing, success another. To win elections, as the party has consistently done in the twentieth century, required a broader appeal. Even if their practice was to choose party over country, the rhetoric of the nationalist agitation eventually suggested that the choice might really be for country too. One basis of the party's subsequent success was its ability to define in partisan terms issues that the agitation had originally raised as ones of potentially nonpartisan scope. The Conservative party was able to fashion a program that went beyond the peerage or Ulster, that addressed the twin concerns of the 1890s, namely, inadequate national defense and the entry of an organized working-class party in domestic politics.

The Conservative party responded by portraying itself as the only party capable of preserving the nation from both external and internal threat, and in doing so it defined the terms of debate (Liberal or Labour pacifism; rapacious socialism). There was no inviolable reason why this had to happen; in point of fact, the Liberal party did maintain British naval supremacy, and its social programs, while progressive, did not pose a Socialist challenge. But as the Conservative party and the nationalist agitation accommodated each other by narrowing the latitude for dissent that could still be permissible and patriotic, the heirs of Burke and Disraeli were able to portray themselves as custodians of more than the rights of privilege or ancient institutions, in other words, as the guarantors of both security and property. Thus, in part with the agitation's assistance, it was the Conservatives who more effectively combined the appeals of party and property in the guise of democracy and country.

Notes

Introduction

1. H. A. Taylor, *Jix: Viscount Brentford* (London, 1933), 89.

2. *Conservative Agents' Journal* (October 1910), 105.

3. The Liberal "faddists" are discussed in D. A. Hamer, *The Politics of Electoral Pressure* (Brighton, 1977).

4. Norbert Soldon, "Laissez-Faire as Dogma: The Liberty and Property Defence League, 1882–1914," in Kenneth Brown, ed., *Essays in Anti-Labour History* (London, 1974), 208–33; Edward J. Bristow, "The Liberty and Property Defence League and Individualism," *Historical Journal* 18 (1975): 761–89.

5. The standard accounts are Benjamin H. Brown, *The Tariff Reform Movement in Great Britain, 1881–1895* (New York, 1943); Sydney H. Zebel, "Fair Trade: An English Reaction to the Breakdown of the Cobden Treaty System," *Journal of Modern History* 12 (1940): 161–85; J. E. Tyler, *The Struggle for Imperial Unity, 1868–1895* (London, 1938), 107–14, 176–98.

6. Robert Beadon, "Why the Imperial Federation League was Dissolved," *National Review* (February 1894), 814–22; W. B. Worsfold, "The Imperial Federation League," *United Empire* 6 (1915): 263–73; M. D. Burgess, "Lord Rosebery and the Imperial Federation League, 1884–1893," *New Zealand Journal of History* 13 (1979): 166–81; Arthur Loring to Rosebery, 26 January 1892, Imperial Federation League MSS; *The Times*, 12 December 1896.

7. *Conservative Agents' Journal* (January–April 1910), 19–20.

8. *Conservative Agents' Journal* (October 1910), 105.

9. Lord Hugh Cecil, *Conservatism* (London, 1912), 8.

10. Lord Willoughby de Broke, "The Tory Tradition," *National Review* (October 1911), 201–13.

11. Dismissed by George Dangerfield in 1935 as being remarkable only in the degree to which his face resembled that of a horse, Willoughby de Broke's career has recently aroused a good deal of attention. On his equestrian features, see Dangerfield's classic *The Strange Death of Liberal England* (New York, 1935), 43–44; on his political views, J. R. Jones, "England," in Hans Rogger and Eugen Weber, eds., *The European Right* (Berkeley, 1966), 29–70; Gregory D. Phillips, "Lord Willoughby de Broke and the Politics of Radical Toryism, 1909–1914," *Journal of British Studies* 20 (1980): 205–24; Alan Sykes, "The Radical Right and the Crisis of Conservatism Before the First

World War," *Historical Journal* 26 (1983): 661–76. The most stimulating studies of the Conservative party's recovery in the later nineteenth century remain those by James Cornford, especially his "The Transformation of Conservatism in the Late Nineteenth Century," *Victorian Studies* 7 (1963–1964): 35–66, and "The Parliamentary Foundations of the Hotel Cecil," in Robert Robson, ed., *Ideas and Institutions in Victorian England* (London, 1967), 268–311.

12. The following works are useful to varying degrees in reconstructing the history of Edwardian England's Conservative pressure groups: Arthur J. Marder, *The Anatomy of British Sea Power* (New York, 1940), 48–55; W. Mark Hamilton, "The Nation and the Navy: Methods and Organization of British Navalist Propaganda, 1889–1914," Ph.D. diss., University of London, 1977; Michael J. Allison, "The National Service Issue, 1899–1914," Ph.D. diss., University of London, 1975; Kenneth D. Brown, "The Anti-Socialist Union, 1908–1949," in Brown, *Essays*, 234–61. While there has been no study specifically focusing upon the Tariff Reform League, much can be gleaned from Alan Sykes' superb *Tariff Reform in British Politics, 1903–1913* (Oxford, 1979) and E. H. H. Green, "Radical Conservatism: The Electoral Genesis of Tariff Reform," *Historical Journal* 28 (1985): 667–92. Two attempts to take a more comprehensive view are Anne Summers' rather compressed essay, "The Character of Edwardian Nationalism," in Paul Kennedy and Anthony Nicholls, eds., *Nationalist and Racialist Movements in Britain and Germany before 1914* (London, 1981), 68–87, and A. J. A. Morris' effort at "thick description," *The Scaremongers* (London, 1984).

13. The two preeminent historians of the party have both specialized in biographies, Norman Gash (Liverpool and Peel) and Lord Blake (Disraeli and Bonar Law). Books on the formal organization can be valuable, such as E. J. Feuchtwanger's *Disraeli, Democracy and the Tory Party* (Oxford, 1968). Some shrewd remarks on the nature of Conservative historiography can be found in Brian Harrison's "Apologia" in his *Separate Spheres* (London, 1978). Unfortunately, both Aaron Friedberg, *The Weary Titan* (Princeton, 1988), and Raphael Samuel, ed., *Patriotism* 3 vols. (London, 1989), arrived too late for their analysis to be addressed here.

Chapter 1

1. N. A. M. Rodger, "The Dark Ages of the Admiralty, 1869–1885," *Mariner's Mirror* 62 (1976): 33–46, 121–28. See also Arthur Marder's fundamental account, *The Anatomy of British Sea Power* (New York, 1940); Paul M. Kennedy, *The Rise and Fall of British Naval Mastery* (New York, 1976), Chapter 8; Peter Padfield, *Rule Britannia: The Victorian and Edwardian Navy* (London, 1981); N. A. M. Rodger, *The Admiralty* (Suffolk, 1979).

2. Lord George Hamilton, *Parliamentary Reminiscences and Reflections*, 2 vols. (London, 1917–1922), 1: 278.

3. Marder, *Anatomy*, 134–35.

4. Admiral Percy Scott, *Fifty Years in the Royal Navy* (London, 1919), 25; Arnold White, "Gunnery vs. Paint," *National Review* (November 1902), 389–96.

5. Quoted in Marder, *Anatomy*, 140.

6. Marder, *Anatomy*, 121–22; William H. McNeill, *The Pursuit of Power* (Chicago, 1982), 268–69.

7. The scare and its repercussions are described in Marder, *Anatomy*, 174–205; Peter Stansky, *Ambitions and Strategies: The Struggle for the Leadership of the Liberal Party in the 1890s* (Oxford, 1964), 19–96.

8. *The Times*, 31 October 1893; Clowes, "Toulon and the French Navy," *Nineteenth Century* (December 1893), 1023–30.

9. W. E. Livesey, *Mahan on Sea Power* (Norman, Okla., 1947); D. M. Schurman, *The Education of a Navy* (Chicago, 1965), 60–82; Paul M. Kennedy, "Mahan Versus Mackinder: Two Interpretations of British Sea Power," *Militärgeschichtliche Mitteilungen* 16 (1974): 39–66.

10. *Hansard's Parliamentary Debates*, 4th Series, vol. 18 (17 November 1893), col. 1151.

11. Lord George Hamilton, a former Unionist First Lord of the Admiralty, introduced a motion demanding immediate action by the Gladstone government, specifically, a "considerable addition" to the Navy to preserve British security. His sharply worded resolution produced a long and heated debate. *Hansard*, 4th Series, vol. 19 (19 December 1893), cols. 1771–1886. Hamilton's Liberal successor, the Earl Spencer, regretted that "a scare is apt to raise false issues and to set a certain number of people against treating the question with sobriety and common sense. After the way in which it was taken up, I am sorry to say, by my predecessor, we shall be in this position, that whatever we do will be claimed as the result of the scare, and our opponents will claim the credit for it while we had all the work and worry." Spencer to Rear Admiral H. F. Stephenson, 14 January 1894, in Peter Gordon, ed., *The Red Earl: The Papers of the Fifth Earl Spencer*, vol. 2, 1885–1910 (Northampton, 1986), 236–37.

12. A sense of the significant changes in the political system between 1883 and 1885 can be gained from Cornelius O'Leary, *The Elimination of Corrupt Practices in British Elections, 1868–1911* (Oxford, 1962); Andrew Jones, *The Politics of Reform, 1884* (Cambridge, 1972); Neal Blewett, "The Franchise in the United Kingdom, 1885–1918," *Past and Present* 32 (1965): 27–56; Mary E. Chadwick, "The Role of Redistribution in the Making of the Third Reform Act," *Historical Journal* 19 (1976): 665–84; Henry Pelling, *Social Geography of British Elections, 1885–1910* (London, 1967).

13. *The Times*, 22 January 1894. Clarke chose to use his pseudonym, "Civis."

14. Dilke to Joseph Chamberlain (copy), 12 February 1894, Dilke MSS 43889, fols. 111–12; Dilke to Gladstone (copy), 12 February 1894, Dilke MSS 43945, fols. 13–29; Stephen Gwynn and G. M. Tuckwell, *Life of Sir Charles Dilke*, 2 vols. (London, 1917) 2: 416–19.

15. Chesney to Dilke (copy), 20 January 1894, Wilkinson MSS 9/4.

16. Dilke to Wilkinson, 23 February 1894, Wilkinson MSS 9/24.

17. *Pall Mall Gazette*, 11 October 1894. Wilkinson's articles were reprinted under the title *The Command of the Sea*, which reflected his dual sense of the word *command*, namely, control of the sea lanes and efficiently exercised authority over the fleet itself.

18. Spenser Wilkinson, *Thirty-Five Years: 1874–1909* (London, 1933), 189. The four Englishmen were H. Lafone, A. W. Lafone, W. L. Ainslie, and E. N. Shackle. On "Harry" Cust, see Stephen Koss, *The Rise and Fall of the Political Press in Britain*, 2 vols. (Chapel Hill, 1981–1984), 1: 337–41. Cust served as a Unionist MP from 1890 to 1895 and from 1900 to 1906, but, in Balfour's view, his party loyalty was "not perhaps above suspicion." Balfour to J. Chamberlain (copy), 19 June 1903, Balfour MSS 49774, fols. 43–47.

19. "Constitution of the Navy League" (Navy League Pamphlet A2); "The Objects of the Navy League" (Navy League Pamphlet A7).

20. Navy League executive committee minutes, 17 January 1895, 4 February 1895, 15 February 1895; Phipps-Hornby to Wilkinson, 11 February 1895, Wilkinson MSS 22/2; Mrs. F. Egerton, *Admiral of the Fleet, Sir Geoffrey Phipps-Hornby* (London, 1896), 393.

21. Ainslie to Wilkinson, 26 May 1919, Wilkinson MSS 22/10.

22. Navy League executive minutes, 4 March 1895.

23. Navy League executive minutes, 11 March 1895. The league justified its decision in a confidential statement to Wilkinson stressing that

> in view of the comparatively small support that the league has received from the public [and] the strong prejudice on the part of influential members of the public against any interference by the league in the organisation of the Admiralty or any of the Government Departments . . . the Executive Committee do not consider that it would be prudent at the present moment to invite controversy by alluding, more prominently than they have done, to the object referred to.

Navy League executive minutes, 8 July 1895.

24. Ainslie to Wilkinson, 12 February 1896, Wilkinson MSS 22/4; *Navy League Annual Report* (1895), 8–12.

25. This theme is lucidly discussed in G. R. Searle, *The Quest for National Efficiency: A Study in British Politics and Political Thought, 1899–1914* (Oxford, 1971).

26. Navy League executive minutes, 17 June 1895; *The Times*, 5 July 1895.

27. *Navy League Journal* (July 1895).

28. *Navy League Journal* (August 1895).

29. Marder, *Anatomy*, 185–88.

30. *The Rise of the Anglo-German Antagonism, 1860–1914* (London, 1980), 464. There is a large and controversial literature about the response of the British economy to both the curious "Great Depression" and foreign competition, much of it conveniently summarized in S. B. Saul, *The Myth of the Great Depression, 1873–1896*, 2nd ed. (London, 1985), and François Crouzet, *The Victorian Economy* (London, 1982), 371–422. Yet, regardless of the outcome of historiographical debates such as that over "entrepreneurial failure," there was a good deal of contemporary support for the pessimistic case, which provided further grist to the navalists' mill. As Spenser Wilkinson warned, "while Great Britain has slept in her dream of prosperity, the whole conditions of the world have changed." *The Command of the Sea* (London, 1894), 19.

31. *The Times*, 2 June 1896.

32. *The Times*, 21 October 1896.

33. *The Times*, 15 September 1897. The league had published C. L. McHardy's *The British Navy for 100 Years*, which advocated reform of the Board of Admiralty and thus renewed the identification of the league with this policy. H. S. Trower, secretary of the league's executive committee, denied that McHardy's book represented official league policy on this point, and he assured readers that "The Navy League are of the opinion that an Admiralty system under which the naval victories of the past 150 years have been won should not be attacked by a civilian body, and the Navy League has no intention of doing so."

34. Navy League executive minutes, 18 July 1898, 15 September 1898, 9 December 1901; *Spectator*, 20 September 1898.

35. Archibald Hurd, "Our Belated Battleships," *Nineteenth Century* (November 1900), 717–29; *Hansard*, 4th Series, vol. 83 (21 May 1900), col. 726; "Seven Years Work," *Navy League Journal* (January 1902), 2–3.

36. Navy League executive minutes, 2 July 1901; Arnold White, "A Message From the Mediterranean," *National Review* (July 1901), 677–89; idem, "Shall the Mediterranean Fleet Remain Unready?" *National Review* (August 1901), 845–54; A. White to H. O. Arnold-Forster, 25 June 1901, Arnold-Forster MSS 50288, fols. 62–64; Arnold-Forster to Selborne (copy), 26 June 1901, Arnold-Forster MSS 50288,

fols. 4–20. White published Beresford's letter in the *Daily Mail*, 21 June 1901. Among his criticisms were inadequate defense of Malta and Egypt, an insufficient number of all types of ships, too few gyroscopes and gunsights, and inedible food. The best brief account of the abrasive White's career is G. R. Searle's introduction to the reprint of White's *Efficiency and Empire*, originally published in 1901 (Brighton, 1973), vii–xxxi.

37. These sentiments were articulated throughout the Navy League's pamphlets and other publications: see, for example, "Ten Years' Work of the Navy League," *Navy League Journal* (February 1905), 34–35; Bernard Semmel, *Liberalism and Naval Strategy* (London, 1986).

38. Lord Beresford's preface to Charles Bathurst, *To Avoid National Starvation* (London, 1912), suggested that only 4.5 million of a population of 44 million were fed on homegrown wheat.

39. *Hansard*, 4th Series, vol. 48 (6 April 1897), cols. 642–51.

40. Some of these issues are touched upon in Richard Soloway, "Counting the Degenerates: The Statistics of Race Deterioration in Edwardian England," *Journal of Contemporary History* 17 (1982): 137–64; idem, *Birth Control and the Population Question in England, 1877–1930* (Chapel Hill, 1982).

41. *Navy League Journal* (July 1895).

42. "Trafalgar and Today," *National Review* (November 1896), 364. Arthur Marder has described Wilson as "one of the three or four most influential moulders of British opinion" on naval matters. *Anatomy*, 215.

43. *Hansard*, 4th Series, vol. 48 (6 April 1897), cols. 652–56.

44. "The Meaning of Defeat" (Navy League Pamphlet C2), 2. See also Wilson, "The Protection of Our Commerce in War," *Nineteenth Century* (February 1896), 218–35; W. C. Crutchley, "The Defence of the British Mercantile Marine in Wartime," *Blackwoods' Magazine* (November 1889), 674–84; Anne Summers, "The Character of Edwardian Nationalism," in Paul Kennedy and Anthony Nicholls, eds., *Nationalist and Racialist Movements in Britain and Germany Before 1914* (London, 1981), 74; Avner Offer, "The Working Classes, British Naval Plans and the Coming of the Great War," *Past and Present* 107 (1985): 204–26.

45. *Hansard*, 4th Series, vol. 48 (6 April 1897), cols. 650; Robert A. Yerburgh, "National Granaries," *National Review* (April 1896), 197–207.

46. *Hansard*, 4th Series, vol. 48 (6 April 1897), cols. 667–75.

47. Chesney to Dilke (copy), 20 January 1894, Wilkinson MSS 9/4.

48. *Navy League Journal* (April 1898).

49. There are valuable descriptions and photographs of the Trafalgar Day celebrations in the *Navy League Journal* (November 1902), 236–37; (November 1905), 275–76. My view of the league's efforts to commemorate Nelson's victory owes much to the essays in Terence Ranger and Eric Hobsbawm, eds., *The Invention of Tradition* (Cambridge, 1983).

50. "Trafalgar and Today." *National Review* (November 1896), 365.

51. *Navy League Journal* (November 1903). In a letter entitled "Too Much Nelson," dated 12 December 1903 and published in the January 1904 issue of the *Navy League Journal*, Jane argued that the "appreciation of past glories is a mistake" and suggested that the league "throw Nelson over board." Yet, from 1898 onward, Nelson's portrait graced each issue of the monthly journal as an integral part of the league's insignia. The Primrose League agreed, noting that "Nelson will have lived in vain for this generation if this generation can only spell his name." *Primrose League Gazette* (May 1909), 7. Nelson, however, did not inspire universal adoration. J. M. Robertson, a staunch Liberal, suspected that "with his tyrannous proclivities, his prestige, and his

grievous lack of human wisdom, he would have become, had he survived Trafalgar, one of the most dangerous political forces in English life." Robertson, *Patriotism and Empire* (London, 1899), 99.

52. *Navy League Journal* (December 1896); Bernard Semmel, *Imperialism and Social Reform: English Social Imperial Thought, 1895–1914* (Cambridge, Mass., 1960).

53. Navy League executive minutes, 27 June 1898, 27 February 1899, 11 January 1904, 2 March 1911.

54. *Spectator*, 13 July 1907.

55. *Navy League Annual Report* (1901), 5.

56. *Western Daily Press*, 30 July 1901, 29 April 1902; S. Humphries, "Hurrah for England: Schooling and the Working Class in Bristol, 1870–1914," *Southern History* 1 (1979): 171–207.

57. Sir John Gray Hill, "An Ideal Sea Training Home," in Alan Burgoyne, ed., *Navy League Annual 1907–1908*, 181.

58. *Navy League Annual Report* (1901), 4–5.

59. *Navy League Journal* (September 1904), 243–45.

60. *Navy League Organisation and Constitution* (1898); W. T. Pike, *Bristol in 1898*, 2 vols. (London, 1898–1899); H. E. Meller, *Leisure and the Changing City, 1870–1914* (London, 1976), 88–89, 96ff.

61. *Navy League Journal* (November 1899, June 1900, August 1904); *Navy League Organisation and Constitution* (1898).

62. *Navy League Journal* (June 1901).

63. Navy League executive minutes, 18 May 1896, 8 June 1896.

64. Navy League executive minutes, 13 June 1898, 11 July 1898. An entry dated 9 February 1903 indicates that, when the league's financial situation finally began to improve, Boyd-Carpenter was paid £200 to improve branch organizations.

65. Bristol regularly returned Unionist candidates for three of its four seats.

66. *Navy League Annual Report* (1901), 7.

67. Navy League executive minutes, 28 March 1898, 24 October 1898, 9 January 1899. The Rugby branch's inactivity in 1902 was cited as an example of "what appears to be a common experience that when the original founder of the movement leaves the locality, the branch languishes." *Navy League Annual Report* (1902), 16.

68. *Navy League Annual Report* (1901), 3.

69. In 1916, the secretary of the league's Bombay branch contacted various Indian educational authorities and urged them to incorporate British naval history into their curricula as had been done for years in the British Isles. The replies were hardly encouraging. The Director of Public Instruction for the Northwest Frontier doubted that education was "sufficiently advanced in this province for any new steps" and added "that not only most of the students but even most of the teachers have never seen the sea." The corresponding official for Poona concurred, his tart rejoinder stressing that "the majority of the teachers and of the pupils in Anglo-vernacular schools have not the least understanding of, or interest in, the sea and shipping." A. M. Reith to Patrick Hannon, 24 July 1916, Hannon MSS 2/3.

70. *Navy League Journal* (November 1898, March 1899, July 1899, August 1899).

71. Navy League executive minutes, 11 December 1894.

72. Navy League executive minutes, 8 February 1895. On 8 April the committee resolved to restrict expenditure only to absolute essentials.

73. Navy League executive minutes, 4, 28 February 1895. Harmsworth had also offered the "medium of his office to facilitate the league's propaganda."

74. Figures are drawn from the league's annual reports for the corresponding years.

75. *Navy League Annual Report* (1895), 6.

76. These remarks are based on a search of local directories, address books, and biographical dictionaries. Names of branch secretaries and committee members are drawn from references in the league's journal or annual reports, its organizational list published in 1898, and notices in the local press. Beyond the three primary occupational groups from which secretaries were drawn at the turn of the century, the following were also represented: an engineer's agent in Hull, a university professor/medical doctor in Birmingham, a surgeon in Cambridge, a costumer/milliner/draper in Penzance, a stationer/paper merchant in Glasgow, and the younger partner in a local shipbuilding firm in Newcastle. The MP solicited was W. V. Faber, who was courted by former Navy League member Harold Wyatt for the rival Imperial Maritime League. This particular example, though, is representative of a widespread practice. Wyatt to Faber (copy), 8 January 1908, Imperial Maritime League documents, vol. 1. An invaluable aid to prosopographical research is H. J. Hanham, "Some Neglected Sources of Information: County Biographical Dictionaries, 1890–1937," *Bulletin of the Institute of Historical Research* 34 (1961): 55–66.

77. For the league as a whole, in 1907 about 2,700 of 20,000 were full members. Harold Wyatt and Lionel Horton-Smith, *The Passing of the Great Fleet* (London, 1909), 213. In Birmingham, 24 of 137 in 1900 were full members; in the Third London branch the comparable figure was 19 of 121. *Navy League Journal* (December 1900, March 1899).

78. *Navy League Annual Report* (1895).

79. The Primrose League's methods have been described as "genteel tea and cakes politics." Ian D'Alton, "Southern Irish Unionism: A Study of Cork Unionists, 1884–1914," *Transactions of the Royal Historical Society* 23 (1973): 85. This is a somewhat misleading evaluation, in view of Primrose League women's contributions as canvassers, but the league emphasized the creation of a sociocultural climate conducive to Conservatism and did not presume to instruct party leaders or field political candidates as was characteristic of the other leagues. The standard work on the subject for many years was Janet Robb, *The Primrose League 1883–1914* (New York, 1942), but it has been superseded by Martin Pugh, *The Tories and the People, 1880–1935* (Oxford, 1985).

80. *Navy League Journal* (January 1898).

81. *Navy League Annual Report* (1901), 7. Apparently the league was as committed to the maintenance of the double standard as it was to the two power standard.

82. *Daily Telegraph*, 21 October 1901.

83. Navy League executive minutes, 18 July 1898, 15 September 1898, 9 December 1901; *Spectator*, 20 September 1898.

84. W. C. Crutchley to Admiralty secretary (copy), 19 November 1901, Arnold White MSS WH1/5.

85. Evan Macgregor to Crutchley (copy), 7 December 1901, White MSS WH1/5.

86. *Hansard*, 4th Series, vol. 123 (9 June 1903), col. 317; *Navy League Annual Report* (1901), 8; *Navy League Journal* (January 1902), 3; *Navy League Annual Report* (1902), 17–18, wherein it reported "there is probably no portion of the league's work which bears better fruit than that pursued in the schools of the kingdom."

87. Navy League executive minutes, 28 November 1898.

88. Navy League executive minutes, 6 February 1899.

89. Navy League executive minutes, 24 September 1900, 8 October 1900.

90. Navy League executive minutes, 1 October 1900.

91. *Navy League Journal* (February 1898). The letter, by Robert Wigglesworth, had originally been published on 7 January 1898 in the *Yorkshire Herald.*

92. In 1891, for example, Beresford had complained that "The Navy is totally unrepresented at Court, in Society, the Clubs, and in Parliament. Neither is it represented in the Country as the fleet is always away." Beresford to Dilke (copy) 12 January 1891, Wilkinson MSS 21/17. Beresford had also given the Navy League his support from the outset. *The Memoirs of Admiral Lord Charles Beresford*, 2 vols. (London, 1914), 2: 397.

93. Arnold White, "Our Silent Navy," *National Review* (March 1902), 78–87.

94. H. Seymour Trower at the league's annual meeting, 26 January 1898, reported in the *Navy League Journal* (March 1898), 41.

95. *The Standard*, 15 January 1902; Navy League executive minutes, 13 January 1902.

96. *Hampstead & Highgate Express*, 18 January 1902.

97. *The Standard*, 17 January 1902; Navy League executive minutes, 17 January 1902, *Hampstead & Highgate Express*, 18 January 1902.

98. *Hampstead & Highgate Express*, 11 January 1902.

99. *Hampstead & Highgate Express*, 25 January 1902.

100. *Navy League Journal* (April 1902), 93.

101. *Navy League Journal* (July 1902), 169.

Chapter 2

1. Cited in Searle, *Quest for National Efficiency*, 5.

2. Ibid., 34–53.

3. Stopford, "The Uses and Limitations of an Army League," *Fortnightly Review* (February 1901), 340.

4. *National Service League Journal* (May 1904). Pilkington served as president of the league's St. Helens branch. See also Anne Summers, "Militarism in Britain Before the Great War," *History Workshop*, 2 (1976): 104–23; A. J. A. Morris, *The Scaremongers*, 108–9; R. J. Q. Adams and Philip Poirer, *The Conscription Controversy in Great Britain, 1900–1918* (London, 1987); Kennedy, *Anglo-German Antagonism*, 371, 380–82.

5. Bentley B. Gilbert, "Health and Politics: The British Physical Deterioration Report of 1904," *Bulletin of the History of Medicine* 39 (1965): 145–53.

6. Marder, *Anatomy*, 65–83; John Gooch, "The Bolt From the Blue" in his *The Prospect of War: Studies in British Defence Policy, 1847–1942* (London, 1981), 1–34.

7. Navy League executive minutes, 24 March 1902; 20, 27 June 1904.

8. *National Service League Journal* (October 1904).

9. Ibid. (November 1903).

10. Herbert Wrigley Wilson, "Trafalgar and Today," *National Review* (November 1896), 364.

11. Notes dated 15 September 1902, Admiralty MSS ADM 116/940 B.

12. Confidential memorandum of 10 October 1902, Cabinet minutes, CAB 37/63/142.

13. E. E. Williams' work is discussed in the introduction to the reprint by Harvester Press of *Made in Germany* (Brighton, 1973); Walter E. Minchinton, "E. E. Williams: Made in Germany and After," *Vierteljahrsschrift für Sozial und Wirtschafts-*

geschichte 62 (1975): 229–42; R. J. S. Hoffman, *Great Britain and the German Trade Rivalry, 1875–1914* (Philadelphia, 1933), 244ff.

14. *Made in Germany*, 1.

15. Ibid., 164–65.

16. Ibid., 167.

17. Brown, *Tariff Reform Movement*, 82, 94.

18. These events have been covered at length in the fifth volume of Julian Amery's biography of Joseph Chamberlain and more incisively in Sykes, *Tariff Reform*, 31–35.

19. George W. E. Russell, *Sir Wilfrid Lawson, A Memoir* (London, 1909), 268–69.

20. Hamilton to Curzon, 7 May 1903, cited in B. H. P. Turner, "Tariff Reform and the Conservative Party, 1895–1906," Ph.D. diss., University of London, 1967, 144.

21. H. C. G. Matthew, *The Liberal Imperialists* (Oxford, 1973).

22. Sydney H. Zebel, "Joseph Chamberlain and the Genesis of Tariff Reform," *Journal of British Studies* 7 (1967): 131–57.

23. Richard Jay, *Joseph Chamberlain: A Political Study* (Oxford, 1981), 275.

24. Leo S. Amery, *My Political Life*, 3 vols. (London, 1953–1955), 1: 236.

25. A. Chamberlain to Mrs. Dugdale, 4 March 1913, Joseph Chamberlain MSS JC 18/18/22.

26. Letter by George Byng in *Morning Post*, 18 February 1908; W. E. Dowding, *The Tariff Reform Mirage* (London, 1913), 7; E. E. Williams, "The Progress Towards Commercial Union of the Empire," in C. H. Mitchell's *Newspaper Press Directory* (1904), 16–17.

27. Williams, "Commercial Union," 17.

28. Ibid., 18–19.

29. Letter by Sir Joseph Lawrence in *Morning Post*, 3 July 1913; Dowding, *Tariff Reform Mirage*, 9–11; *Westminster Gazette*, 20 February 1908; *Morning Post*, 18 February 1908; Chamberlain to J. Parker Smith, 5 July 1903, Parker Smith MSS TD 1/116.

30. *The Times*, 22 July 1903; Amery, *My Political Life*, 1: 238–39.

31. The reference is to the German Customs Union of 1834, which foreshadowed the eventual consolidation of the German Empire under Prussian leadership. It attracted the tariff reformers' admiration as a precedent that revealed how a loose affiliation of states could be united into a formidable world power through (in part) economic measures.

32. Chamberlain to Collings, 18 July 1903, as cited in Julian Amery, *Joseph Chamberlain and the Tariff Campaign* (London, 1969), 307.

33. Edward Nettlefold simultaneously served as treasurer for the Imperial Tariff committee and the local Liberal Unionist Association. C. A. Vince, the secretary, was another Liberal Unionist associate. Dowding, *Tariff Reform Mirage*, 16–17; *Liberal Magazine* (August 1903), 436.

34. Chamberlain to W. A. S. Hewins, 25 July 1903, Hewins MSS 49/183.

35. Alfred Gollin, *Balfour's Burden: Arthur Balfour and Imperial Preference* (London, 1965); idem, "Historians and the Great Crisis of 1903," *Albion* 8 (1976): 83–97; Sykes, *Tariff Reform*, 44–53.

36. A. J. Marrison, "The Development of a Tariff Reform Policy During Joseph Chamberlain's First Campaign, May 1903–February 1904," in W. H. Chaloner and B. M. Ratcliffe, eds., *Trade and Transport: Essays in Economic History in Honour of T. S. Willan* (Manchester, 1977), 214–41; Charles W. Boyd, ed., *Mr. Chamberlain's Speeches*, 2 vols. (New York, 1914); Sykes, *Tariff Reform*, 55–62.

37. *Conservative Agents' Journal* (July 1903), 70.

38. Ibid., 70–71.

39. A. W. Coats, "Political Economy and the Tariff Reform Campaign of 1903," *Journal of Law and Economics* 11 (1968): 184, 188–90.

40. Richard Rempel, *Unionists Divided: Arthur Balfour, Joseph Chamberlain and the Unionist Free Traders* (Newton Abbot, 1972), 71. Lord Selborne was only one of a number of politicians to predict that "the Duke's action" would "have far reaching consequences." Selborne to Balfour, 21 December 1903, Balfour MSS 49707, fols. 149–51. Not that Devonshire's action was entirely unexpected, for he had warned Chamberlain earlier that year that "the Liberal Unionist organisation cannot be employed in the active support of the policy [tariff reform] without serious risk if not the certainty of breaking it up." Devonshire to Chamberlain, 29 May 1903, Joseph Chamberlain MSS JC 18/18/43.

41. Rempel, *Unionists Divided*, 72–74.

42. *The Times*, 13 January 1904.

43. *Conservative Agents' Journal* (April 1904), 51. The agent identified himself only as "F. N. S."

44. "Work Accomplished by the League in Croydon, and Typical of the Work Undertaken in Every Free Trade Unionist's Constituency" (undated report compiled by Organization Committee), Blagdon MSS ZR1 25/99.

45. *The Times*, 30 July 1904; "Work Accomplished by the League," Blagdon MSS ZR1 25/99; *Croydon Guardian*, 23 January 1904, 30 April 1904.

46. Rempel, *Unionists Divided*, 142–43; *The Times*, 6, 8 February 1905; R. Cecil to Sandars, 18 February 1905, Balfour MSS 49737, fols. 27–32.

47. Rempel, "Lord Hugh Cecil's Parliamentary Career"; *The Times*, 9 February 1905; R. Cecil to Sandars, 18 February 1905, Balfour MSS 49737, fols. 27–32.

48. J. Chamberlain to Ridley, 18 February 1905, Blagdon MSS ZRI 25/99; H. Cecil to Balfour, n.d., Balfour MSS 49759, fols. 135–36. It was rumored that the league was spending £50 a week in Greenwich to dethrone Cecil.

49. *The Times*, 30 July 1904.

50. J. Chamberlain to Selborne, 16 September 1904, Selborne MSS 9, fols. 136–37.

51. Selborne to Balfour, 20 December 1904, Balfour MSS 49708, fols. 29–31.

52. Selborne to Balfour, 22 December 1904, Balfour MSS 49708, fols. 37–38.

53. Balfour to Selborne (copy), 28 December 1904, Balfour MSS 49708, fol. 49; Sandars to Short, 30 December 1904, Balfour MSS 49762, fols. 227–30.

54. J. Chamberlain to Ridley (copy), 28 November 1904, Joseph Chamberlain MSS JC 19/7/72; J. Chamberlain to Maxse, 21 January 1904, Maxse MSS 452/734.

55. J. Chamberlain to Hewins, 3 February 1905, Hewins MSS 47/104.

56. J. Chamberlain to Hewins, 9 February 1905, Hewins MSS 47/110.

57. Pearson had only spent mornings at the league's Victoria Street offices and devoted the remainder of his time to his newspaper responsibilities. Sidney Dark, *The Life of Sir Arthur Pearson* (London, 1922), 102.

58. J. Chamberlain to Ridley, 18 February 1905, Blagdon MSS ZRI 25/99; *Monthly Notes on Tariff Reform* (November 1905).

59. W. Maxwell Lyte to Cecil, 18 December 1905, Lord Robert Cecil MSS 51158, fols. 30–31.

60. Arthur Dart to Bowles (copy), 19 October 1905, Balfour MSS 49860, fols. 57–62.

61. Bowles to Dart (copy), 22 October 1905, Balfour MSS 49860.

62. See the frequent correspondence between Bowles and Dart (secretary of the Norwood branch of the Tariff Reform League) throughout October and November 1905.

63. Arthur Haig to Balfour, 6 August 1905, Balfour MSS 49857, fols. 269–70.

64. *Hansard*, 4th Series, vol. 18 (6 April 1897), col. 650.

65. Ibid., col. 663.

66. Wolfgang Mock, "The Function of 'Race' in Imperial Ideologies: The Example of Joseph Chamberlain," *Nationalist and Racialist Movements*, 190–203.

67. See the crisp analysis of P. J. Cain, "Political Economy in Edwardian England: The Tariff Reform Controversy," in Alan O'Day, ed., *The Edwardian Age: Conflict and Stability, 1900–1914* (London, 1979), 34–59.

68. Chamberlain is, of course, a difficult personality to penetrate, and any ascription of motive to his tortuous career might be thought hazardous. But there is a valuable assessment of him in Jay, *Joseph Chamberlain*, and further insights can be gleaned from Michael Balfour's otherwise disappointing *Britain and Joseph Chamberlain* (London, 1985).

69. Peter Clarke, *Liberals and Social Democrats* (Cambridge, 1978).

70. Marrison, "Development of a Tariff Reform Policy," 224.

71. Herbert Wrigley Wilson, "Mr. Chamberlain's New Policy" (pamphlet, 1903).

72. *Hansard*, 4th Series, vol. 48 (6 April 1897), col. 669.

73. Balfour to J. Chamberlain (copy), 18 February 1905, Balfour MSS 49794, fols. 61–65.

74. J. Chamberlain to Parker Smith, 9 September 1903, Parker Smith MSS TD 1/116.

75. John M. MacKenzie, *Propaganda and Empire: The Manipulation of British Public Opinion, 1880–1960* (Manchester, 1984); John MacKenzie, ed., *Imperialism and Popular Culture* (Manchester, 1986).

76. *Hansard*, 4th Series, vol. 48 (6 April 1897), cols. 667–68.

77. Ibid., (29 April 1897), cols. 1174–75.

78. *The Campaign Guide 1904: A Handbook for Unionist Speakers* (London, 1904), 705.

79. R. Cecil to Sandars, 7 December 1904, Balfour MSS 49737, fols. 22–23.

80. Estimates varied not just because of Balfour's deliberate efforts at ambiguity but also in response to the twists and turns of the fiscal debate and the consequent vacillation of many MPs or prospective candidates. In late 1904 the Tariff Reform League divided Unionists into 205 tariff reformers, 103 retaliationists, and 42 free fooders. Herbert Gladstone was advised of another count that "included 22 Chamberlainites who are not sufficiently advanced for the TR list and also 8 Free Traders which they class as retaliationists." A list in the Selborne papers drawn up for Balfour involved further subtleties. Some 245 MPs were classified as tariff reformers, of whom 172 were said publicly to have supported imperial preference and a further 73 who would do so if it became government policy. Another 98 were placed in Balfour's camp as retaliationists, with 27 free fooders and 4 unclassified MPs accounting for the remainder. Whatever the discrepancies, and it is misleading to presume one can settle on a precise, final calculation, it seems fair to conclude that tariff reformers significantly outnumbered Unionist Free Traders, but that there remained a large body of MPs who reserved any further commitment until a stronger lead from Balfour or other political circumstances dictated so. Considering the relatively brief period for which the fiscal issue had again been under debate, the extent of the tariff reform advance is quite impressive. Ponsonby to H. Gladstone, 21 December 1904, Herbert Gladstone MSS 46023, fols. 176–177; undated memorandum, Selborne MSS 1, fols. 58–65.

81. Sandars to Balfour, 21 February 1904, Balfour MSS 49762, fols. 75–81.

82. H. Cecil to Balfour, 24 May 1903, Balfour MSS 49759, fols. 23–36.

83. Ritchie to Balfour, 4 October 1904, Balfour MSS 49857, fols. 64–66.

84. R. Cecil to Sandars, 18 February 1905, Balfour MSS 49737, fols. 27–32.

85. Sandars to Balfour, 25 October 1905, Balfour MSS 49764, fols. 83–84.

86. Sandars to Balfour, 13 December 1905, Balfour MSS 49764, fols. 121–25.

87. Acland-Hood to Sandars, 22 December 1905, Balfour MSS 49771, fols. 131–32. See also A. K. Russell, *Liberal Landslide: The General Election of 1906* (Newton Abbot, 1973). It is interesting that Hood chose the analogy of domestic service to convey the hierarchical structure of the party's organization.

88. R. Cecil to Sandars, 18 February 1905, Balfour MSS 49737, fols. 27–28.

89. Letter dated 9 November 1905, Balfour MSS 49858, fols. 12–18.

90. Draft provisionally dated 23 December 1904 (marked "not sent"), Balfour MSS 49857, fols. 112–14.

91. *Daily Mail*, 3 October 1903; W. A. S. Hewins, *The Apologia of an Imperialist*, 2 vols. (London, 1929), 1: 73–81; Pearson to Hewins, 14 November 1903, Hewins MSS 46/94.

92. Ritchie to Balfour, 4 October 1904, Balfour MSS 49857, fols. 64–66; Herbert Gladstone to Hewins (copy), 18 March 1904, Herbert Gladstone MSS 46061, fols. 187–88; Francis Channing, *Memories of Midland Politics, 1885–1910* (London, 1918), 284; Cobden Club, *Budget and Tariff Compared* (London, 1909).

93. Amery, *Joseph Chamberlain*, 529.

94. Pearson to Hewins, 2 December 1903, Tariff Commission MSS TC 6/1/26.

95. Hewins to Pearson (copy), 24 December 1903, Tariff Commission MSS TC 6/1/26.

96. Recollections by Sir H. Brittain, n.d., Joseph Chamberlain MSS JC 19/7/5; Amery, *Joseph Chamberlain*, 533.

97. Hewins, *Apologia*, 86: J. Chamberlain to Hewins (copy), 5 November 1910, Tariff Commission MSS TC 6/8/2.

98. See discussion at beginning of this section, "Fiscal Fictions and Factions"; M. M. Barrie, "Free Trade and Protection From the Workman's Point of View," *Nineteenth Century* (August 1903), 202–15. The critical role of class in politics at the turn of the century is incisively argued in P. F. Clarke, *Lancashire and the New Liberalism* (Cambridge, 1971), and has been widely, if not universally, accepted. In contrast, the role of religion is stressed in Kenneth D. Wald, *Crosses on the Ballot: Patterns of British Voter Alignment Since 1885* (Princeton, 1983).

99. *Monthly Notes on Tariff Reform* (July, August, October 1904, May 1907); Semmel, *Imperialism and Social Reform*, 114–15; K. D. Brown, "The Trade Union Tariff Reform Association," *Journal of British Studies* 9 (1970): 141–53.

100. *Monthly Notes on Tariff Reform* (July 1904, July 1905); *The Times*, 22 July 1904.

101. Leaflet, Shiffner MSS 3238.

102. Aubrey-Fletcher to Shiffner, 14, 19 February 1904; F. S. Shenstone to Shiffner, 4 December 1903; G. Holman to Shiffner, 6 December 1903, Shiffner MSS 3238; P. Blackwell, "An Undoubted Jewel: A Case Study of Five Sussex Country Houses, 1880–1914," *Southern History* 3 (1981): 183–200; *Monthly Notes on Tariff Reform* (July 1905). In 1907 Hewins delivered an address "at an admirable meeting at Lewes" with "excellent results." Hewins to Balfour, 26 November 1907, Balfour MSS 49779, fols. 129–30.

103. *Monthly Notes on Tariff Reform* (July 1905, November 1905, November 1906).

104. Circular by Leconfield, 6 March 1905, Petworth Archives 5476; Leconfield to Maxse, 17 March 1907, Maxse MSS 457/497.

105. Cornford, "Hotel Cecil," 311; John Ramsden, *The Age of Balfour and Baldwin, 1902-1940* (London, 1978), 97.

106. Semmel, *Imperialism and Social Reform*, 102-5.

107. Ibid., 102.

108. A. J. Marrison, "Businessmen, Industries and Tariff Reform in Great Britain, 1903-1930," *Business History* 25 (1983): 148-78; *Report of the Tariff Commission, vol. I: The Iron and Steel Trades* (1904).

109. *Fiscal Reform: A Popular, Verbatim, and Unabridged Report of the Recent Fiscal Debate between Mr. Samuel Storey and Mr. J. M. Robertson in Newcastle-Upon-Tyne on November 28th, 29th, and 30th, 1905* (Sunderland, n.d.), 8-9.

110. *Hansard*, 4th Series, vol. 129 (9 February 1904), col. 742.

111. *Hansard*, 4th Series, vol. 129 (2 February 1904), col. 48.

112. Neal Blewett, "Free Fooders, Balfourites, Whole Hoggers. Factionalism Within the Unionist Party, 1906-10," *Historical Journal* 11 (1968): 95-124. See also Rempel, *Unionists Divided*, 94-104.

Chapter 3

1. Iwan-Muller to Balfour, 13 February 1906, Balfour MSS 49796, fols. 115-59.

2. Russell, *Liberal Landslide*, 179.

3. *The Times*, 30 January 1906.

4. Blewett, "Free Fooders," 96-97; Rempel, *Unionists Divided*, 166-69.

5. Fisher to Rosebery, 10 May 1901, as cited in Jon Tetsuro Sumida, "British Capital Ship Design and Fire Control in the Dreadnought Era: Sir John Fisher, Arthur Hungerford Pollen, and the Battle Cruiser," *Journal of Modern History* 51 (1979): 207.

6. Marder, *From the Dreadnought to Scapa Flow*, 5 vols. (London, 1961-1970), 1: 14-18; idem, *Anatomy*.

7. Rhodri Williams, "Arthur James Balfour, Sir John Fisher and the Politics of Naval Reform, 1904-10," *Historical Research* 60 (1987): 87. Williams' article provides a concise analysis of many of the points raised in this paragraph.

8. *Navy League Journal* (February 1905), 35. See also *English Review* (June 1925) and *Navy League Annual Report* (1902), 14, for more on Wyatt's contributions. Wyatt had stood for election in 1906 as "an avowed supporter of Mr. Chamberlain." Navy League executive minutes, 6 November 1905.

9. Navy League executive minutes, 29 October 1906, 5 November 1906; Wyatt and Horton-Smith, *The Passing of the Great Fleet* (London, 1909); T. C. Knox to Horton-Smith, 27 November 1906, Horton-Smith MSS HSM/8.

10. *The Times*, 22 January 1907, as cited in Williams, "Arthur James Balfour, Sir John Fisher and the Politics of Naval Reform," 88.

11. Circular by W. C. Crutchley, 28 February 1907, Horton-Smith MSS HSM/8.

12. Navy League executive minutes, 6 May 1907.

13. Pollock to Crutchley (copy), 6 May 1907, Horton-Smith MSS HSM/8.

14. *Navy League Journal* (June 1907), 152. *Spectator*, 11 May 1907; Wyatt and Horton-Smith, *Passing of the Great Fleet*, 60-62. Among the specific examples he cited were the abandonment of naval stations in the West Indies and Falklands, the withdrawal of cruisers from many areas, the reduction in dockyard workers and naval

personnel, and the failure to build sufficient destroyers or establish a naval base on England's eastern coast.

15. *Navy League Journal* (June 1907), 152.

16. Ibid.

17. Wyatt and Horton-Smith, *Passing of the Great Fleet*, 81. The actual vote was 44–27.

18. *Navy League Journal* (June 1907), 152.

19. *Spectator*, 6 July 1907.

20. Grace Wyatt to Horton-Smith, 30 May 1907, Horton-Smith MSS HSM/8.

21. Crutchley to Horton-Smith, 4 June 1907, 13 and 23 July 1907, Horton-Smith MSS HSM/8. The files on the Navy League maintained by the Board of Trade under the Companies Registration Act are disappointing, listing only a handful of subscribers. Board of Trade BT 31/10358/77970.

22. Circular by Yerburgh, 1 July 1907, Horton-Smith MSS HSM/8; *The Times*, 29 June 1907.

23. Many of the proxies themselves can be found in the Horton-Smith MSS HSM/8. I had hoped that they might be used to provide occupational data on league members, but only the witnesses, not the signatories, were required to state their occupations. Very few signatories were themselves also witnesses, suggesting that decisions regarding which policy to support during the dissension were taken in private, rather than at group meetings at which other league members would be available as witnesses.

24. *Navy League Journal* (August 1907), 220.

25. Ibid., 222.

26. Ibid.

27. *Sunday Sun*, 10 April 1904; Navy League executive minutes, 13 April 1904; *Navy League Journal* (August 1907), 223.

28. *Navy League Journal* (August 1907), 223.

29. Ibid., 224.

30. Ibid., 223–25.

31. Ibid., 226.

32. Ibid., 226–27.

33. Ibid., 229.

34. Ibid., 231.

35. Ibid., 230. The speaker was J. J. Jackson.

36. Ibid.

37. Ibid.

38. Ibid., 226.

39. Ibid., 228. Hayes Fisher admitted to hoping "to detach" Liberals on the naval issue, but saw "no sign of that yet."

40. Ibid., 227.

41. Ibid.

42. Ibid., 231.

43. Ibid., 227.

44. Navy League executive minutes, 16 December 1907.

45. Navy League executive minutes, 9 December 1907.

46. Navy League executive minutes, 27 January 1908; "A Collection of pamphlets and documents forming a history of the Imperial Maritime League, brought together by L. G. H. Horton-Smith," pamphlet vol. 1. The Third London branch of the Navy League had been "composed mainly of railway employees" and maintained a "high

standard of business capacity and unflagging attention to the needs of the Navy." *Navy League Annual Report* (1901), 7. See also *Navy League Annual Report* (1902), 17, and *Navy League Journal* (July 1905) for similar testimonials.

47. "Imperial Maritime League documents," passim; Wyatt and Horton-Smith, *Passing of the Great Fleet*, passim.

48. Hopkins to Esher (copy), 7 February 1908, Admiralty MSS ADM 1/7990.

49. Arnold-Forster to Maxse, 27 July 1907, Maxse MSS 457/552.

50. Navy League executive minutes, 11 November 1907, 27 January 1908.

51. Navy League executive minutes, 28 January 1908, 10 February 1908.

52. Navy League executive minutes, 17 February 1908.

53. Navy League executive minutes, 16 March 1908, 6 April 1908.

54. Press statement, 29 October 1908, and circular by W. F. Lord, 2 November 1908, both in "Imperial Maritime League Documents," vol. 1; *Ealing Gazette* 7 November 1908. Action with regard to the Ealing meeting is noted but not explained in Navy League executive minutes, 4 November 1908.

55. Rempel, *Unionists Divided*, 167-69; Sykes, *Tariff Reform*, 100-14; Amery, *Joseph Chamberlain*, 821ff.; Peter Fraser, "Unionism and Tariff Reform: The Crisis of 1906," *Historical Journal* 5 (1962): 149-66; David Dutton, "Unionist Politics and the Aftermath of the General Election of 1906: A Reassessment," *Historical Journal* 22 (1979): 861-76.

56. Alfred Moseley to J. Chamberlain, 27 July 1906, Joseph Chamberlain MSS JC 21/2/67.

57. Ridley to J. Chamberlain (copy), 22 January 1906, Joseph Chamberlain MSS JC 21/2/82. Bagley, a former Unionist agent for Rye, had the reputation of being one of the party's more progressive and effective organizers.

58. Maxse to Bonar Law, 2 January 1907, Bonar Law MSS 18/3/28.

59. Blewett, "Free Fooders," 118; Alan Sykes, "The Confederacy and the Purge of the Unionist Free Traders 1906-1910," *Historical Journal* 18 (1975): 349-66.

60. Sandars to Balfour, 2 April 1907, Balfour MSS 49765, fols. 34-38.

61. Balfour to Sandars (copy), 5 April 1907, Balfour MSS 49765, fols. 46-51.

62. Sandars to Balfour, 22 January 1907, Balfour MSS 49765, fols. 11-16.

63. George Lane Fox to Sandars, 10 January 1907, J. S. Sandars MSS c. 753, fols. 39-40.

64. Balfour to Austen Chamberlain, 23 October 1907, cited in Blewett, "Free Fooders," 108.

65. Balfour to Sandars (copy), 24 January 1907, Balfour MSS 49765, fols. 23-25.

66. *The Times*, 15 November 1907; Sykes, *Tariff Reform*, 141-44; P. F. Clarke, *Lancashire and the New Liberalism* (Cambridge, 1971), 349-55.

67. *Tariff Reform League Speaker's Handbook* (6th ed., 1910), xiv. Leo Amery was another tariff reformer accustomed to regarding the Empire as "a unit and as the final object of patriotic emotion and action." *My Political Life*, 1: 253.

68. Cited in Clarke, *Lancashire*, 352.

69. *Hansard*, 4th Series, vol. 129 (12 February 1904), col. 1242.

70. Ibid. (15 February 1904), col. 1382.

71. A. Chamberlain to Balfour, 9 March 1905, Balfour MSS 49735, fols. 176-179.

72. Neal Blewett, *The Peers, the Parties and the People: The General Elections of 1910* (London, 1972), 66. "Paddy" Goulding was also "a capital watchdog." Jesse Collings to J. Chamberlain, 8 November 1908, Joseph Chamberlain MSS JC 22/44.

73. Bowles to Cecil, 26 December 1907, Lord Robert Cecil MSS 51072, fols. 107-108, and 6 January 1908, Lord Robert Cecil MSS 51072, fols. 120-21; Sykes, *Tariff*

Reform, 161; P. F. Clarke, "British Politics and Blackburn Politics, 1900–1910," *Historical Journal* 12 (1969): 302–27.

74. Bowles to Cecil, 14 April 1908, Lord Robert Cecil MSS 51072, fols. 134–35; R. Cecil to Balfour, 19 January 1908, Balfour MSS 49737, fols. 86–87.

75. Goulding to J. Chamberlain, 25 March 1908, Joseph Chamberlain MSS JC 22/80.

76. Blewett, "Free Fooders," 119.

77. *Morning Post*, 19 January 1909.

78. Goulding to Bonar Law, 25 January 1909, Bonar Law MSS 18/5/87. Publication upset delicate negotiations between Goulding and Law on the one hand and Cecil and Bowles on the other about retaining their seats. Eventually, any hope of a further "concordat" collapsed, and the latter left to contest Blackburn. K. Waterson to Sandars, 23 August 1909, Balfour MSS 49860, fols. 135–49; Clarke, "British Politics and Blackburn Politics."

79. A. W. Coats, "Political Economy and the Tariff Reform Campaign of 1903," *Journal of Law and Economics* 11 (1968): 181–229; W. J. Ashley to Bonar Law, 21 December 1904, Bonar Law MSS 18/1/5. Hewins recalled that the "Conservative, especially the Conservative politician, likes to have the economic aspects of some complicated question summed up for him in a ten minute conversation, and if the impressions he derives last long enough to enable him to make a speech, he is quite well satisfied." Hewins, *Apologia of an Imperialist*, 1: 163.

80. Carter to Cecil, 5 March 1908, Lord Robert Cecil MSS 51158, fols. 177–81.

81. T. J. MacNamara, *The Political Situation: Letters to a Working Man* (London, 1909), 8.

82. *Worcester Echo*, 28 January 1908, cited in Dowding, *Tariff Reform Mirage*, 23–24. This account would appear to substantiate points a and b of Carter's memorandum to Cecil.

83. Memorandum, April 1910, Walter Long MSS 947/449/4.

84. Sir Joseph Lawrence to Balfour, 6 November 1907, Balfour MSS 49791, fols. 226–29; R. Cecil to Long, 8 March 1908, Walter Long MSS 947/444.

85. Acland-Hood to Sandars, 11 January 1908, Balfour MSS 49771, fols. 170–71.

86. Lawrence to Balfour, 6 November 1907, Balfour MSS 49791, fols. 226–29.

87. *Unionist Organization Committee Index of Proceedings to 31 March 1911*, 52. Unfortunately, no verbatim transcript of the evidence referred to in the index was ever published, only brief interim and final reports in April and June 1911. Copies of the index may be found in the Conservative Research Department Library and in the Walter Long MSS 947/450/12.

88. Clarke, "British Politics and Blackburn Politics," 314.

89. Lord Hugh Cecil in *Hansard*, 4th Series, vol. 129 (12 February 1904), cols. 1245–46.

90. Portland to Balfour, 20 October 1907, Balfour MSS 49736, 38–39.

91. *Monthly Notes on Tariff Reform* (December 1905). The *Standard*, 29 March 1910, claimed that the league operated 161 such dump shops, while the league itself claimed that nearly 100,000 people attended the Dumped Goods Exhibition at Manchester's Midland Hotel in November 1910 and that similar, if smaller, exhibitions drew 70,000 in Warrington, 40,000 in Blackburn, and 20,000 in Nottingham. *Tariff Reform League Annual Report* (1912), 140.

92. Gwynne to Bonar Law, 11 February 1908, Bonar Law MSS 18/4/53. The subject is well discussed by A. J. A. Morris, *The Scaremongers*, 148–63; Christopher

Andrew, *Her Majesty's Secret Service* (New York, 1986), 34–49; David French, "Spy Fever in Britain 1900–1915," *Historical Journal* 21 (1978): 355–70.

93. *The War Inevitable* (London, 1908), 14. See, more generally, Samuel Hynes, *The Edwardian Turn of Mind* (Princeton, 1968), 34–53; I. F. Clarke, *Voices Prophesying War* (London, 1966).

94. Steel-Maitland to Guy Speir (copy), 15 July 1911, Steel-Maitland MSS GD 193/155/2/148; "Alien Immigration" (Tariff Reform League pamphlet No. 65); the key study is Colin Holmes, *Anti-Semitism in British Society, 1876–1939* (London, 1979).

95. Amery, *My Political Life*, 1: 236.

96. Lawrence to Balfour, 6 November 1907, Balfour MSS 49791, fols. 226–29.

97. Croft, *My Life of Strife* (London, 1948), 46–47.

98. A. Chamberlain to Balfour (copy), 26 January 1910, Austen Chamberlain MSS AC 8/5/2.

99. Lawrence to T. M. Horsfall (copy), 3 January 1908, Tariff Commission MSS TC 6/4/18. Although even Austen Chamberlain admitted in private to being baffled by the intractability of the evidence, as in the case of meat duties (taxing dead or live meat more heavily). Chamberlain, *Politics From Inside: An Epistolary Chronicle, 1906–1914* (New Haven, 1937), 159.

100. Hewins to Balfour, 14 December 1908, Balfour MSS 49779, fols. 202–3.

101. Amery to Steel-Maitland, 5 March 1909, Steel-Maitland MSS GD 193/141/1–2.

102. John Barnes and David Nicholson, eds., *The Leo Amery Diaries* (London, 1980), 64.

103. Balfour to Northcliffe (copy), 17 January 1906, Balfour MSS 49858, fols. 149–50.

104. Sykes, *Tariff Reform*, 138.

105. A. M. Gollin, *Proconsul in Politics: A Study of Lord Milner in Opposition and in Power* (London, 1964); Robert J. Scally, *The Origins of the Lloyd George Coalition* (Princeton, 1975), 87, 100–3.

106. Malmesbury, ed., *The New Order* (London, 1908), 4–5.

107. Ibid., 3.

108. Ibid., 224, 177; Burgoyne, *The War Inevitable*, 89; Burgoyne to Long, 10 January 1911, Walter Long MSS 947/445/12. Burgoyne hoped to credit any profit from sales of the book to the Tariff Reform League. A. J. Barnham to Steel-Maitland, 2 December 1908, Steel-Maitland MSS GD 193/139/64.

109. *The New Order*, 177.

110. Ibid., 7.

111. "The Confederacy," esp. 354–55.

112. David Clark, *Colne Valley: Radicalism to Socialism* (London, 1981), 141–61; Pelling, *Popular Politics and Society*, 130–46; Stanley Pierson, *British Socialists: The Journey From Fantasy to Politics* (Cambridge, Mass., 1979), 131–38.

113. National Union executive minutes, 10 July 1907, Conservative Party Archive.

114. A thorough study of the London Municipal Society is Ken Young, *Local Politics and the Rise of Party* (Leicester, 1975).

115. London Municipal Society executive minutes, 31 July 1907, Guildhall Library MSS 19528/1.

116. *Daily Express*, 25 October 1907. The society had approached Acland-Hood and Percival Hughes of the Unionist party, but they were not listed among those in attendance. London Municipal Society executive minutes, 19 September 1907. Balfour

himself conducted extensive discussions on Socialism with Hewins during the first week of November. Memoranda of conversations of 1, 3, 4 November 1907, Balfour MSS 49779, fols. 117–28.

117. *The Times*, 25 October 1907.

118. Cited in Brown, "The Anti-Socialist Union," 236.

119. London Municipal Society, *Conference on the Progress of Socialism* (London, 1907), 7.

120. Stanley Salvidge, *Salvidge of Liverpool* (London, 1934), 76.

121. Ralph D. Blumenfeld, *R. D. B.'s Diary 1887–1914* (London, 1930), 224–25.

122. Mallock to Hood, ? September 1908, J. S. Sandars MSS, c. 757, fols. 15–16.

123. Ashley to Blumenfeld, 13 November 1912, Blumenfeld MSS Mou. 10; Memorandum, December 1911, Steel-Maitland MSS GD 193/108/3/47–61. Clearly Mallock's letter and Steel-Maitland's memorandum both contradict Kenneth Brown's account, which minimizes the financial relations between the Unionist party and the Anti-Socialist Union. Brown relied too heavily on the fallible (or selective) memory of Sir Harry Brittain, who recalled that "the Unionist Party gave not a bob to the ASU." Brown, "The Anti-Socialist Union," 251. Yet another Union member, Claude Lowther, had wanted "lots of money from the Party," and Acland-Hood testified to the Unionist Organization Committee that he subsidized the union. Lowther to Blumenfeld, 7 September 1907, Blumenfeld MSS LOWT. 1; Young, *Local Politics*, 110, which first drew attention to the discrepancy between Brown's account and Steel-Maitland's decision; F. Coetzee, "Pressure Groups, Tory Businessmen, and the Aura of Political Corruption Before the First World War," *Historical Journal* 29 (1986): 833–52.

124. Ashley to Sandars, 16 July 1909, J. S. Sandars MSS c. 759, fols. 23–24.

125. For example, Hammersmith, West Ham, and Battersea.

126. *The Anti-Socialist*, March 1909.

127. *The Anti-Socialist*, February 1909.

128. *Anti-Socialist Union Speaker's Handbook* (1911), iv.

129. *The Anti-Socialist*, March 1909, 22.

130. "The Workman's Dream," *The Anti-Socialist*, February 1909, 5.

131. Brown, "The Anti-Socialist Union," 241. Jessel had stressed that "Conservatives and Liberals" were "equally welcome" and promised that the executive committee would not be "composed of men serving under a party banner."

Chapter 4

1. Morris, *The Scaremongers*, 146–47.

2. V. R. Berghahn, *Germany and the Approach of War in 1914* (London, 1973), 62–65.

3. Marder, *From the Dreadnought to Scapa Flow*, 1: 151–85; Donald C. Gordon, "The Lengthy Shadow of H. H. Mulliner," in Robert W. Love, ed., *Changing Interpretations and New Sources in Naval History* (New York, 1980), 309–24; Alfred Gollin, *The Observer and J. L. Garvin* (London, 1960), 64–92.

4. See Blewett, *Peers, the Parties, and the People*, 51–52.

5. G. J. Marcus, "The Naval Crisis of 1909 and the Croydon By-Election," *Journal of the Royal United Service Institution* 103 (1958): 500–14.

6. *Morning Post*, 17 March 1909.

7. *Croydon Advertiser*, 20 March 1909.

8. *Croydon Times*, 17 March 1909; *Croydon Guardian*, 20, 27 March 1909; *The Times*, 19 March 1909; *Morning Post*, 20 March 1909.

9. As Fisher explained in another context, the naval agitation would "bear good fruit. . . . We are very much stronger than anyone supposes but yet we are not too strong for as Nelson said, *we can never be!*" Fisher to Bonar Law, 27 July 1912, Bonar Law MSS 26/5/42.

10. *The Navy* (August 1909), 229.

11. Ibid.

12. Ibid.

13. Ibid., 241. Wilfrid Ashley praised Ridley as someone "who, of anybody, ought to know how a widespread organisation should be run."

14. Ibid., 240. All quotations are taken from the verbatim account published in the August 1909 issue of *The Navy*.

15. Ibid., 242. The speaker was Gerard Fiennes.

16. In this sense, it is likely that the proposed reforms were also a direct result of the executive committee's experience with Wyatt, Horton-Smith, and the other dissidents in 1907.

17. Major Anstruther-Gray in *The Navy* (August 1909), 243.

18. Ibid.

19. J. Alex Mitchell, ibid., 244.

20. A. A. Somerville, ibid.

21. Violet Brooke-Hunt, ibid., 243–44.

22. See, above all, Bruce Murray's fine study, *The People's Budget 1909/10* (Oxford, 1980).

23. Quoted in Morris, *The Scaremongers*, 224.

24. *National Service League Annual Report* (1908); *National Service League Journal* (May 1906); *Nation in Arms* (October, December 1908).

25. *National Service League Annual Report* (1908). The league did maintain strong urban branches in Birmingham and Warrington.

26. *The Patriot* (August 1908, August 1909). This was a monthly journal published by the Essex association.

27. *Nation in Arms* (May 1908).

28. *The Times*, 6 April 1909. Morris provides a concise account of the by-election in *The Scaremongers*, 235–37.

29. Milner to Balfour (copy), 6 April 1909, Milner MSS 35, fols. 169–70.

30. For example, Rowland Hunt wrote Acland-Hood stressing the symbolic importance of Kincaid-Smith's candidacy, but, upon finding Hood unimpressed, then appealed to Maxse for assistance in smoothing relations between the National Service League and Conservative Central Office. Hunt to Maxse, 18 April 1909, Maxse MSS 459, fols. 112–14.

31. *The Times*, 7 April 1909. Similar sentiments were expressed in a letter from J. H. Howell, a vice president of the Tariff Reform League, Navy League, and National Service League. Kincaid-Smith's defeat,

> even by a supporter of Mr. Balfour's naval and Mr. Chamberlain's fiscal policy, at this juncture would be hailed with delight by the Little Englanders, who would assuredly misrepresent its cause and glory in its consequence abroad . . . the false impression . . . that on the first appeal since the naval crisis to a British electorate by the man who sacrificed his seat in order to test the opinion of his constituents on the question of naval defence, the verdict had been in favour of restricting the building of our Dreadnoughts and encouraging Germany to increase and accelerate the building of hers.

The Times, 12 April 1909. Howell stressed his admiration for Kincaid-Smith's "British pluck" and "manliness."

32. Indeed, *The Times'* special correspondent in Stratford reported that while local Unionists appreciated the suggestion "that all parties should unite in supporting a national defense candidate, they have any number of reasons why such an indisputable general principle should not count in this particular case." *The Times*, 7 April 1909.

33. Sandars to Balfour, 12 April 1909, Balfour MSS 49765, fols. 217–20.

34. *The Times*, 6 May 1909.

35. Murray, *The People's Budget*; idem, "The Politics of the 'People's Budget,'" *Historical Journal* 16 (1973): 555–70.

36. Quoted in Bentley B. Gilbert, *David Lloyd George: A Political Life* (London, 1987), 381.

37. Quoted in Murray, *The People's Budget*, 176.

38. These included Mid-Devon in January 1908 and Goulding's victory at Worcester in February 1908.

39. *Monthly Notes on Tariff Reform* (April 1909).

40. *Monthly Notes* (May 1907, September 1909). All too often, however, these reports failed to quote specific figures.

41. Tariff Reform League estimated expenses for 1905 (memorandum of February 1905), Blagdon MSS ZR1 25/99; Sandars to Balfour, 26 January 1907, Balfour MSS 49765, fol. 26; Chamberlain, *Politics From Inside*, 131. See also my article, "Pressure Groups, Tory Businessmen and the Aura of Political Corruption Before the First World War," *Historical Journal* 29 (1986): 833–52.

42. Tariff Reform League Cash Book, 1909, Tariff Commission MSS TC 11/2/1. Ridley was also to dispatch two agents on a private 2 month foray to elicit further contributions. Ridley to Maxse, 9 December 1910, Maxse MSS 462, fols. 781–82.

43. Murray, *The People's Budget*, 86.

44. This theme was persistently articulated in the league's journal, *Monthly Notes*, its *Speaker's Handbook*, and encapsulated in the phrase, "England expects that every foreigner will pay his duty" (a reference to Nelson's famous signal at Trafalgar). See Walter Arnstein, "Edwardian Politics: Turbulent Spring or Indian Summer?" in O'Day, *The Edwardian Age*, 73. A sense of platform arguments can be gleaned from E. Ashton Bagley, *Question Time: Being a Series of Answers to Questions Asked at Indoor and Outdoor Tariff Reform and Unionist Meetings*, published by the league in December 1909. Bagley was a Unionist candidate for Leicester.

45. Murray, *The People's Budget*, 209–10; Ramsden, *Age of Balfour and Baldwin*, 28–33.

46. Peter Clarke, "The Edwardians and the Constitution," in Donald Read, ed., *Edwardian England* (London, 1982), 40–55. A full account, based on an awesome mastery of the sources, is to be found in Blewett, *The Peers, the Parties, and the People*, 68–102.

47. Milner to Roberts (copy), 24 November 1909, Milner MSS 15, fol. 188.

48. Quoted in Morris, *The Scaremongers*, 213. See also Blewett, *The Peers, the Parties, and the People*, 125–28; Marder, *From the Dreadnought to Scapa Flow*, 1: 156–59.

49. Gwynne to Sandars, 30 March 1909, Balfour MSS 49797, fols. 89–90.

50. Quoted in Gollin, *The Observer and J. L. Garvin*, 129–30.

51. *The Navy* (December 1909).

52. A complete list was published in *The Navy* (February 1910), 41–42. The six

Liberals were Lord Clonmell (Rugby), F. Coysh (Kindswinford), George Greenwood (Peterborough), G. Jackson (Handsworth), Sir George Kemp (Manchester NW), and Colonel Ivor Phillips (Southampton).

53. Ibid., 42.

54. Ibid. (January 1910).

55. Ibid.

56. Navy League executive minutes, 2 November 1896.

57. By 1906 the two leagues were even being confused with each other in rural districts. *Navy League Journal* (July 1906).

58. Nunburnholme to McKenna, 7 April 1909, McKenna MSS 3/14/18.

59. McKenna to Nunburnholme (copy), 20 April 1909, McKenna MSS 3/14/18 (2). On at least one occasion Balfour examined Navy League posters relayed to him by Admiral Fisher. Fisher to Balfour, 3 January 1908, Balfour MSS 49712, fols. 30–31. The Unionist party leader also declined an invitation to join the Navy League, although he expressed sympathy with its aims and appreciation of its work. Balfour to Field (copy), 6 March 1908, Balfour MSS 49859, fols. 233–34.

60. *Standard*, 4 January 1910.

61. Quoted in Morris, *The Scaremongers*, 227.

62. Goulding's various notes for speeches (n.d.), Wargrave MSS A 3/6/2. Ironically, the Irish-born Goulding was nicknamed "Paddy."

63. Croft, *My Life of Strife*, 41–42.

64. Quoted in Peter Bull, *Bulls in the Meadows* (London, 1957), 26. "The Meadows" was the family home in Uxbridge Road.

65. *Evening Standard*, 29 September 1909; *Liberty* (March 1911).

66. "Duello With Fists," *Daily Telegraph*, 7 January 1910; *Illustrated London News*, 15 January 1910. Both references are from cuttings in Bull Collection H 920, BUL HAM 2086.

67. See, for examples, the references to rowdiness at Victoria Park and Finsbury Park in *The Anti-Socialist* (August 1909) or the hospitalization of a borough organizer (Mr. Gauld) after a beating during the Dumfries by-election. Brown, "The Anti-Socialist Union," 248.

68. *Liberty* (November 1910).

69. *The Anti-Socialist* (April 1909).

70. Ibid. (March 1910).

71. Ibid. (January 1910).

72. Herbert Wrigley Wilson, "What Capitalism Has Done for the Worker" (Anti-Socialist Union [ASU] pamphlet No. 4).

73. "Success Without Socialism" (ASU pamphlet No. 76).

74. "Tampering With the Army and Navy" (ASU pamphlet No. 22). Similar points were advanced in the Union's *Speaker's Handbook* (1911), 12–15.

75. One qualified for the franchise by meeting requirements of property and residential stability. It was commonly assumed that the more mobile elements of the population were working class and that the earlier in a calendar year an election was held, the larger the proportion of these individuals who would still be eligible to vote. Given that such workers probably voted Liberal (this was the assumption of contemporaries), the Asquith ministry would be well advised to delay polling from December 1909 until January 1910. The same assumptions inform Blewett, "The Franchise," and the important article by H. C. G. Matthew, R. McKibbin, and J. Kay, "The Franchise Factor in the Rise of the Labour Party," *English Historical Review* 91 (1976): 723–52.

They have since been refined by Duncan Tanner, "The Parliamentary Electoral System, the 'Fourth' Reform Act and the Rise of Labour in England and Wales," *Bulletin of the Institute of Historical Research* 56 (1983): 205–19.

76. Blewett, *The Peers, the Parties, and the People*, 377–415.

77. *Tariff Reform League Annual Report* (1913), 8.

78. *The Times*, 12 January 1910.

79. "Short Account of Work Done by the Union," supplement to *The Anti-Socialist* (March 1910). All quotations are drawn from this source.

80. *Monthly Notes on Tariff Reform* (February 1910), 126–27.

81. *The Anti-Socialist* (March 1910); *The Times*, 16 April 1910.

82. Murray, *The People's Budget*, passim.

83. Salisbury to Austen Chamberlain (copy), 1 February 1910, Austen Chamberlain MSS AC 8/5/5.

84. Austen Chamberlain to Balfour, 29 January 1910, Balfour MSS 49736, fols. 63–65.

85. Quoted in Blewett, *The Peers, the Parties, and the People*, 160.

86. Austen Chamberlain to Balfour, 29 January 1910, Balfour MSS 49736, fols. 63–65; Salisbury to Austen Chamberlain, 2 February 1910, Austen Chamberlain MSS AC 8/5/6.

87. Circular of 2 December 1910, Walter Long MSS 947/450/4.

88. Parker-Smith to Balfour, 28 January 1907, Balfour MSS 49859, fols. 131–36; Hugh Elliot to Austen Chamberlain, 5 August 1910, Austen Chamberlain MSS AC 8/6/7.

89. Lancashire's pivotal position as the "cockpit" of late Victorian and Edwardian elections is emphasized throughout Clarke's *Lancashire and the New Liberalism*.

90. Salisbury to Austen Chamberlain, 2 February 1910, Austen Chamberlain MSS AC 8/5/6.

91. Ware to Austen Chamberlain, 25 January 1910, Austen Chamberlain MSS AC 8/3/12.

92. Blewett, *Peers, the Parties, and the People*, 161. Milner summarized the dilemma, noting that "it is indisputable that we could have carried tariff reform before now, and could carry it tomorrow, without the food taxes. But we won't drop them because they give us the only real chance of asserting the principle of preference." Milner to Willison (copy), 8 May 1910, Milner MSS 37, fols. 5–7. To Milner, national regeneration was inconceivable without the greater imperial unity that preference would promote.

93. Cecil to Northcliffe (copy), 3 August 1909, Robert Cecil MSS 51159, fols. 224–33.

94. John D. Fair, *British Interparty Conferences* (Oxford, 1980), 77–102.

95. Robert J. Scally, *The Origins of the Lloyd George Coalition: The Politics of Social Imperialism 1900–1918* (Princeton, 1975) is an unreliable work that persistently exaggerates the extent of prewar sentiment in favor of coalition government.

96. Balfour likened dealing with the Irish to "eating dirt." Blewett, *The Peers, the Parties, and the People*, 161.

97. The phrase is Peter Clarke's in *Lancashire and the New Liberalism*, 343.

98. Austen Chamberlain to Balfour (copy), 23 September 1910, Austen Chamberlain MSS AC 8/6/16. Even Austen had to admit being "flooded with letters from 'ardent' but wobbly Tariff Reformers begging us to play hankypanky somehow with the Food Taxes," a tide that emanated above all from the north. It was "in the cotton districts of Lancashire [that] the cause of Tariff Reform has not yet achieved the victory

it deserves," observed the Tariff Reform League, attributing the lack of progress to undue Irish influence and to it having been "industriously dinned into Lancashire ears that Tariff Reform will raise the cost of food and diminish the amount of employment." Thus even whole-hoggers linked food taxes and disappointing electoral performance in pivotal Lancashire, even if they left it to others to draw the obvious conclusion, that the latter would improve only in direct relation to the reduction of the former. Chamberlain, *Politics From Inside*, 300; *Monthly Notes on Tariff Reform* (March 1910), 237.

99. Blewett, *The Peers, the Parties, and the People*, 178–88; Clarke, *Lancashire and the New Liberalism*, 297–298; Gollin, *The Observer and J. L. Garvin*, 258ff.; Bonar Law to Balfour (copy), 26 November 1910, Bonar Law MSS 18/8/14; Bonar Law to Balfour (copy), 29 November 1910, Bonar Law MSS 18/8/15.

100. *The Times*, 30 November 1910.

101. Ibid.

102. See Maxse's remarks in *National Review* (November 1910), 367–69; Lansdowne to Willoughby de Broke, 11 October 1910, Willoughby de Broke MSS WB/1/8.

103. Ashley to Sandars, 4 May 1910, J. S. Sandars MSS c. 760, fols. 131–32.

104. Ashley to Sandars, 28 August 1910, J. S. Sandars MSS c. 760, fols. 284–85.

105. Horton-Smith to Blumenfeld, 30 August 1910, Blumenfeld MSS HORT 1; "The Peril Involved to the Empire by the Continued Existence of the Navy League," pamphlet of December 1910, Imperial Maritime League documents, vol. 2; T. C. Knox to Maxse, 11 October 1909, Maxse MSS 460, fols. 420–21.

106. Wyatt and Horton-Smith, *Keep the Flag Flying*, 51.

107. Circular of 6 July 1909, Imperial Maritime League documents, vol. 1. The league later claimed to have collected 140,203 signatures.

108. Wyatt and Horton-Smith, *Keep the Flag Flying*, 45.

109. Ibid., 46.

110. Election poster, March 1909, Imperial Maritime League documents, vol. 1.

111. Wyatt and Horton-Smith, *Keep the Flag Flying*, 65–66.

112. Bagley to Ridley, 23 November 1910, Blagdon MSS ZRI 25/99.

113. *The Times*, 25 November 1910; Bagley to Ridley, 26 November 1910, Blagdon MSS ZRI 25/99; Ridley to Weardale (copy), 27 November 1910, Blagdon MSS ZRI 25/99.

114. Weardale to Ridley, 30 November 1910, Blagdon MSS ZRI 25/99.

115. Ridley to Austen Chamberlain, 12 December 1910, Austen Chamberlain MSS AC 8/7/25.

116. Ridley to Austen Chamberlain, 16 December 1910, Austen Chamberlain MSS AC 8/7/26.

117. Ridley to Bonar Law, 27 December 1910, Bonar Law MSS 18/6/150.

118. Maxse to Goulding, 19 December 1910, Wargrave MSS A/3/2.

119. Maxse to Goulding, 10 December 1910, Wargrave MSS A/3/2.

120. See the references in note 3 to the Introduction.

Chapter 5

1. Rowland Hunt to Willoughby de Broke, 14 August 1911, Willoughby de Broke MSS WB/3/34; Sykes, *Tariff Reform*, 245ff.; Selborne to Wyndham (copy), 22 August 1911, Selborne MSS 74, fols. 190–93; Phillips, *The Diehards*, 142–47; Peter Fraser, "The Unionist Debacle of 1911 and Balfour's Retirement," *Journal of Modern History*, 35 (1963): 354–65.

2. See Phillips, *The Diehards*, passim; Sykes, "Radical Right."

3. *Standard*, 22 October 1908; Navy League executive minutes, 5 July 1912; *The Navy* (November 1913).

4. *Navy League Annual Report* (1912), 79–81.

5. Figures are drawn from the corresponding issues of *The Navy* and, in the case of Birmingham, also from *Navy League Annual Report* (1912), 48–50.

6. "The National Need for a Reformed Navy League," memorandum dated January 1911, by "Reformer," Arnold White MSS WHI/136.

7. Ibid.

8. Bellairs to Maxse, 2 February 1910, Maxse MSS 461, fols. 569–70.

9. Arthur Griffith-Boscawen, *Fourteen Years in Parliament* (London, 1907), 135.

10. Clarke, *Lancashire and the New Liberalism*, 290.

11. E. Ashton Bagley to Bonar Law, 23 December 1912, Bonar Law MSS 28/1/81; Yerburgh to Long, 26 December 1912, Walter Long MSS 947/446/24.

12. White to Hannon, 28 December 1916, Hannon MSS 2/3. Yerburgh was temporarily detained in Germany as a British citizen after the outbreak of the First World War, but so low was his profile that Hannon presumed the Germans would be unaware of his role as Navy League president! Hannon to Walter Page (copy), 29 September 1914, Hannon MSS 2/1.

13. "The National Need for a Reformed Navy League."

14. Ibid.

15. W. H. Williams to Hannon, 22 December 1910, and Testimonial to Hannon, 25 February 1911, Hannon MSS 5/1.

16. *Navy League Annual Report* (1912), 41; *Navy League Annual Report* (1911), 51.

17. Fisher to Winston Churchill, 30 December 1911, cited in the companion volume to Randolph Churchill, *Winston S. Churchill* (London, 1969), vol. 2, 1366.

18. *Navy League Annual Report* (1911), 23.

19. Ampthill to Hewitt, 12 April 1911, Hannon MSS 2/1.

20. *The Navy* (March 1914). I am most grateful to J. W. Sloan Allison, Secretary of the Glasgow branch of the Sea Cadet Association (as the Navy League has been renamed) for sending me a photocopy of the list, which I then checked against various Glasgow directories and W. S. Murphy, *Captains of Industry* (Glasgow, 1901). Concerning the view of a businessman from Liverpool that fellow businessmen had little to gain from any association with the Navy League, see the correspondence by "Lancastrian" in the *Journal of Commerce*, 25 October 1910, 26 November 1910, 4 January 1911.

21. *Navy League Annual Report* (1911), 11; *Navy League Annual Report* (1912), 11–12; *Navy League Annual Report* (1913), 11.

22. *The Navy* (July 1913), 189.

23. Ibid.

24. Navy League executive minutes, 20 September 1911.

25. *The Navy* (August 1913), 225.

26. Ibid. All quotations in the following paragraph are also drawn from this source. For the political sympathies and associational activities of English clerks, see Richard Price, "Society, Status and Jingoism: The Social Roots of Lower Middle Class Patriotism, 1870–1900," in Geoffrey Crossick, ed., *The Lower Middle Class in Britain 1870–1914* (London, 1977), 89–112; Gregory Anderson, *Victorian Clerks* (Manchester, 1976), 74–88.

27. *Navy League Annual Report* (1911), 22; *Navy League Annual Report* (1913).

In 1912 the league decided to appeal to "rich men" for further financial support. Navy League executive minutes, 9 October 1912.

28. *Standard*, 10 February 1913; Navy League executive minutes, 2 March 1911, 16 July 1913; Navy League general purposes committee minutes, 6 December 1911.

29. *Bristol Times and Mirror*, 4 March 1913.

30. Clipping of 15 March 1913, "Imperial Maritime League documents," vol. 5.

31. Horton-Smith to Morrison (copy), 18 March 1913, "Imperial Maritime League documents," vol. 5.

32. Circular dated 10 January 1913, "Imperial Maritime League documents," vol. 5.

33. Wyatt and Horton-Smith, *Keep the Flag Flying*, 78–79.

34. O. L. Mathias to branch secretaries (copy), 16 July 1914, "Imperial Maritime League documents," vol. 6.

35. Circular dated October 1913, "Imperial Maritime League documents," vol. 5.

36. For example, Croft informed Bonar Law that the reveille movement had "unanimously decided to bank fires and funds and to cease independent action in the country . . . as a mark of our esteem and confidence in yourself." Croft to Bonar Law, 30 November 1911, Bonar Law MSS 24/4/92. Similar confidence was expressed by the Tariff Reform League. Ridley to Bonar Law, 12 November 1911, Bonar Law MSS 24/3/20.

37. Tariff Reform League cash book, Tariff Commission MSS TC 11/2/1.

38. Ridley to Bonar Law, 27 December 1910, Bonar Law MSS 18/6/150.

39. Chamberlain, *Politics From Inside*, 366.

40. Tariff Commission Balance Sheets, Tariff Commission MSS TC 9/1/7. Already in 1909 the Commission's treasurer was "afraid our resources will be at an end shortly, if I cannot obtain further support." W. Burbridge to John W. Dennis (copy), 25 November 1909, Tariff Commission MSS TC 6/1/3.

41. T. W. A. Bagley to Bonar Law, 9 October 1911, Bonar Law MSS 18/7/196.

42. *Monthly Notes*, November 1911, 263; *Morning Post*, 12, 13 October 1911. As early as December 1910, in the wake of Balfour's referendum pledge, Ridley had broached the issue to Austen Chamberlain: "There is also the question of the publication of our funds. I should like the committee seriously to consider the question of how far we could do so." Ridley to Chamberlain, 12 December 1910, Austen Chamberlain MSS AC 8/7/25.

43. *Monthly Notes*, November 1911, 263–65.

44. George Wyndham to Joseph Chamberlain, 31 July 1912, Joseph Chamberlain MSS JC 22/152; circular dated 10 September 1912, Lord Robert Cecil MSS 51160, fols. 177–86. The most generous donor was the Duke of Bedford, giving £5,000.

45. Lord Bayford diary, 13 October 1912.

46. Lawrence to Maxse, 14 June 1912, Maxse MSS 466, fols. 97–98.

47. *Tariff Reform League Annual Report* (1912), 144.

48. Ibid., 91.

49. Ibid., 96.

50. Ibid., 92–93.

51. Amery to Ridley, 21 October 1910, Blagdon MSS ZRI 25/99.

52. Amery to Steel-Maitland, 5 March 1909, Steel-Maitland MSS GD 193/141/1–2.

53. Long to Bonar Law, n.d., Bonar Law MSS 26/1/76.

54. H. S. Stavely-Hill to Long, 25 November 1912, Walter Long MSS 947/446/1.

55. Canon Edward Rees to Chamberlain, 13 December 1912, Austen Chamberlain

MSS AC 10/3/46; Lord Galway to Chamberlain, 5 January 1913, Austen Chamberlain MSS AC 9/5/25.

56. Croft to Max Aitken, 29 October 1912, Beaverbrook MSS BBK C/101.

57. Long to Bonar Law, March 1912, Bonar Law MSS 26/1/76. In October 1912 the Tariff Reform League elected to suspend the formation of new branches in the West Riding. Tariff Reform League executive minutes, 15 October 1912, Tariff Commission MSS TC 11/1/1.

58. *Yorkshire Post*, 7 September 1912.

59. Ibid.

60. Long to Bonar Law, enclosing memorandum of 29 February 1912, Bonar Law MSS 26/1/76. Tom Smith stood twice as a Unionist workingman's candidate, but without success. Clarke, *Lancashire and the New Liberalism*, 302.

61. T. W. A. Bagley to Bonar Law, 8 October 1912, Bonar Law MSS 27/3/18.

62. Arbuthnot to Sandars, 26 July 1909, Sandars MSS c. 759, fols. 42–44.

63. Arbuthnot to Bonar Law, 16 August 1912, Bonar Law MSS 27/1/41.

64. Bonar Law to Chaplin (copy), 31 December 1912, Bonar Law MSS 33/4/86.

65. Ibid.

66. Ibid.

67. This final act in the tariff reform drama is discussed in greater detail in Sykes, *Tariff Reform*, 258–84; Clarke, *Lancashire and the New Liberalism*, 305–8; Ramsden, *Age of Balfour and Baldwin*, 75ff.; Robert Blake, *The Unknown Prime Minister: The Life and Times of Andrew Bonar Law, 1858–1923* (London, 1955), 105–18.

68. *Tariff Reform League Annual Report* (1913), 87–88.

69. Ibid., 83.

70. For example, Bootle (1911) or Altrincham (1913). T. W. A. Bagley to Bonar Law, 31 March 1911, Bonar Law MSS 18/7/165; Tariff Reform League executive minutes, 10 June 1913, Tariff Commission MSS TC 11/1/1; George Hamilton to Duncannon (copy), 31 May 1913, enclosed in Duncannon to Bonar Law, 6 June 1913, Bonar Law MSS 29/5/11. Viscount Duncannon succeeded Goulding as chairman of the league's influential organization committee.

71. Lawrence to Chamberlain, 5 January 1913, Austen Chamberlain MSS AC 9/5/49. The young secretary, E. Ashton Bagley, was, nonetheless, in his estimation, "a veritable Moltke." Lawrence to Long, 22 December 1910, Walter Long MSS 947/445/9.

72. Ridley to Chamberlain, 29 December 1912, Austen Chamberlain MSS AC 10/3/48.

73. Ridley to Chamberlain, 2 January 1913, Austen Chamberlain MSS AC 9/5/72.

74. Ridley to Chamberlain, 21 January 1913, Austen Chamberlain MSS AC 9/5/73.

75. Pelling, *Social Geography*, 276–77; *The Times*, 14 March 1913.

76. *The Times*, 8 March 1913.

77. Sykes, "The Confederacy," 353–54; Bentinck to Duke of Portland (copy), 11 October 1908, enclosed in Portland to Balfour (copy), 20 October 1907, Balfour MSS 49737, fols. 38–40.

78. Chamberlain, *Politics From Inside*, 532.

79. *The Times*, 15–20 March 1913.

80. *The Times*, 20 March 1913.

81. *Tariff Reform League Annual Report* (1912), 14. The report for 1912 was not adopted until the league's annual meeting in March 1913.

82. Ibid.

83. Ibid., 24.

84. Ibid., 25–26.

85. Ibid., 40–41.

86. Ibid., 52, 55.

87. Ibid., 48.

88. Ibid.

89. Thomas Cox, secretary of the National Union, ensured that party officials conferred "with the Tariff Reform League in regard to the production of leaflets dealing with tariff reform," and Steel-Maitland later confirmed this arrangement, which had been undertaken "in order to prevent unnecessary overlapping." Likewise the tariff section of the party's 1909 *Campaign Guide* was prepared with the league's assistance. Cox to Steel-Maitland, 23 March 1910, Steel-Maitland MSS GD 193/147/2/7; Steel-Maitland to Cecil, 17 April 1912, Lord Robert Cecil MSS 51071, fols. 77–78. An example of branch fusion occurred at Bexhill. *Morning Post*, 14 January 1909.

90. Amery, *My Political Life*, 1: 255.

91. Ibid., 254–55.

92. Croft to Bonar Law, 8 November 1913, Bonar Law MSS 30/4/17.

93. This issue has been the subject of considerable historical debate. Some of the key contributions include Ross McKibbin, *The Evolution of the Labour Party, 1910–1924* (Oxford, 1974); Clarke, *Lancashire and the New Liberalism*, especially 311–39; idem, "The Electoral Position of the Liberal and Labour Parties 1910–1914," *English Historical Review* 90 (1975): 828–36; Martin Pugh, *The Making of Modern British Politics 1867–1939* (Oxford, 1982), 111–57; George L. Bernstein, "Liberalism and the Progressive Alliance in the Constituencies, 1900–1914: Three Case Studies," *Historical Journal* 26 (1983): 617–40; idem, *Liberalism and Liberal Politics in Edwardian England* (London, 1986); Blewett, *The Peers, the Parties, and the People*, 234–65, 391–95.

94. Wolmer to Steel-Maitland, 29 January 1910, Steel-Maitland MSS GD 193/147/8/43. Official Unionist support for working-class candidacies was reluctant at best. Blewett, *The Peers, the Parties, and the People*, 272; Ramsden, *Age of Balfour and Baldwin*, 104–5.

95. Some speakers were quite effective and "gave great satisfaction." Sandars to Acland-Hood (copy), 4 May 1910, Sandars MSS c. 760, fols. 125–27.

96. *Liberty*, 7 June 1911, 2 August 1911, 6 December 1911.

97. *The Times*, 25 October 1909; *The Anti-Socialist*, November 1909, 118.

98. *The Times*, 19 November 1909, 2 March 1910.

99. *Liberty*, May 1910.

100. *Liberty*, March 1911, 45.

101. Ibid., 55.

102. *Liberty*, August 1910, 55. A. E. Beck, a Unionist candidate for Derby, claimed in July 1910 that "between sixty and seventy branches of the Union" had recently been founded in Warwickshire, Worcestershire, Staffordshire and Derbyshire, each "representing active operations." Most likely, though, these branches were strongest on paper.

103. Lowther to Blumenfeld, 7 September 1909, Blumenfeld MSS LOWT 1.

104. *Liberty*, August 1910.

105. *Anti-Socialist Union Speakers' Handbook* (1911). Many of the union's activists tended to be younger men, like Lowther, Wilfrid Ashley, or Harman Grisewood, the secretary, whose "loathing for the Liberals was ferocious and exuberant." Harman Grisewood [the secretary's son], *One Thing at a Time: An Autobiography* (London, 1968), 10–11. I am grateful to Mr. Grisewood for informing me that none of his father's papers has survived. The union also encouraged the formation of an affiliated Noncon-

formist Anti-Socialist Union (headed by Reverend George Freeman), an Education branch (which attracted some 900 teachers), and a Civil Service Anti-Socialist League. *The Anti-Socialist*, September 1909; *The Times*, 13 August 1910; *Liberty*, January 1910; C. W. Spiller to Arnold White, 12 September 1910, Arnold White MSS WHI/34. Spiller, the secretary of the Civil Service Socialist Society, estimated his organization's membership at 1,500. The Anti-Socialist Union also maintained a Women's Auxiliary, which first met on 2 December 1909 under the auspices of the Primrose League, and trained some 260 female speakers by July 1910. On the impact of female participation in the Primrose League, see Pugh, *The Tories and the People*, 43–69; Linda Walker, "Party Political Women: A Comparative Study of Liberal Women and the Primrose League, 1890–1914," in Jane Rendall, ed., *Equal or Different: Women's Politics 1800–1914* (Oxford, 1987), 165–91.

106. Memorandum of December 1911?, Steel-Maitland MSS GD 193/108/3/ 47–61.

107. The underlying motive was expressed by Bonar Law, who wrote that "in the troubles ahead of us connected with labour we are moving very fast in the direction of revolution; and though I am sure you will consider my hope a baseless one, I still entertain it—that it is by means of Tariff Reform that we might, so to speak, get the train for a time at least shifted onto other lines. . . ." Bonar Law to Salisbury (copy), 3 May 1912, Bonar Law MSS 33/4/34.

108. *The Campaign Guide 1914*, vi.

109. *The Navy* (February 1915); *Navy League Annual Report* (1915), 18, 29; Anti-Socialist Union leaflets, dated 1915, Mount Temple MSS 27M60/BR 81; pamphlet of October 1915, "Imperial Maritime League Documents," vol. 7. For example, the Imperial Maritime League claimed that its efforts with the Navy League had attracted up to 130,000 new recruits, while, on the local level, the women of the Navy League's Richmond branch sewed 210 garments for British destroyer crews by May 1916.

110. *Navy League Annual Report* (1914), 79.

111. *Navy League Annual Report* (1915), 18. See also Nicholas Hiley, "Counter-Espionage and Security in Great Britain During the First World War," *English Historical Review*, 101 (1986): 635–70; G. R. Searle, *Corruption in British Politics, 1895–1930* (Oxford, 1987), 241ff.

112. *Navy League Annual Report* (1915), 13; Navy League executive minutes, 15 February 1917, 21 June 1917, 5 July 1917, 9 May 1918. Likewise, the Imperial Maritime League's posters drew a sharp rebuke from the secretary of the National Transport Workers' Federation, who complained that

> There are two suggestive illustrations in the advertisement—one of a silent factory, and the other of a battery silent presumably from want of ammunition. The former illustration is intended to convey that the guns are silent because the workers who should be making shells are on strike. Later in your advertisement it is suggested that the workers of this country are being used to serve the purposes of agents of the German government.

The secretary, Robert Williams, challenged league president Willoughby de Broke to produce any evidence in support of this startling and offensive accusation. *Daily News and Leader*, 15 June 1915, cutting in "Imperial Maritime League Documents," vol. 7.

113. Hannon claimed to have evidence that efforts were underway "to form local committees of soldiers and workmen after the Russian model, and that labour unrest, especially in the Tyne area, is being exploited by pacifists and I. L. P. [Independent Labour party] propagandists with the object of bringing about a limitation of output of

war material." Hannon believed that if £5,000 was secretly placed at the league's disposal, it could "render most valuable service to the Government. . . . [and] counteract the activities of the peacemongers and anti-war plotters. . . ." Hannon to Winston Churchill (copy), 24 July 1917, Mount Temple MSS 27M60/BR 82. For the Tariff Reform League's campaign, see *Tariff Reformer and Empire Monthly* (June 1917).

114. *War Notes for Members*, 15, 30 September 1915; *Tariff Reformer and Empire Monthly* (May 1918), 81–82.

115. Biscoe Tritton to Hannon, 21 February 1917, Hannon MSS 2/3.

116. *Navy League Annual Report* (1917), 36; Hannon to Yerburgh (copy), 21 November 1916, Hannon MSS 2/3; Tariff Reform League special committee minutes, 18 February 1919, Tariff Commission MSS TC 11/1/2.

117. Navy League executive minutes, 15 May 1919. Fulham's branch, for example, formerly quite active, held no meetings during 1916, while the Slindon branch met only once between September 1914 and October 1922. Arnold White found one meeting at Dulwich fruitless and, at Eastbourne, felt "humiliated by the fact that there was no audience to hear me." *The Navy* (February 1917); Slindon branch minute book, West Sussex Record Office Add. MSS 13449; White to Hannon, 19 June 1916, Hannon MSS 5/2. The Tariff Reform League appealed during the war to the Unionist party for financial support, but without success, and, by the conflict's end, "the old TRL was derelict." Austen Chamberlain to Croft, 24 October 1917, Croft MSS CH/7; Amery, *My Political Life*, vol. 2, 291.

118. John Stubbs, "The Impact of the Great War on the Conservative Party," in Chris Cook and Gillian Peele, eds. *The Politics of Reappraisal 1918–1939* (New York, 1975), 14–38; John Turner, "The British Commonwealth Union and the General Election of 1918," *English Historical Review* 93 (1978): 528–59; W. D. Rubinstein, "Henry Page Croft and the National Party, 1917–22," *Journal of Contemporary History* 9 (1974): 129–48; C. J. Wrigley, "In the Excess of Their Patriotism: The National Party and Threats of Subversion," in Wrigley, ed., *Warfare, Diplomacy and Politics: Essays in Honour of A. J. P. Taylor* (London, 1986), 93–119. See also the essays in John Turner, ed., *Businessmen and Politics* (London, 1984), and R. P. T. Davenport-Hines, *Dudley Docker* (Cambridge, 1984).

Conclusion

1. Many of these works are discussed in John D. Fair and John A. Hutcheson, Jr., "British Conservatism in the Twentieth Century: An Emerging Ideological Tradition," *Albion* 19 (1987): 549–78.

2. Austen Chamberlain to Steel-Maitland, 10 October 1907, Steel-Maitland MSS GD 193/134/119.

3. W. H. Mallock, *Memoirs of Life and Literature* (London, 1920), 254. Mallock responded that clouds, "when taken together, make not clouds, but lightning."

4. Hewins, *Apologia of an Imperialist*, vol. 1, 163; Willoughby de Broke, *The Passing Years* (London, 1924), 182; Maxse to Bonar Law, 11 November 1911, Bonar Law MSS 24/3/9.

5. Willoughby de Broke, *The Passing Years*, 182.

6. Maxse to Bonar Law, 11 November 1911, Bonar Law MSS 24/3/9.

7. Balfour to Long (copy), 2 June 1911, Balfour MSS 49777, fols. 99–103. Likewise, Alan Burgoyne stressed the role of fellow young men in movements like the reveille. Burgoyne to Long, 10 January 1911, Walter Long MSS 947/445/12. See also

Jane Ridley, "The Unionist Social Reform Committee, 1911–1914: Wets Before the Deluge," *Historical Journal* 30 (1987): 391–413, especially 392.

8. Leo Amery was a persistent critic on this score, including his classic denunciation of Acland-Hood that until "he is poisoned or pensioned, we shall not get a step forward." Amery to Bonar Law, 16 December 1910, Bonar Law MSS 18/6/146; Amery to Sandars, 31 January 1911, Balfour MSS 49775, fols. 149–60. Many of Amery's charges were confirmed by Steel-Maitland in his memorandum for Bonar Law, Steel-Maitland MSS GD 193/108/3/47–61. See also Blewett, *The Peers, the Parties, and the People*, 266–76; Ramsden, *Age of Balfour and Baldwin*, 46, 58ff. This attitude, I believe, marks off the nationalistic associations from the Primrose League, whose archaic trappings, deference to traditional hierarchy, and established issues all make it rather more difficult to regard that league as having been devoted to transforming the style and substance of Unionist politics. The rhetoric of democratization, efficiency, and so forth does, however, sound similar to the assault on *Honoratiorenpolitik* advertised by the nationalist pressure groups of Wilhelmine Germany. I have deliberately excluded any comparative study of the topic here, but interested readers may turn to Geoff Eley's massive *Reshaping the German Right* (New Haven, 1980) and the subsequent revision of his arguments by Roger Chickering's *We Men Who Feel Most German* (London, 1984) and Marilyn Shevin Coetzee's "The Mobilization of the Right? The Deutscher Wehrverein and Political Activism in Württemberg, 1912–1914," *European History Quarterly* 15 (1985): 431–52 and *The Germany Army League: Popular Nationalism in Wilhelmine Germany* (Oxford, 1990), as well as our joint article, "Rethinking the Radical Right in Germany and Britain Before 1914," *Journal of Contemporary History* 21 (1986): 515–73.

9. Lawrence to Balfour, 13 June 1908, Balfour MSS 49791, fols. 246–49. It is possible that the proliferation of nationalist leagues owed something to the inclusion in Unionist/Liberal Unionist ranks of former Liberals, who brought with them the characteristically Liberal habit of forming voluntary associations. One might also consider whether the leagues acted as harbingers of the new group politics and "corporate bias" of postwar Britain. This argument, however, would seem to be on firmer ground with regard to the British Commonwealth Union or the Unionist Business Committee.

10. *Toryism: A Political Dialogue*, 5.

11. Ibid., 10–11.

12. Lawrence to Long, 22 December 1910, Walter Long MSS 947/444/9.

13. Paul Smith, *Disraelian Conservatism and Social Reform* (London, 1967).

14. The Navy League was wracked by further dissension in 1921–1922 over whether to accept British parity with the United States Navy at the Washington Naval Conference, and it eventually opted to concentrate solely upon educational work as the Sea Cadet Association. The Tariff Reform League was wound up in 1922, only to be succeeded by the Empire Development Union. The Anti-Socialist Union was not dissolved until the Attlee government in 1949, by which time its independent efforts were clearly ineffectual.

15. See Fair and Hutcheson, "British Conservatism in the Twentieth Century."

16. Cecil to Northcliffe (copy), 3 August 1909, Lord Robert Cecil MSS 51159, fols. 224–33.

17. Feiling, *Toryism*, 99.

18. Lord Bayford diary, 15 November 1911.

19. For example, Salvidge to Long, 23 December 1912, Walter Long MSS 947/446/5; Lawrence to Balfour, 6 November 1907, Balfour MSS 49791, fols. 226–29; Aitken to Rev. F. H. Burrows (copy), 17 December 1912, Beaverbrook MSS BBK B/

39. This also seemed to be one of the lessons of the abortive constitutional conference of 1910.

20. See John D. Fair, "From Liberal to Conservative: The Flight of the Liberal Unionists After 1886," *Victorian Studies* 29 (1986): 291–314; Hugh Berrington, "Partisanship and Dissidence in the Nineteenth-Century House of Commons," *Parliamentary Affairs* 21 (1967–1968): 338–74.

21. Steel-Maitland memorandum, n.d. (December 1911), Steel-Maitland MSS GD 193/108/3/47–61.

22. Ibid.

23. In addition to the works cited in note 3 of the Introduction, the following are of particular significance: G. R. Searle, "Critics of Edwardian Society: The Case of the Radical Right," in O'Day, ed., *The Edwardian Age*, 79–96; idem, "The 'Revolt From the Right' in Edwardian Britain," in Kennedy and Nicholls, eds., *Nationalist and Racialist Movements*, 21–39; Alan Sykes, "The Radical Right and the Crisis of Conservatism Before the First World War," *Historical Journal* 26 (1983): 661–76; Kennedy, *Rise of the Anglo-Germany Antagonism*, 361–85; idem, "The Pre-War Right in Britain and Germany," in Kennedy and Nicholls, *Nationalist and Racialist Movements*, 1–20.

24. J. H. Grainger's *Patriotisms: Britain 1900–1939* (London, 1986) is instructive in this regard.

Bibliography

Archival Sources

Birmingham University Library
  Austen Chamberlain MSS
  Joseph Chamberlain MSS

Bodleian Library, Oxford
  Conservative Party Archive
  Lord Milner MSS
  J. S. Sandars MSS
  2nd Earl of Selborne MSS
  3rd Earl of Selborne MSS

British Library, London
  Althorp MSS
  Lord Avebury MSS
  A. J. Balfour MSS
  Lord Robert Cecil MSS
  Herbert Gladstone MSS
  Sir Charles Dilke MSS
  H. O. Arnold-Forster MSS
  Walter Long MSS
  Lord Northcliffe MSS
  C. T. Ritchie MSS
  Imperial Federation League MSS

British Library of Political and Economic Science, London
  Clapham Conservative Association MSS
  Metropolitan Conservative Agents' Association MSS
  Tariff Commission MSS

Christ Church, Oxford
  Geoffrey Drage MSS

Churchill College, Cambridge
  Sir William Bull MSS
  Henry Page Croft MSS
  Reginald McKenna MSS

Conservative Research Department, London
  Lord Bayford Diary
  London Unionist Members Committee, minute book

East Sussex Record Office, Lewes
  Sir John Shiffner MSS

Guildhall Library, London
  London Municipal Society MSS

Hammersmith Public Library
  Sir William Bull MSS

Hampshire Record Office, Winchester
  Lord Mount Temple MSS

House of Lords Record Office, London
  Lord Beaverbrook MSS
  Andrew Bonar Law MSS
  Ralph Blumenfeld MSS
  Sir William Bull MSS
  Patrick Hannon MSS
  J. St. Loe Strachey MSS
  Lord Wargrave MSS
  Lord Willoughby de Broke MSS

Kent Archives Office, Maidstone
  Chilston MSS

National Army Museum, Ogilby Trust
  Spenser Wilkinson MSS

National Maritime Museum, Greenwich
  Leslie Cope-Cornford MSS
  Lionel Horton-Smith MSS
  Geoffrey Phipps-Hornby MSS
  Arnold White MSS

Northumberland Record Office, Newcastle
  Blagdon MSS

Public Record Office, Kew
  Admiralty MSS
  Board of Trade MSS
  Cabinet MSS
  Lord Cromer MSS

Royal Commonwealth Society, London
  Imperial Federation League MSS

Sea Cadet Association, Wimbledon
  Navy League, minute books

Scottish Record Office, Edinburgh
  Arthur Steel-Maitland MSS

Sheffield Central Library
  Sheffield Central Conservative Association, minute books
  Wentworth Woodhouse Muniments

Sheffield University Library
  W. A. S. Hewins MSS

Strathclyde Regional Archives, Glasgow
  James Parker-Smith MSS

West Sussex Record Office, Chichester
  Viscount Bessborough MSS
  Leo Maxse MSS
  Petworth Archives
  Slindon Navy League, minute book

Westminster Public Libraries, Archives Department
  National Society of Conservative Agents, minute books
  Westminster Conservative Association, minute books

Wiltshire Record Office, Trowbridge
  Walter Long MSS

Primary Sources

Books and Articles

Angell, Norman. *"Two Keels to One Not Enough": A Reply to the President of the Navy League*. London: War and Peace Pamphlet No. 4, 1914.
Anti-Socialist Union. Pamphlets and leaflets.
———. Courses of Tuition by Correspondence.
———. *Speaker's Handbook*, 1911.
Ashley, William J. *The Tariff Problem*. London: P. S. King, 1903.
Bagley, E. Ashton. *Question Time: Being a Series of Answers to Questions Asked at Indoor and Outdoor Tariff Reform and Unionist Meetings*. London: Tariff Reform League, 1909.
Bathurst, Charles. *To Avoid National Starvation*. London: Hugh Rees, 1912.
Beadon, Robert. "Why the Imperial Federation League Was Dissolved." *National Review*, February 1894, 814–22.
Bellairs, Carlyon. "The Standard of Strength for Imperial Defence." *Journal of the Royal United Service Institution*, September 1904, 3–31.
———. "The Cobden Club and the Navy." *National Review*, June 1907, 614–26.
Blumenfeld, Ralph D. *Twenty-Five Years Ago 1908–1933: The Record of the Anti-Socialist and Anti-Communist Union*. London: Anti-Socialist Union, n.d.
Boyd, C. W., ed. *Mr. Chamberlain's Speeches*. 2 vols. New York: Houghton-Mifflin, 1914.
Burgoyne, Alan H., ed. *The Navy League Annual*. London: Navy League, 1907–1914.
Caillard, Vincent. "Some Considerations on Imperial Finance." *National Review*, February 1902, 871–95.
———. "Foreign Trade and Home Markets." *National Review*, March 1902, 51–77.
———. "Some Suggestions Towards an Imperial Tariff." *National Review*, April 1902, 209–27.
Cambray, Philip. *Politics Retold 1880–1924*. London: Philip Allan, 1925.
Cecil, Lord Hugh. *Conservatism*. London: Williams & Norgate, 1912.

Clowes, William Laird. "Toulon and the French Navy." *Nineteenth Century*, December 1893, 1023–30.

Cobden Club. *Budget and Tariff Compared*. London, 1909.

Crutchley, W. C. "The Defence of the British Mercantile Marine in Wartime." *Blackwoods' Magazine*, November 1889, 674–84.

Dowding, W. E. *The Tariff Reform Mirage*. London: Methuen, 1913.

Egerton, Hakluyt [Arthur Boutwood]. *Patriotism: An Essay Towards a Constructive Theory of Politics*. London: George Allen, 1905.

Elliott, Walter. *Toryism and the Twentieth Century*. London: Philip Allan, 1927.

Empire Industries Association. *Empire Industries Association and British Empire League: History and Constitution*. London, n.d.

Farrer, J. A. *Liberalism and the National Service League*. London: T. Fisher Unwin, 1911.

Feiling, Keith. *Toryism: A Political Dialogue*. London: C. Bell, 1913.

Gardiner, A. G. *Pillars of Society*. London: James Nisbet, 1913.

Grant, Daniel. *Free Food and Free Trade*. London: T. Fisher Unwin, 1904.

Grisewood, Harman, and Ellis Robbins. *Land and the Politicians*. London: Duckworth, 1914.

Hewins, W. A. S. "Why We Should Concentrate on the Empire." *Nineteenth Century*, November 1922, 720–29.

Hirst, F. W. *The Six Panics and Other Essays*. London: Methuen, 1913.

Hurd, Archibald. "Our Belated Battleships." *Nineteenth Century*, November 1900, 717–29.

———. "The Navy That We Need." *Fortnightly Review*, August 1903, 277–87.

Imperial Federation League. *Annual Report*, London, 1892.

Jane, Fred T. "The Navy—Is All Well?" *Fortnightly Review*, April 1902, 445–57.

Kennedy, J. M. *Tory Democracy*. London: Stephen Swift, 1911.

Low, Sydney. "The Breakdown of Voluntary Enlistment." *Nineteenth Century*, March 1900.

Lucy, Henry W. *The Balfour Parliament 1900–1905*. London: Hodder & Stoughton, 1906.

Mackinder, Halford J. *Britain and the British Seas*. London: Heinemann, 1902.

MacNamara, T. J. *The Political Situation: Letters to a Working Man*. London: Hodder & Stoughton, 1909.

———. *Tariff Reform and the Working Man*. London: Hodder & Stoughton, 1910.

Mahan, Alfred Thayer. *The Influence of Sea Power Upon History, 1660–1783*. Boston: Little, Brown & Co., 1890.

Malmesbury, Lord, ed. *The New Order: Studies in Unionist Policy*. London: Francis Griffiths, 1908.

National Service League. *Annual Report and Balance Sheet*, 1908.

———. Pamphlets and leaflets, 1909–1915.

———. *Hints and Instructions for Honorary Helpers*. 3rd ed., 1910.

Navy League. *Annual Reports*, 1895–1920.

———. *Constitution and Membership*, 1898.

———. Pamphlets and leaflets.

Reynolds, Stephen, Bob Woolley, and Tom Woolley. *Seems So! A Working Class View of Politics*. London: Macmillan, 1911.

Roberts, Lord. *A Nation in Arms*. London: John Murray, 1907.

———. *Fallacies and Facts*. London: John Murray, 1911.

Robertson, J. M. *Patriotism and Empire*. London: Grant Richards, 1899.

Scott, Admiral Percy. *Fifty Years in the Royal Navy*. London: John Murray, 1919.

Shee, George F. *The Briton's First Duty: The Case for Conscription*. London: Grant Richards, 1901.

Smith, F. E. *Unionist Policy and Other Essays*. London: Williams & Norgate, 1913.

Stopford, J. G. B. "The Uses and Limitations of an Army League." *Fortnightly Review*, February 1901.

Tariff Commission. *Reports*. London: P. S. King, 1904–1907.

Tariff Reform League. *Annual Reports*, 1905, 1912–1913.

————. Pamphlets and leaflets, 1905–1921.

————. *The Tariff Reformer's Pocket Book and Vade Mecum*, 1906–1914.

————. *Speaker's Handbook*. 6th ed., 1910.

Union Defence League. *Irish Facts for British Platforms*, 1907–1916.

Unionist Party. *National Union Gleanings*, 1894–1912.

————. Pamphlets and leaflets, 1894–1914.

————. *The Campaign Guide: A Handbook for Unionist Speakers*, 1904, 1909, 1914.

————. *The Unionist Record 1895–1905: A Fighting Brief for Unionist Candidates and Speakers*, 1905.

————. *Gleanings and Memoranda*, 1912–1914.

White, Arnold. "A Message From the Mediterranean." *National Review*, July 1901, 677–89.

————. "Shall the Mediterranean Fleet Remain Unready?" *National Review*, August 1901, 845–54.

————. "The Silent Navy." *National Review*, March 1902, 78–87.

————. "Gunnery vs. Paint." *National Review*, November 1902, 389–96.

————. *Efficiency and Empire*. Brighton: Harvester Press, 1973, reprint.

Wilkinson, Spenser. *The Command of the Sea*. Westminster: Archibald Constable, 1894.

————. "Our Preparations for War," *National Review*, April 1902, 197–208.

————. *Britain at Bay*. New York: G. P. Putnam's Sons, 1909.

Wilkinson, William J. *Tory Democracy*. New York: Columbia University Press, 1925.

Williams, E. E. "The Progress Towards Commercial Union of the Empire." In *The Newspaper Press Directory*. London: C. H. Mitchell & Co., 1904, 16–19.

————. *Made in Germany*. Brighton: Harvester Press, 1973, reprint.

Williamson, A. *British Industries and Foreign Competition*. London: Simpkin, Marshall & Hamilton, 1894.

Willoughby de Broke, Lord. "The Tory Tradition." *National Review*, October 1911, 201–13.

————, ed. *National Revival: A Restatement of Tory Principles*. London: Herbert Jenkins Ltd., 1913.

Wilson, Herbert Wrigley. "The Protection of Our Commerce in War." *Nineteenth Century*, February 1896, 218–35.

————. "Trafalgar and Today." *National Review*, November 1896, 354–69.

————. "Naval Questions of the Day." *Fortnightly Review*, August 1901, 239–48.

————. *Mr. Chamberlain's New Policy*. London: Swan Sonnenschein, 1903.

Worsfold, W. Basil. "The Imperial Federation League 1884–1893." *United Empire*, February 1915, 263–73.

Wyatt, Harold F. "England's Threatened Rights at Sea." *Journal of the Royal United Services Institution*, January 1910, 5–33.

Wyatt, Harold F., and Lionel Horton-Smith. *The Passing of the Great Fleet*. London: Imperial Maritime League, 1909.

————. *Keep the Flag Flying*. London: Imperial Maritime League, 1910.
Yerburgh, Robert A. "National Granaries." *National Review*, April 1896, 197–207.

Journals

The Anti-Socialist
Conservative Agents' Journal
Liberal Magazine
Liberty
Monthly Notes on Tariff Reform
The Nation
The Nation in Arms
National Review
National Service League Journal

The Navy
Navy League Journal
Nineteenth Century
Primrose League Gazette
Quarterly Review
Spectator
Tariff Reform League Notes for Speakers
Tariff Reform League War Notes
Tariff Reformer and Empire Monthly

Newspapers

Bristol Times and Mirror
Daily Express
Daily Mail
Daily Telegraph
Journal of Commerce (Liverpool)
Manchester Courier
Morning Post

Observer
Pall Mall Gazette
Standard
The Times
Western Daily Press (Bristol)
Westminster Gazette
Yorkshire Post (Leeds)

Government Publications and Reference Works

Debrett's House of Commons and Judicial Bench
Directory of Directors
Dod's Parliamentary Companion
Hansard's Parliamentary Debates
Kelly's Directories (various counties)
W. T. Pike's New Century Series (various counties)
Stock Exchange Yearbook
Who's Who

Secondary Sources

Biographies, Memoirs, and Published Letters

Alexander, Eric, 3rd Viscount Chilston. *Chief Whip: The Political Life and Times of Aretas Akers-Douglas, 1st Viscount Chilston*. London: Routledge & Kegan Paul, 1961.
Amery, Leopold S. *My Political Life*. 3 vols. London: Hutchinson, 1953–1955.
Barnes, John, and David Nicholson, eds. *The Leo Amery Diaries*. Vol. 1. London, Hutchinson, 1980.

Beresford, Admiral Lord. *The Memoirs of Admiral Lord Beresford.* 2 vols. London: Methuen, 1914.

Blake, Robert. *The Unknown Prime Minister: The Life and Times of Andrew Bonar Law 1858–1923.* London: Eyre & Spottiswoode, 1955.

Blouet, Brian W. *Sir Halford Mackinder 1861–1947: Some New Perspectives.* Oxford: Oxford University School of Geography, Research Paper No. 13.

Blumenfeld, Ralph D. *R. D. B.'s Diary 1887–1914.* London: William Heinemann, 1930.

Campbell, John. *F. E. Smith: First Earl of Birkenhead.* London: Jonathan Cape, 1983.

Chamberlain, Austen. *Politics From Inside: An Epistolary Chronicle 1906–1914.* New Haven: Yale University Press, 1937.

Channing, Francis. *Memories of Midland Politics 1885–1910.* London: Constable, 1918.

Clarke, Alan, ed. *A Good Innings: The Private Papers of Viscount Lee of Fareham.* London: John Murray, 1974.

Croft, Henry Page. *My Life of Strife.* London: Hutchinson, 1948.

Crutchley, William Caius. *My Life at Sea.* London: Chapman & Hall, 1912.

Dark, Sidney. *The Life of Sir Arthur Pearson.* London: Hodder & Stoughton, 1922.

Davenport-Hines, R. P. T. *Dudley Docker: The Life and Times of a Trade Warrior.* Cambridge: Cambridge University Press, 1984.

Davies, P. N. *Sir Alfred Jones.* London: Europa, 1978.

Dugdale, Blanche. *Arthur James Balfour.* 2 vols. London: Hutchinson, 1936.

Dutton, David. *Austen Chamberlain: Gentleman in Politics.* Bolton: Ross Anderson, 1985.

Egerton, Mrs. F. *Admiral of the Fleet Sir Geoffrey Phipps-Hornby.* London: William Blackwood & Sons, 1896.

Eardley-Wilmot, Sir Sydney. *An Admiral's Memories.* London: Sampson, Low & Marsden, 1927.

Fraser, Peter. *Joseph Chamberlain: Radicalism and Empire, 1868–1914.* London: Cassell & Company, 1966.

Garvin, J. L., and Julian Amery. *The Life of Joseph Chamberlain.* 6 vols. London: Macmillan, 1932–1969.

Gilbert, Bentley B. *David Lloyd George: A Political Life.* Vol. 1. London: Batsford, 1987.

Gollin, Alfred M. *The Observer and J. L. Garvin 1908–1914.* Oxford: Oxford University Press, 1960.

———. *Proconsul in Politics: A Study of Lord Milner in Opposition and in Power.* London: Anthony Blond, 1964.

———. *Balfour's Burden: Arthur Balfour and Imperial Preference.* London: Anthony Blond, 1965.

Gordon, Peter, ed. *The Red Earl: The Papers of the Fifth Earl Spencer.* Vol. 2, 1885–1910. Northamptonshire Record Society, 1986.

Griffith-Boscawen, Arthur. *Fourteen Years in Parliament.* London: John Murray, 1907.

———. *Memories.* London: John Murray, 1925.

Grigg, John. *Lloyd George: The People's Champion.* Berkeley: University of California Press, 1978.

———. *Lloyd George: From Peace to War.* Berkeley: University of California Press, 1985.

Hamilton, Lord George. *Parliamentary Reminiscences and Reflections.* 2 vols. London: John Murray, 1917–1922.

Hewins, W. A. S. *The Apologia of an Imperialist*. 2 vols. London: Constable, 1929.

Hutchinson, Horace. *Life of Sir John Lubbock, Lord Avebury*. 2 vols. London: Macmillan, 1914.

Jay, Richard. *Joseph Chamberlain: A Political Study*. Oxford: Oxford University Press, 1981.

Jeyes, S. H. *The Life of Sir Howard Vincent*. London: George Allen, 1912.

Judd, Denis. *Radical Joe: A Life of Joseph Chamberlain*. London: Hamish Hamilton, 1977.

Kennedy, Aubrey. *Salisbury, 1830–1903: Portrait of a Statesman*. London: John Murray, 1953.

Koss, Stephen. *Asquith*. London: Allen Lane, 1976.

Londonderry, Marchioness of. *Henry Chaplin: A Memoir*. London: Macmillan, 1926.

Long, Walter. *Memories*. London: Hutchinson, 1922.

Lowther, James. *A Speaker's Commentaries*. 2 vols. London: Edward Arnold, 1925.

Lyttelton, Edith. *Alfred Lyttelton: An Account of His Life*. London: Longmans, Green & Company, 1923.

Mackail, J. W., and Guy Wyndham. *Life and Letters of George Wyndham*. 2 vols. London: Hutchinson, n.d.

Mackay, Ruddock F. *Fisher of Kilverstone*. Oxford: Oxford University Press, 1973.

Mallock, W. H. *Memoirs of Life and Literature*. London: Chapman & Hall, 1920.

Marder, Arthur J., ed. *Fear God and Dread Nought: The Correspondence of Admiral Fisher*. 3 vols. Cambridge, Mass.: Harvard University Press, 1952–1960.

Maxwell, Sir Herbert. *Evening Memories*. London: Alexander Maclehose, 1932.

Petrie, Sir Charles. *Walter Long and His Times*. London: Hutchinson, 1936.

——. *The Life and Letters of the Right Hon. Sir Austen Chamberlain*. 2 vols. London: Cassell & Company, 1939–1940.

Repington, Charles à Court. *Vestigia*. London: Constable, 1919.

Russell, George W. E. *Sir Wilfrid Lawson: A Memoir*. London: Smith, Elder, 1909.

Salvidge, Stanley. *Salvidge of Liverpool*. London: Hodder & Stoughton, 1934.

Taylor, H. A. *Jix: Viscount Brentford*. London: Stanley Paul, 1933.

Thornton, Percy. *Some Things We Have Remembered*. London: Longmans, Green & Co., 1912.

Vincent, John, ed. *The Crawford Papers: The Journals of David Lindsay, Twenty-Seventh Earl of Crawford and Tenth Earl of Balcarres 1871–1940 During the Years 1892 to 1940*. Manchester: Manchester University Press, 1984.

Wilkinson, Spenser. *Thirty-Five Years: 1874–1909*. London: Constable, 1933.

Willoughby de Broke, Lord. *The Passing Years*. London: Constable, 1924.

Winterton, Lord. *Pre-War*. London: Macmillan, 1932.

Zebel, Sydney H. *Balfour: A Political Biography*. Cambridge: Cambridge University Press, 1973.

Books and Articles

Adams, R. J. Q., and Philip Poirer. *The Conscription Controversy in Great Britain, 1900–1918*. London: Macmillan, 1987.

Aldcroft, Derek, ed. *The Development of British Industry and Foreign Competition 1875–1914*. London: George Allen & Unwin, 1968.

Allen, Robert C. "International Competition in Iron and Steel, 1850–1913." *Journal of Economic History* 39 (1979): 911–37.

Allison, Michael J. *The National Service Issue 1899–1914*. Ph.D. diss., University of London, 1975.

Anderson, Gregory. *Victorian Clerks*. Manchester: Manchester University Press, 1976.

Ashworth, William. "Economic Aspects of Late Victorian Naval Administration." *Economic History Review* 22 (1969): 491–505.

Auspos, Patricia. "Radicalism, Pressure Groups, and Party Politics: From the National Education League to the National Liberal Federation." *Journal of British Studies* 20 (1980): 184–204.

Baylen, J. O. "The New Journalism in Late Victorian Britain." *Australian Journal of Politics and History* 18 (1972): 367–85.

Bernstein, George L. "Liberalism and the Progressive Alliance in the Constituencies." *Historical Journal* 26 (1983): 617–40.

———. *Liberalism and Liberal Politics in Edwardian England*. London: Allen & Unwin, 1986.

Berrington, Hugh. "Partisanship and Dissidence in the Nineteenth-Century House of Commons." *Parliamentary Affairs* 21 (1967–1968): 338–74.

Best, Geoffrey. "Militarism and the Victorian Public School." In *The Victorian Public School*, eds. Brian Simon and Ian Bradley, 129–46. Dublin: Gill & Macmillan, 1975.

Blackwell, P. "An Undoubted Jewel: A Case Study of Five Sussex Country Houses, 1880–1914." *Southern History* 3 (1981): 183–200.

Blake, Lord, and Hugh Cecil, eds. *Salisbury: The Man and His Policies*. London: Macmillan, 1987.

Blake, Robert. *The Conservative Party From Peel to Thatcher*. 2nd ed. London: Fontana, 1985.

Blanch, Michael. "Imperialism, Nationalism and Organized Youth." In *Working-Class Culture*, eds. John Clarke, C. Critcher, and Richard Johnson, 103–20. London: Hutchinson, 1979.

———. "British Society and the War." In *The South African War*, ed. Peter Warwick, 210–38. London: Longman, 1980.

Blewett, Neal. "The Franchise in the United Kingdom, 1885–1918." *Past and Present* 32 (1965): 27–56.

———. "Free Fooders, Balfourites, Wholehoggers: Factionalism Within the Unionist Party, 1906–10." *Historical Journal* 11 (1968): 95–124.

———. *The Peers, the Parties, and the People: The General Elections of 1910*. London: Macmillan, 1972.

Boswell, J. S., and B. R. Johns. "Patriots or Profiteers? British Businessmen and the First World War." *Journal of European Economic History* 11 (1982): 423–45.

Boyle, T. "The Liberal Imperialists 1892–1906." *Bulletin of the Institute of Historical Research* 52 (1979): 48–82.

Bristow, Edward J. "The Liberty and Property Defence League and Individualism." *Historical Journal* 18 (1975): 761–89.

Brown, Benjamin H. *The Tariff Reform Movement in Great Britain, 1881–1895*. New York: Columbia University Press, 1943.

Brown, Kenneth D. "The Trade Union Tariff Reform Association 1904–1913." *Journal of British Studies* 9 (1970): 141–53.

———, ed. *Essays in Anti-Labour History*. London: Macmillan, 1974.

Burgess, M. D. "Lord Rosebery and the Imperial Federation League 1884–1893." *New Zealand Journal of History* 13 (1979): 166–81.

Burk, Kathleen, ed. *War and the State: The Transformation of British Government, 1914–1919*. London: Allen & Unwin, 1982.

Burn, W. L. "English Conservatism." *Nineteenth Century* 145 (1949): 1–11, 67–76.

Butler, Lord, ed. *The Conservatives: A History From Their Origins to 1965*. London: George Allen & Unwin, 1977.

Cain, P. J. "Political Economy in Edwardian England: The Tariff Reform Controversy." In *The Edwardian Age*, ed. Alan O'Day, 34–59. London: Macmillan, 1979.

———. *Economic Foundations of British Overseas Expansion 1815–1914*. London: Macmillan, 1980.

Capie, F. "The Pressure for Tariff Protection in Britain 1917–1931." *Journal of European Economic History* 9 (1980): 431–47.

Carew, Anthony. *The Lower Deck of the Royal Navy 1900–1939*. Manchester: Manchester University Press, 1981.

Chadwick, Mary E. "The Role of Redistribution in the Making of the Third Reform Act." *Historical Journal* 19 (1976): 665–84.

Checkland, Sydney. "The Mind of the City." *Oxford Economic Papers* 9 (1957): 261–78.

Chickering, Roger. *We Men Who Feel Most German: A Cultural Study of the Pan-German League 1886–1914*. London: Allen & Unwin, 1984.

Clark, David. *Colne Valley: Radicalism to Socialism. The Portrait of a Northern Constituency in the Formative Years of the Labour Party, 1890–1910*. London: Longman, 1981.

Clarke, P. F. "British Politics and Blackburn Politics, 1900–1910." *Historical Journal* 12 (1969): 302–27.

———. *Lancashire and the New Liberalism*. Cambridge: Cambridge University Press, 1971.

———. "The Electoral Sociology of Modern Britain." *History* 57 (1972): 31–55.

———. "The End of Laissez Faire and the Politics of Cotton." *Historical Journal* 15 (1972): 493–512.

———. "The Electoral Position of the Liberal and Labour Parties 1910–1914." *English Historical Review* 90 (1975): 828–36.

———. *Liberals and Social Democrats*. Cambridge: Cambridge University Press, 1978.

Coats, A. W. "Political Economy and the Tariff Reform Campaign of 1903." *Journal of Law and Economics* 11 (1968): 181–229.

Coetzee, Frans. "Pressure Groups, Tory Businessmen and the Aura of Political Corruption Before the First World War." *Historical Journal* 29 (1986): 833–52.

Coetzee, Frans, and Marilyn Shevin Coetzee. "Rethinking the Radical Right in Germany and Britain Before 1914." *Journal of Contemporary History* 21 (1986): 515–37.

Colls, Roger, and Phillip Dodd, eds. *Englishness: Politics and Culture 1880–1920*. London: Croom Helm, 1986.

Cook, Chris. "Labour and the Downfall of the Liberal Party 1906–1914." In *Crisis and Controversy: Essays in Honour of A. J. P. Taylor*, eds. C. Cook and Alan Sked, 38–65. London: Macmillan, 1976.

Cornford, James. "The Transformation of Conservatism in the Late Nineteenth Century." *Victorian Studies* 7 (1963): 35–66.

———. "The Parliamentary Foundations of the Hotel Cecil." In *Ideas and Institutions in Victorian England*, ed. Robert Robson, 268–311. London: Bell, 1967.

Crossick, Geoffrey, ed. *The Lower Middle Class in Britain 1870–1914*. London: Croom Helm, 1977.

Crouzet, François. "Trade and Empire: The British Experience From the Establishment of Free Trade Until the First World War." In *Great Britain and Her World 1750–1914: Essays in Honour of W. O. Henderson*, ed. B. M. Ratcliffe, 209–35. Manchester: Manchester University Press, 1975.

———. *The Victorian Economy*. London: Methuen, 1982.

Cunningham, Hugh. "The Language of Patriotism 1750–1914." *History Workshop* 12 (1981): 8–33.

———. "The Conservative Party and Patriotism." In *Englishness: Politics and Culture 1880–1920*, ed. Phillip Dodd, 283–307. London: Croom Helm, 1986.

D'Alton, Ian. "Southern Irish Unionism: A Study of Cork Unionists 1884–1914." *Transactions of the Royal Historical Society* 23 (1973): 71–88.

Dangerfield, George. *The Strange Death of Liberal England*. New York: Capricorn, 1961.

Davin, Anna. "Imperialism and Motherhood." *History Workshop* 5 (1978): 9–65.

Davis, Lance, and Robert Huttenback. *Mammon and the Pursuit of Empire: The Political Economy of British Imperialism, 1860–1912*. Cambridge: Cambridge University Press, 1986.

Douglas, Roy. "Voluntary Enlistment in the First World War and the Work of the Parliamentary Recruiting Committee." *Journal of Modern History* 42 (1970): 564–85.

———. "The National Democratic Party and the British Workers' League." *Historical Journal* 15 (1972): 533–52.

Dunbabin, J. P. D. "Parliamentary Elections in Great Britain, 1868–1900: A Psephological Note." *English Historical Review* 81 (1966): 82–99.

———. "British Elections in the Nineteenth and Twentieth Centuries, a Regional Approach." *English Historical Review* 95 (1980): 241–67.

Dutton, David. "Unionist Politics and the Aftermath of the General Election of 1906: A Reassessment." *Historical Journal* 22 (1979): 861–76.

———. "Lancashire and the New Unionism: The Unionist Party and the Growth of Popular Politics 1906–1914." *Transactions of the Historic Society of Lancashire and Cheshire* 130 (1981): 131–48.

———. "The Unionist Party and Social Policy 1906–1914." *Historical Journal* 24 (1981): 871–84.

Eccleshall, Robert. "English Conservatism as Ideology." *Political Studies* 25 (1977): 62–83.

Eley, Geoff. *Reshaping the German Right*. New Haven: Yale University Press, 1980.

Emy, H. V. "The Impact of Financial Policy on English Party Politics Before 1914." *Historical Journal* 15 (1972): 103–31.

———. *Liberals, Radicals and Social Politics 1892–1914*. Cambridge: Cambridge University Press, 1973.

Englander, David, and James Osborne. "Jack, Tommy, and Henry Dubb: The Armed Forces and the Working Class." *Historical Journal* 21 (1978): 593–621.

Ensor, Sir Robert C. K. *England 1870–1914*. Oxford: Oxford University Press, 1936.

———. "Some Political and Economic Interactions in Later Victorian England." *Transactions of the Royal Historical Society* 31 (1949): 17–28.

Fahey, David M. "Brewers, Publicans and Working Class Drinkers: Pressure Group Politics in Late Victorian and Edwardian England." *Histoire Sociale* 13 (1980): 85–103.

Fair, John D. *British Interparty Conferences*. Oxford: Oxford University Press, 1980.

———. "From Liberal to Conservative: The Flight of the Liberal Unionists After 1886." *Victorian Studies* 29 (1986): 148–78.

Fawcett, Arthur. *Conservative Agent*. London: National Society of Conservative and Unionist Agents, 1967.

Feuchtwanger, E. J. *Disraeli, Democracy, and the Tory Party*. Oxford: Oxford University Press, 1968.

Floud, Roderick, and Donald McCloskey, eds. *The Economic History of Britain Since 1700*. 2 vols. Cambridge: Cambridge University Press, 1981.

Foster, R. F. "Tory Democracy and Political Elitism: Provincial Conservatism and Parliamentary Tories in the Early 1880s." In *Parliament and Community*, eds. Art Cosgrove and J. I. McGuire, 147–75. Belfast: Appletree Press, 1983.

Fraser, Peter. "The Liberal Unionist Alliance: Chamberlain, Hartington and the Conservatives, 1886–1904." *English Historical Review* 77 (1962): 53–78.

———. "Unionism and Tariff Reform: The Crisis of 1906." *Historical Journal* 5 (1962): 149–66.

———. "The Unionist Debacle of 1911 and Balfour's Retirement." *Journal of Modern History* 35 (1963): 354–65.

French, David. "Spy Fever in Britain 1900–1915." *Historical Journal* 21 (1978): 355–70.

———. *British Economic and Strategic Planning 1905–1915*. London: Allen & Unwin, 1982.

———. "The Edwardian Crisis and the Origins of the First World War." *International History Review* 4 (1982): 207–21.

Fussell, G. E. "The Tariff Commission Report." *Agricultural History Review* 30 (1982): 137–42.

Gainer, Bernard. *The Alien Invasion: The Origins of the Alien Act of 1905*. London: Heinemann, 1972.

Gilbert, Bentley B. "Health and Politics: The British Physical Deterioration Report of 1904." *Bulletin of the History of Medicine* 39 (1965): 145–53.

———. *The Evolution of National Insurance in Great Britain*. London: Joseph, 1966.

Glickman, Harvey. "The Toryness of English Conservatism." *Journal of British Studies* 1 (1961–1962): 111–43.

Gollin, Alfred M. "Historians and the Great Crisis of 1903." *Albion* 8 (1976): 83–97.

Goodman, Gordon L. "Liberal Unionism: The Revolt of the Whigs." *Victorian Studies* 3 (1959): 173–89.

Gordon, Donald C. *The Dominion Partnership in Imperial Defence, 1870–1914*. Baltimore: Johns Hopkins University Press, 1965.

———. "The Lengthy Shadow of H. H. Mulliner." In *Changing Interpretations and New Sources in Naval History*, ed. Robert William Love, 309–24. New York: Garland Press, 1980.

Gordon, Michael. "Domestic Conflict and the Origins of the First World War: The British and German Cases." *Journal of Modern History* 46 (1974): 191–226.

Gourevitch, Peter Alexis. "International Trade, Domestic Coalitions and Liberty: Comparative Responses to the Crisis of 1873–1896." *Journal of Interdisciplinary History* 8 (1977): 281–313.

Grainger, J. H. *Patriotisms: Britain 1900–1939*. London: Routledge & Kegan Paul, 1986.

Green, E. H. H. "Radical Conservatism: The Electoral Genesis of Tariff Reform." *Historical Journal* 28 (1985): 667–92.

Guttsman, W. L. *The British Political Elite*. New York: Basic Books, 1963.

Halévy, Elie. *Imperialism and the Rise of Labour 1895–1905*. London: Ernest Benn, 1929.

———. *The Rule of Democracy 1905–1914*. London: Ernest Benn, 1934.

Halpern, Paul. *The Mediterranean Naval Situation 1908–1914*. Cambridge. Mass.: Harvard University Press, 1971.

Hamer, D. A. *The Politics of Electoral Pressure*. Brighton: Harvester Press, 1977.

Hammerton, Elizabeth, and David Cannadine. "Conflict and Consensus on a Ceremonial Occasion: The Diamond Jubilee in Cambridge in 1897." *Historical Journal* 24 (1981): 111–46.

Hamilton, W. Mark. *The Nation and the Navy: Methods and Organisation of British Navalist Propaganda 1889–1914*. Ph.D. diss., University of London, 1977.

———. "The New Navalism and the British Navy League." *Mariner's Mirror* 64 (1978): 37–43.

Hanham, H. J. "Some Neglected Sources of Information: County Biographical Dictionaries 1890–1937." *Bulletin of the Institute of Historical Research* 34 (1961): 55–66.

———. *Elections and Party Management: Politics in the Time of Disraeli and Gladstone*. 2nd ed. Brighton: Harvester Press, 1978.

Harrison, Brian. *Separate Spheres: The Opposition to Women's Suffrage in Britain*. London: Croom Helm, 1978.

Hearnshaw, F. J. C. *Conservatism in England*. London: Macmillan, 1933.

Heyck, T. W. *The Dimensions of British Radicalism: The Case of Ireland, 1874–95*. Urbana: University of Illinois Press, 1974.

Hiley, Nicholas. "Counter-Espionage and Security in Great Britain During the First World War." *English Historical Review* 101 (1986): 635–70.

Hoffman, R. J. S. *Great Britain and the German Trade Rivalry 1875–1914*. Philadelphia: University of Pennsylvania Press, 1933.

Holmes, Colin. *Anti-Semitism in British Society 1876–1939*. London: Edward Arnold, 1979.

Howkins, Alun. "Edwardian Liberalism and Industrial Unrest: A Class View of the Decline of Liberalism." *History Workshop* 4 (1977): 143–61.

Humphries, S. "Hurrah for England: Schooling and the Working Class in Bristol 1870–1914." *Southern History* 1 (1979): 171–207.

Hynes, Samuel. *The Edwardian Turn of Mind*. Princeton: Princeton University Press, 1968.

Jalland, Patricia. *The Liberals and Ireland: The Ulster Question in British Politics to 1914*. Brighton: Harvester Press, 1980.

Jessop, B. *Traditionalism, Conservatism and British Political Culture*. London: Allen & Unwin, 1974.

Joyce, Patrick. *Work, Society, and Politics: The Culture of the Factory in Late Victorian England*. Brighton: Harvester Press, 1980.

Jones, Gareth Stedman. "Working-Class Culture and Working-Class Politics in London, 1870–1900: Notes on the Remaking of a Working Class." *Journal of Social History* 7 (1974): 460–508.

Jones, Grace. *National and Local Issues in Politics: A Study of East Sussex and the Lancashire Spinning Towns, 1906–1910*. Ph.D. diss., University of Sussex, 1965.

Jones, J. R. "England." In *The European Right: A Historical Profile*, eds. Hans Rogger and Eugen Weber, 29–70. Berkeley: University of California Press, 1966.

Jones, R. B. "Balfour's Reform of Party Organisation." *Bulletin of the Institute of Historical Research* 38 (1965): 94–101.

Jordan, Gerald H. S. "Pensions not Dreadnoughts: The Radicals and Naval Retrenchment." In *Edwardian Radicalism 1900–1914*, ed. A. J. A. Morris, 162–79. London: Routledge & Kegan Paul, 1974.

Kavanagh, Dennis. "The Deferential English: A Comparative Critique." *Government and Opposition* 6 (1971): 333–60.

Kennedy, Paul M. "Mahan Versus Mackinder: Two Interpretations of British Sea Power." *Militärgeschichtliche Mitteilungen* 16 (1974): 39–66.

———. *The Rise and Fall of British Naval Mastery*. New York: Scribners, 1976.

———. *The Rise of the Anglo-German Antagonism 1860–1914*. London: Allen & Unwin, 1980.

Kennedy, Paul M., and Anthony Nicholls, eds. *Nationalist and Racialist Movements in Britain and Germany Before 1914*. London: Macmillan, 1981.

Kindleberger, Charles. "Germany's Overtaking of England 1806–1914." In *Economic Response: Comparative Studies in Trade, Finance, and Growth*, ed. Charles Kindleberger, 185–236. Cambridge, Mass.: Harvard University Press, 1978.

Kinnear, Michael. *The British Voter: An Atlas and Survey Since 1885*. London: Batsford, 1968.

Koss, Stephen. *The Rise and Fall of the Political Press in Britain*. 2 vols. Chapel Hill: University of North Carolina Press, 1981–84.

Lammers, Donald. "Arno Mayer and the British Decision for War: 1914." *Journal of British Studies* 12 (1973): 137–65.

Langan, Mary, and Bill Schwarz, eds. *Crises in the British State 1880–1930*. London: Hutchinson, 1985.

Layton-Henry, Z. "Democracy and Reform in the Conservative Party." *Journal of Contemporary History* 13 (1978): 653–70.

Lee, A. J. "Conservatism, Traditionalism and the British Working Class. 1880–1918." In *Ideology and the Labour Movement*, eds. David Martin and David Rubinstein, 84–102. London: Croom Helm, 1979.

Lloyd, Trevor. "The Whip as Paymaster: Herbert Gladstone and Party Organization." *English Historical Review* 89 (1974): 785–813.

Lunn, Kenneth, and Richard C. Thurlow, eds. *British Fascism: Essays on the Radical Right in Interwar Britain*. London: Croom Helm, 1980.

Mace, Rodney. *Trafalgar Square: Emblem of Empire*. London: Lawrence & Wishart, 1976.

MacKenzie, John M. *Propaganda and Empire: The Manipulation of British Public Opinion, 1880–1960*. Manchester: Manchester University Press, 1984.

———, ed. *Imperialism and Popular Culture*. Manchester: Manchester University Press, 1986.

Marsh, Peter. *The Discipline of Popular Government: Lord Salisbury's Domestic Statecraft 1881–1902*. Brighton: Harvester Press, 1978.

Mason, J. W. "Political Economy and the Response to Socialism in Britain 1870–1914." *Historical Journal* 23 (1980): 565–87.

Matthew, H. C. G. *The Liberal Imperialists*. Oxford: Oxford University Press, 1973.

Matthew, H. C. G., R. McKibbin, and J. Kay. "The Franchise Factor in the Rise of the Labour Party." *English Historical Review* 91 (1976): 723–52.

Mayer, Arno. *The Persistence of the Old Regime: Europe to the Great War*. New York: Pantheon, 1981.

McCloskey, Donald N. "Did Victorian Britain Fail?" *Economic History Review* 23 (1970): 446–59.

McCready, H. W. "The Revolt of the Unionist Free Traders." *Parliamentary Affairs* 16 (1962–1963): 188–206.

McDowell, R. B. *British Conservatism 1832–1914*. London: Faber & Faber, 1959.

McEwen, J. M. "The Coupon Election of 1918 and Unionist Members of Parliament." *Journal of Modern History* 34 (1962): 294–306.

McKibbin, Ross. *The Evolution of the Labour Party 1910–24*. Oxford: Oxford University Press, 1974.

McNeill, William H. *The Pursuit of Power: Technology, Armed Force, and Society Since A.D. 1000*. Chicago: University of Chicago Press, 1982.

Meacham, Standish. *A Life Apart: The English Working Class 1890–1914*. Cambridge. Mass.: Harvard University Press, 1977.

Middlemas, Keith. *Politics in Industrial Society: The Experience of the British System Since 1911*. London: Andre Deutsch, 1979.

Minchinton, Walter E. "E. E. Williams: Made in Germany and After." *Vierteljahrsschrift für Sozial und Wirtschaftsgeschichte* 62 (1975): 229–242.

Mock, Wolfgang. *Imperiale Herrschaft und nationales Interesse: "'Constructive Imperialism' oder Freihandel in Grossbritannien vor dem Ersten Weltkrieg*. Stuttgart: Klett-Cotta, 1982.

Morris, A. J. A. *Radicalism Against War*. London: Longman, 1972.

———. *The Scaremongers: The Advocacy of War and Rearmament, 1896–1914*. London: Routledge & Kegan Paul, 1984.

Murray, Bruce K. "The Politics of the 'People's Budget.'" *Historical Journal* 16 (1973): 555–70.

———. *The People's Budget 1909/10*. Oxford: Oxford University Press, 1980.

Newby, Howard. "The Deferential Dialectic." *Comparative Studies in Society and History* 17 (1975): 139–64.

Norton, Philip, and Arthur Aughey. *Conservatives and Conservatism*. London: Temple Smith, 1981.

Nowell-Smith, S., ed. *Edwardian England 1901–1914*. Oxford: Oxford University Press, 1964.

O'Day, Alan, ed. *The Edwardian Age: Conflict and Stability 1900–1914*. London: Macmillan, 1979.

Offer, Avner. *Property and Politics, 1870–1914: Landownership, Law, Ideology, and Urban Development in England*. Cambridge: Cambridge University Press, 1981.

———. "Empire and Social Reform: British Overseas Investment and Domestic Politics, 1908–1914." *Historical Journal* 26 (1983): 119–38.

———. "The Working Classes, British Naval Plans and the Coming of the Great War." *Past and Present* 107 (1985): 204–26.

———. "Morality and Admiralty. 'Jacky' Fisher, Economic Warfare and the Laws of War." *Journal of Contemporary History* 23 (1988): 99–119.

O'Leary, Cornelius. *The Elimination of Corrupt Practices in British Elections, 1868–1911*. Oxford: Oxford University Press, 1962.

Padfield, Peter. *Rule Britannia: The Victorian and Edwardian Navy*. London: Routledge & Kegan Paul, 1981.

Parkin, Frank. "Working Class Conservatives: A Theory of Political Deviance." *British Journal of Sociology* 18 (1967): 278–90.

Pelling, Henry. *The Origins of the Labour Party 1880–1900*. 2nd ed. Oxford: Oxford University Press, 1965.

———. *Social Geography of British Elections 1885-1910*. London: Macmillan, 1967.

———. *Popular Politics and Society in Late Victorian Britain*. 2nd ed. London: Macmillan, 1979.

———. "The Politics of the Osborne Judgement." *Historical Journal* 25 (1982): 889–909.

Perkin, Harold. *The Structured Crowd: Essays in English Social History*. Brighton: Harvester Press, 1981.

Perry, P. J., ed. *British Agriculture 1875-1914*. London: Methuen, 1973.

Phillips, Gregory D. *The Diehards: Aristocratic Society and Politics in Edwardian England*. Cambridge. Mass.: Harvard University Press, 1979.

———. "Lord Willoughby de Broke and the Politics of Radical Toryism, 1909-1914." *Journal of British Studies* 20 (1980): 205–24.

Pinto-Duschinsky, Michael. *British Political Finance 1830-1980*. Washington, D. C.: American Enterprise Institute for Public Policy Research, 1981.

Playne, Caroline. *The Pre-War Mind in Britain*. London: George Allen & Unwin, 1928.

Pollard, Sidney, and Paul Robertson. *The British Shipbuilding Industry, 1870-1914*. Cambridge. Mass.: Harvard University Press, 1979.

Porter, Dilwyn. *The Unionist Tariff Reformers 1903-1914*. Ph.D. diss., University of Manchester, 1976.

Price, Richard N. *An Imperial War and the British Working Class*. London: Routledge & Kegan Paul, 1972.

———. "Society, Status and Jingoism: The Social Roots of Lower Middle Class Patriotism, 1870-1900." In *The Lower Middle Class in Britain 1870-1914*, ed. G. Crossick, 89–112. London: Croom Helm, 1977.

Pugh, Martin. *Electoral Reform in War and Peace 1906-1918*. London: Routledge & Kegan Paul, 1978.

———. "New Light on Edwardian Voters: The Model Elections of 1906-12." *Bulletin of the Institute of Historical Research* 51 (1978): 103–9.

———. "Yorkshire and the New Liberalism?" *Journal of Modern History* 50 (1978): D1139-55.

———. *The Making of Modern British Politics 1867-1939*. Oxford: Basil Blackwell, 1982.

———. *The Tories and the People 1880-1935*. Oxford: Basil Blackwell, 1985.

Purdue, A. W. "The Liberal and Labour Parties in North-East Politics 1900-1914: The Struggle for Supremacy." *International Review of Social History* 26 (1981): 1–24.

———. "Jarrow Politics, 1885-1914: The Challenge to Liberal Hegemony." *Northern History* 18 (1982): 182–98.

Ramsden, John. *The Age of Balfour and Baldwin 1902-1940*. London: Longman, 1978.

Ranft, Bryan, ed. *Technical Change and British Naval Policy*. London: Hodder & Stoughton, 1977.

Read, Donald, ed. *Edwardian England*. London: Croom Helm, 1982.

Rempel, Richard A. "Lord Hugh Cecil's Parliamentary Career, 1900-1914: Promise Unfulfilled." *Journal of British Studies* 11 (1972): 104–30.

———. *Unionists Divided: Arthur Balfour, Joseph Chamberlain and the Unionist Free Traders*. Newton Abbot: David & Charles, 1972.

Ridley, Jane. "The Unionist Social Reform Committee, 1911-1914: Wets Before the Deluge." *Historical Journal* 30 (1987): 391–413.

Robb, Janet H. *The Primrose League 1883-1914*. New York: Columbia University Press, 1942.

Rodger, N. A. M. "The Dark Ages of the Admiralty 1869–1885." *Mariner's Mirror* 62 (1976): 33–46, 121–28.

———. *The Admiralty*. Lavenham, Suffolk: Terrence Dalton, 1979.

Rubinstein, W. D. "Henry Page Croft and the National Party 1917–22." *Journal of Contemporary History* 9 (1974): 129–48.

———. *Men of Property: The Very Wealthy in Britain Since the Industrial Revolution*. London: Croom Helm, 1981.

Russell, A. K. *Liberal Landslide: The General Election of 1906*. Newton Abbot: David & Charles, 1973.

Saul, S. B. "The Economic Significance of Constructive Imperialism." *Journal of Economic History* 17 (1957): 173–92.

———. *Studies in British Overseas Trade 1870–1914*. Liverpool: Liverpool University Press, 1960.

———. *The Myth of the Great Depression, 1873–96*. 2nd ed. London: Macmillan, 1985.

Scally, Robert J. *The Origins of the Lloyd George Coalition: The Politics of Social Imperialism 1900–1918*. Princeton: Princeton University Press, 1975.

Searle, G. R. *The Quest for National Efficiency*. Oxford: Basil Blackwell, 1971.

———. "Critics of Edwardian Society: The Case of the Radical Right." In *The Edwardian Age*, ed. Alan O'Day, 79–96. London: Macmillan, 1979.

———. "The 'Revolt from the Right' in Edwardian Britain." In *Nationalist and Racialist Movements*, eds. P. Kennedy and A. Nicholls, 21–39. London: Macmillan, 1981.

———. "The Edwardian Liberal Party and Business." *English Historical Review* 98 (1983): 28–60.

———. *Corruption in British Politics, 1895–1930*. Oxford: Clarendon Press, 1987.

Semmel, Bernard. *Imperialism and Social Reform: English Social–Imperial Thought 1895–1914*. Cambridge. Mass.: Harvard University Press, 1960.

———. *Liberalism and Naval Strategy*. London: Allen & Unwin, 1986.

Shevin Coetzee, Marilyn. "The Mobilization of the Right? The Deutscher Wehrverein and Political Activism in Württemberg, 1912–1914." *European History Quarterly* 15 (1985): 431–52.

Smith, Paul. *Disraelian Conservatism and Social Reform*. London: Routledge & Kegan Paul, 1967.

Soloway, Richard. *Birth Control and the Population Question in England, 1877–1930*. Chapel Hill: University of North Carolina Press, 1982.

———. "Counting the Degenerates: The Statistics of Race Deterioration in Edwardian England." *Journal of Contemporary History* 17 (1982): 137–64.

Southgate, Donald, ed. *The Conservative Leadership, 1832–1932*. London: Macmillan, 1974.

Springhall, John O. *Youth, Empire and Society: British Youth Movements, 1883–1940*. London: Croom Helm, 1977.

Stansky, Peter. *Ambitions and Strategies: The Struggle for the Leadership of the Liberal Party in the 1890's*. Oxford: Oxford University Press, 1964.

Steele, E. D. "Imperialism and Leeds Politics c.1850–1914." In *A History of Modern Leeds*, ed. Derek Fraser, 327–52. Manchester: Manchester University Press, 1980.

Steinberg, Jonathan. "The Copenhagen Complex." *Journal of Contemporary History* 1 (1966): 23–46.

Steiner, Zara. *Britain and the Origins of the First World War*. London: Macmillan, 1977.

Stokes, Eric. "Milnerism." *Historical Journal* 5 (1962): 47–60.

Stubbs, John. "Lord Milner and Patriotic Labour, 1914–1918." *English Historical Review* 87 (1972): 717–54.

———. "The Impact of the Great War on the Conservative Party." In *The Politics of Reappraisal 1918–1939*, eds. Chris Cook and Gillian Peele, 14–38. New York: St. Martin's Press, 1975.

Sumida, Jon T. "British Capital Ship Design and Fire Control in the Dreadnought Era: Sir John Fisher, Arthur Hungerford Pollen, and the Battle Cruiser." *Journal of Modern History* 51 (1979): 205–30.

Summers, Anne. "Militarism in Britain Before the Great War." *History Workshop* 2 (1976): 104–23.

———. "The Character of Edwardian Nationalism: Three Popular Leagues." In *Nationalist and Racialist Movements*, eds. P. Kennedy and A. Nicholls, 68–87. London: Macmillan, 1981.

Sykes, Alan. "The Confederacy and the Purge of the Unionist Free Traders 1906–1910." *Historical Journal* 18 (1975): 349–66.

———. *Tariff Reform in British Politics 1903–1913*. Oxford: Oxford University Press, 1979.

———. "The Radical Right and the Crisis of Conservatism Before the First World War." *Historical Journal* 26 (1983): 661–76.

Tanner, Duncan. "The Parliamentary Electoral System, the 'Fourth' Reform Act and the Rise of Labour in England and Wales." *Bulletin of the Institute of Historical Research* 56 (1983): 205–19.

Thomas, J. A. *The House of Commons 1832–1901: A Study of Its Economic and Functional Character*. Cardiff: University of Wales Press, 1939.

Thompson, Paul. *Socialists, Liberals and Labour: The Struggle for London 1885–1914*. London: Routledge & Kegan Paul, 1967.

———. *The Edwardians: The Remaking of British Society*. London: Weidenfeld & Nicholson, 1975.

Trebilcock, Clive. "Legends of the British Armaments Industry: A Revision." *Journal of Contemporary History* 5 (1970): 2–19.

———. *The Vickers Brothers: Armaments and Enterprise, 1854–1914*. London: Europa, 1977.

Tucker, Albert V. "W. H. Mallock and Late Victorian Conservatism." *University of Toronto Quarterly* 31 (1962): 223–41.

Turner, B. H. P. *Tariff Reform and the Conservative Party 1895–1906*. Ph.D. diss., University of London, 1967.

Turner, J. A. "The British Commonwealth Union and the General Election of 1918." *English Historical Review* 93 (1978): 528–59.

———, ed. *Businessmen and Politics: Studies of Business Activity in British Politics, 1900–1945*. London: Heinemann, 1984.

Tyler, J. E. *The Struggle for Imperial Unity 1868–1895*. London: Longman, 1938.

Urwin, Derek W. "The Development of the Conservative Party Organisation in Scotland until 1912." *Scottish Historical Review* 44 (1965): 89–111.

Wald, Kenneth D. "Class and the Vote Before the First World War." *British Journal of Political Science* 8 (1978): 441–57.

———. *Crosses on the Ballot: Patterns of British Voter Alignment Since 1885*. Princeton: Princeton University Press, 1983.

Walker, Linda. "Party Political Women: A Comparative Study of Liberal Women and the Primrose League, 1890–1914. In *Equal or Different? Women's Politics 1800–1914*, ed. Jane Rendall, 165–91. Oxford: Basil Blackwell, 1987.

Waller, P. J. *Democracy and Sectarianism: A Political and Social History of Liverpool 1868–1939*. Liverpool: Liverpool University Press, 1981.

Warren, Allen. "Sir Robert Baden-Powell, the Scout Movement and Citizen Training in Great Britain, 1900–1920." *English Historical Review* 101 (1986): 376–98.

Weinroth, Howard. "Left-Wing Opposition to Naval Armaments in Britain Before 1914." *Journal of Contemporary History* 6 (1971): 93–120.

———. "Norman Angell and the Great Illusion: An Episode in Pre-1914 Pacifism." *Historical Journal* 17 (1974): 551–74.

Wiener, Martin J. *English Culture and the Decline of the Industrial Spirit 1850–1980*. Cambridge: Cambridge University Press, 1981.

Williams, Rhodri. "Arthur James Balfour, Sir John Fisher and the Politics of Naval Reform, 1904–10." *Historical Research* 60 (1987): 80–99.

Wood, J. C. "Alfred Marshall and the Tariff Reform Campaign of 1903." *Journal of Law and Economics* 23 (1980): 481–95.

———. *British Economists and the Empire, 1860–1914*. London: Croom Helm, 1983.

Wrigley, C. J., ed. *A History of British Industrial Relations 1875–1914*. Brighton: Harvester Press, 1982.

———. "In the Excess of Their Patriotism: The National Party and Threats of Subversion." In *Warfare, Diplomacy and Politics: Essays in Honour of A. J. P. Taylor*, ed. C. J. Wrigley, 93–119. London: Hamish Hamilton, 1986.

Young, K. *Local Politics and the Rise of Party: The London Municipal Society and the Conservative Intervention in Local Elections 1894–1963*. Leicester: Leicester University Press, 1975.

Zebel, Sydney H. "Fair Trade: An English Reaction to the Breakdown of the Cobden Treaty System." *Journal of Modern History* 12 (1940): 161–85.

———. "Joseph Chamberlain and the Genesis of Tariff Reform." *Journal of British Studies* 7 (1967): 131–57.

Index